TEXAS
SAYINGS & FOLKLORE

Mavis Parrott Kelsey, Sr.

bright sky press
HOUSTON, TEXAS

bright sky press
HOUSTON, TEXAS

2365 Rice Boulevard, Suite 202
Houston, Texas 77005

www.brightskypress.com

Library of Congress Cataloging-in-Publication Data on file with publisher.

10 9 8 7 6 5 4 3 2 1

ISBN 978-1-936474-92-9

Editorial Direction, Lucy Herring Chambers
Creative Direction, Ellen Peeples Cregan
Design, Marla Garcia
Printed in Canada through Friesens

Dedicated to all my family
who look after me.

The sun has riz and the sun has set,
and here we is in Texas yet

Table *of* Contents

Introduction

*T**here are a thousand thoughts lying within a man that he does not know till he picks up a pen to write.* (W. M. Thackeray)

Once a word leaves your mouth you cannot chase it back, even with the swiftest horse. (Chinese proverb)

I am a one-hundred-year-old retired general internist with little to look forward to, so I enjoy looking back to my past. I'm not a scholar, but in spite of it, I continue to write, even if poorly. In 2009 I started collecting the words and sayings of my people. I found it so interesting that I published the limited first edition book entitled *Texas Sayings and Folklore.*

Since then I have collected thousands more sayings and have combined them with those in the first book to compile a second edition with the same title. I have done it for fun. This title doesn't mean that all these sayings originated in Texas or are used only in Texas. It means they are used in Texas. The book represents almost a century of my memories. No longer can I recite all these sayings, but I can recognize them when I see or hear them. This shows the amazing capacity of the human brain. The brain is one huge memory book.

I found that many of these sayings are as old as language. Some have their origin in ancient Sumerian as early as 5,000 B.C.; in Sanskrit, the source of the Indo-European languages; or in ancient Chinese and African tongues; and later in Hebrew, Greek and Latin. Many are transmitted in the Holy Bible. They bear the wisdom of the ancients, handed down through the centuries.

It's not surprising that our vernacular speech, which is passed down outside of our formal education, contains this wisdom. These sayings have formed today's speech. Reading them in their ancient

form reveals they have changed very little to this day. Sayings are loaded with time-tested good sense, valuable advice and truisms. Some are light-hearted, funny, and even silly. Other sayings express our deepest emotions about our joys, our sorrows, life and death, major events of life and human frailties. They include profound axioms, proverbs and the words of great philosophers.

Many sayings are closely connected with my boyhood and youth. There was as much folk life involved as there was folk speech. I have described some of my own experiences as well as the sayings. I started recalling the expressions I learned from my family and neighbors as a child and youth in the small Northeast Texas town of Deport, Lamar County, Texas, located in the Black Land Cotton Belt. Dozens of our ancestral families were Old South plantation folks of English and Scotch Irish ancestry who migrated to Virginia and the Carolina colonies between 1611 and 1767. After the American Revolution they began migrating westward, stopping over in Kentucky, Tennessee, Alabama, Mississippi and the Indian Territory before some of them reached Texas between 1833 and 1872. We are often described as White Anglo-Saxon Protestants or WASPS, the original settlers of America who constituted a majority of the North American population. Such was our family background until my sons and grandchildren began intermarrying with people who had the added ancestry of New Englanders and Northern Europeans (German, French and Scandinavian).

I first became interested in metaphors but soon found these expressions took other forms. Many familiar proverbs and sayings were not metaphors. Neither were some axioms, and there were slang, vulgarisms and euphemisms. I am now too old to study any more than what's in my *Webster's Collegiate Dictionary,* Fifth Edition, Merriam Co., Springfield, Mass: 1948, and *Roget's International Thesaurus,* 32nd Printing, Crowell Co: 1961.

Centuries after the ancients came the words of Shakespeare and Samuel Johnson, the great lexicographer who published the first useful dictionary. In America, Benjamin Franklin, David Crockett and Mark Twain became famous for their remarks. Yogi Berra and Will Rogers contributed some of our sayings. Even my friends, Susan G. Baker and former Texas Lieutenant Governor Bill Hobby, have contributed sayings. Vernacular speech is loaded with good sense and valuable advice. People writing their memoirs like to repeat the folk sayings of their youth.

People I know have their favorite sayings and enjoy using them. For example, my friend David Chapman who headed the Cushing Library at Texas A&M University informed me that the expression **shake a leg** had its origin in the British Navy two hundred years ago. David said that *a flash in the pan* dates back to the days of flintlock guns: if the spark failed to fire the gun, it was called a flash in the pan.

Some lexicographers say there are millions of sayings, and there are sayings that are used by millions of people. The media will never run out of sayings and phrases. I collect several known to me every day when I read the *Houston Chronicle* and the *Wall Street Journal.* These sayings and phrases are popular, useful and save space in headlines. They provide nuances and special meaning to communication. A picture may say more than a thousand words. A metaphor may also say more than a thousand words. Today's ever expanding new technology has already spawned thousands of new expressions. They will stay with us as long as they are useful.

Collecting proverbs and other sayings is a popular hobby, resulting in hundreds of books. There are websites and blogs where people list many forms of sayings and sell their books. Millions, probably billions, of people have their favorite expressions and every craft and profession has its own expressions. My friends remember and collect them and often send me lists of sayings. Unfortunately my friend of seventy years, Angus Anderson, has died and is no longer here to add sayings and proofread the book. Angus died in October 2010 at the age of ninety-three years. As I write this book in my ninety-ninth year, not a one of my school or Air Force buddies is alive.

Folk language, or the vernacular as linguists call it, was the predominant speech in my country town. People seemed to be divided into two groups: those who said "ain't" for "is not" or "are not" and those who did not.

I was born in 1912 before sound movies, the phonograph, and rapid transportation had become popular. Before there were automobiles and good roads, not many people traveled far from home. Some never left their home county. My friend Sarah Bryant's father said he wouldn't go to Europe if it was across the street. Radio was just getting started and TV only started in the 1940s. Therefore, people developed their local sayings and pronunciations. I remember a linguist saying that he could tell which East Texas county people came from by listening to their speech.

There were still a number of illiterate people whose children were learning proper English in the Deport Public School. The county school superintendent was an elected official who was teaching people proper English and not to say "ain't". My parents had attended college. My two grandmothers had been school teachers. My paternal grandfather and maternal great grandfathers were doctors, so we didn't say "ain't". But I grew up among people of old folkways and learned many expressions which I still use every day.

In my time I have seen the horse and buggy sayings like *"Get a horse!"* become obsolete due to the advent of automobiles. I remember the Great Influenza Epidemic and World War I when I was six years old. My grandfather, Dr. J. B. Kelsey, came out of retirement to treat the sick. Many died. I still have a quarantine sign like those that were posted on the doors of the afflicted. My Uncle Russell Kelsey was wounded in France during the war and I remember our family praying together for his safe return. Fortunately he survived. I remember a few words of a song that was popular during World War I. The song was written by Irving Berlin for the soldiers:

> *"Oh! How I hate to get up in the morning,*
> *Oh, how I love to remain in bed*
> *For the hardest blow of all is to hear the bugler call:*
> *'You've got to get up, you've got to get up,*
> *You've got to get up this morning!"*

The song was accompanied by a bugler playing Reveille. I remember it so well because Uncle Russell was a bugler for his infantry company.

I heard the sayings of The Great Depression which lasted from 1929 until World War II in 1941, including such words as the *Dust Bowl,* the *Okies,* the *soup kitchen,* the *Bonus Army, CCC camps,* the *WPA* and the *PWA. People were so poor they didn't have a pot to piss in.* Only the last expression has survived.

When the Japanese attacked Pearl Harbor in December 1941, we declared war on Japan and Germany. World War II then lasted four years. I heard sayings about the women who entered the workforce for the first time: *Rosie the Reviter* and the *WACs.* Most of us can remember the nursery rhymes we learned as small

children. I also remember the church hymns and the patriotic songs we sang in the Deport Public School. My father's family loved music. Dad played a cornet. He gave me a bugle, but I never learned to play it because I can't carry a tune in a bucket. In addition to being a bugler, Uncle Russell also played the saxophone and the clarinet. Uncle Joe played a cornet. Aunt Lucille, with a degree in music from Kidd Key College, taught piano and voice while her husband, Dean Oliver, played the violin.

I listened with rapture to the family musicals at my grandfather's house. They all played together on Sunday afternoons. They joined with other musicians to sing and play at the Methodist Church, the Deport High School Auditorium and at other events.

Most people don't remember *"Reach for a Lucky instead of a sweet"*, *Cracker Jacks, chocolate covered cherries, lemon sours, Tom Brown shoes* and *Barbasol.*

I encountered and already knew many vulgarities and dirty words, the kind that are not accepted in polite society. I am not printing them. However, dirty language is thriving today while morality, ethics and religion are declining. I agree with the scientists who say our planet is declining. The human race is one of the principal causes of the decline. In the past century the rate of decline has increased at a tremendous rate.

Metaphors and clichés are tempting to use because they can save many words. There are many time-proven expressions in this book. They are here because they are very useful and will be here for a long time to come.

Time is running out on me so I do not have time to organize these thousands of sayings into a form that makes the sayings readily accessible for the reader. If you're looking for a favorite saying, there's no index; you will just have to dig it out of the book.

I mentioned that I am familiar with most of these sayings. I was reminded of many by reading several books described in the bibliography.

Mary Wilson Kelsey's parents, Cooke and Mary Wilson, in the back seat of a surrey. Spindletop Oil field, 1908.

As Solomon said 3,000 years ago (Eccl. 1:9), ***"...there's nothing new under the sun."*** Many of today's sayings are a rehash of ancient proverbs, written to fit today's world. Others have been polished by the elite. There will be a list of examples of folk language of the uneducated, or vernacular, of early twentieth century Northeast Texas. Then you will find listed the proverbs, phrases and other sayings I learned from all my people during my youth and later years, even up until today.

My assistant, Becky Ayers, has great patience and she has nursed this book to its conclusion. I couldn't do it without her. To quote some old sayings, she's ***the apple of my eye, one of my blessings,*** and she works ***beyond the call of duty.*** With Becky ***it's no sooner said than done.*** She's got plenty of ***know-how.*** She's ***ship shape, true blue*** and ***sticks with it.*** She has ***infectious enthusiasm*** and ***goes full throttle.*** She knows ***the art of living*** and has ***the can-do spirit.*** She ***goes at it with eyes wide open.*** She ***shoots from the hip.*** She's ***happy as a lark.*** She's ***ready, willing and able.*** She's not ***on the wild side*** and ***doesn't have a mean streak in her.***

DEFINITION OF FORMS OF SAYINGS AND EXPRESSIONS

A saying is a statement, especially a proverbial one. The sayings in this book take many forms. Learning these forms has been helpful in enjoying and understanding the sayings. This is a list defining briefly the forms of our sayings, most of which are taken from Noah Webster's dictionary. I have used this dictionary for sixty-five years. Incidentally, Webster was a friend of George Washington during the American Revolution.

Acronym: The use of initials for words. Example: *BYOB – Bring your own booze.*

Adage: A saying which has obtained credit by long use. A synonym of axiom. Example: *You can't take it with you.*

Aphorisms: A short pithy sentence stating a doctrine or truth, loosely a maxim or synonym. Example: *All men are created equal.*

Axiom: A statement of self-evident truth. Example: *Haste makes waste.*

Cliché: A trite phrase or a hackneyed expression. Phrases too often used. Examples: *In the lap of luxury. The run of the mill.*

Conundrum: A kind of riddle or puzzling quotation of which the answer is a pun or involves a pun. Example: *What's pink when it's green and red when it's black? A blackberry.*

Expression: A form of prose or phrase which manifests a thought. Example: *Everybody loves a lover.*

Euphemism: The substitution of an inoffensive or mild expression for one that may offend or suggest something unpleasant. Examples: *She's pleasingly plump.*

Generic: Using a name, place or thing to identify or express a meaning. Example: *A good time Charley.*

Jargon: Gibberish, or confused or unintelligible language. Example: *Squaniferous.*

Jest and joke: A jeering or satirical remark; something done or said in banter or raillery; a joke or a thing not to be taken seriously, sometimes taunting or ill-natured. A sportive sally designed to promote good humor without offending the feeling of another; to make merriment of words in action. Example, from the sayings of the ancients: *Jests often decide matters of importance more effectively than seriousness.* (Horace 45-8 BC).

Limerick: A nonsense poem of five anapestic lines, of which lines 1, 2 and 5 are of three feet and rhyme and lines 3 and 4 are two feet and rhyme. Example:

In the Garden of Eden sat Adam
Disporting himself with his madam
She was filled with elation
For in all creation
There was only one man and she had him

Maxim: A general truth or rule of conduct expressed in sententious form or as a proverb; an axiom. Example: *Pride goeth before a fall.*

Metaphor: To carry over, as rhetoric; use of a word or phrase literally denoting one kind of object or idea in place of another by way of suggesting a likeness or analogy between them. Example: *Don't bite off more than you can chew.*

Neologism: The use of a new word for an old word in a new or different sense. Example: *Cowboy up or horn in.*

Omens: An occurrence or phenomenon supposed to portend some future event. To foretell by signs or portends. Example: *Finding a coin is good luck to the finder and bad luck to the loser.*

Oxymoron: A combination for epigrammatic effect of contradictory or incongruous words or expressions. Examples: *Deadly serious comedy. Whims of iron. My dearest enemy. Perfectly rotten.*

Paraprosdokian: A figure of speech in which the latter part of a sentence or phrase is surprising or unexpected. Frequently used in a humorous situation. Example: *Where there's a will, I will want to be in it.*

Phrase: A short, pithy expression, especially one often used. Example: *Out on a limb.*

Pleonasm: Using more words than necessary. Redundancy of language in speaking or writing. Can be a synonym with tautology. Examples: *Submerged under water. The far distant future. A free gift. A fighting warrior.*

Proverb: A profound maxim (chiefly Biblical); a parable (often a metaphor), a truth couched obtrusively, a brief epigrammatic saying that is popular by word. Example: *"There's nothing new under* the sun." (Solomon – 1,000 BC) ***"Wealth is hard to come by, but poverty is always with us."*** (A Sumerian, 5,000-3000 BC)

Pun: Different meaning words that say the same thing. A play of words of the same sound but of different meaning or different application of words for a witty effect. Example: ***Lettuce cut up without dressing. Bare with us. I'm a frayed knot.***

Punch line: An effectively aimed, forceful saying. Example: ***Take that and smoke it in your pipe.***

Quip: A smart, sarcastic term or jest; a witty sally; a quibble. Example: ***Zip your lip.***

Rhetoric: The art of expressive speech or discourse, especially in writing prose. Elegance of language. Example: ***What a spendthrift he is of his tongue.*** (Shakespeare)

Rhyme: A composition in verse having correspondence of terminal sounds. Examples: ***Those who wait may be too late. She shopped till she dropped.***

Riddle: An enigma proposed for guessing. Example: ***Why does the chicken cross the road? To get to the other side.***

Saying: A statement, especially a proverbial one. Example: ***You do what you gotta do.*** (President Bill Clinton)

Simile: A figure of speech by which one thing is likened or compared to something of different kind or quality or comparing two things that are the same or similar. Example: ***He is fat as a pig.***

Slang and slang shorthand: The jargon of a class or a calling or a society; widely current terms of forced, fantastic, grotesque meaning or eccentric humor or fancy or vulgar abuse. Carl Sandburg says slang is a language that takes off its coat, spits on its hands and goes to work. Examples: ***Dadburnit. SNAFU.***

Tautology: Needless repetition of meaning in other words. Examples: ***The exact same spot.***

Tongue Twisters: Sentences difficult to pronounce. Examples: ***Pick a peck of pickled peppers. She sells sea shells by the seashore. Spending spree sparks splurge.***

Vernacular: The spoken word belonging to a particular region; the native or indigenous speech of the common man, instead of speech of literary language. Example: ***Don't never fool with nothin' that ain't none of your business.***

Vulgarity: Words of the common people, the vernacular, offensive to good taste, coarse; but some are not offensive. Example: ***He doesn't have a pot to piss in.*** "Aggravating" for "provoking" is an inoffensive vulgarism of the common people, or the vernacular.

Wisecrack: A jocular smart remark; all slang; a wiseacre is one making undue pretensions of wisdom. Example: ***It's greater than riches to scratch where it itches.***

There are many other forms of expression or sayings in this book: platitudes, invectives, cynicisms, one-liners, buzz words, colloquialisms, put downs, expletives, dirty words, profundities, exclamations, greetings, sermons, lingo and erotica.

Mavis Parrott Kelsey, age three, and his mother, Bonita Parrott Kelsey. Deport, Texas, 1915.

CHAPTER ONE

Folk Speech *of* Northeast Texas

DON'T NEVER FOOL WITH NOTHING THAT AIN'T NONE OF YOUR BUSINESS.

Using the word **"ain't"** for the negative *"is not"* or *"have not"* may be the most significant part of speech which distinguishes the uneducated speaker in Northeast Texas during the early 1900s. There are also thousands of words and sayings which make up the **vernacular** or **folk language** of our area.

Vernacular speech may be passed down by word of mouth for generations. Today frequent and widespread use of vernacular speech by the media is leading much of it to meld into accepted language. Many of our everyday expression are the vernacular. The media, especially the writers of headlines, could not do without vernacular speech.

VERNACULAR SPEECH USING "AIN'T"

Eighty ain't old, just fully matured.	H'aint so (It isn't so). Ain't she sweet.
How come he ain't ready?	I ain't et yet. Say it ain't so.
It ain't too much. It ain't too bad.	If it ain't one thing, it's another.
T'aint nuthin fancy (it isn't fancy).	It ain't gonna rain no more.
She ain't likely to do nuthin wrong.	Women and kids ain't easy to handle.
There ain't no such a thing (or animal).	If it ain't broke, don't fix it.

Ain't it aggravating? Aint' that the truth?

H'aint never seen it (I have never seen it).

He ain't worth two bits (or the powder to blow him to Hell).

He ain't got no sense. He ain't getting' nowheres.

I ain't never seed the like. It ain't worth a continental.

It ain't no telling. No use telling. It ain't that way.

Is you is or is you ain't? She is or she ain't.

Shucks, that ain't nuthin. That ain't hay. It ain't no different.

The old grey mare, she ain't what she used to be.

The creek ain't never got this high before.

There ain't a ace on the bottom of the deck, is they?

You ain't seen nuthin yet. It just ain't right. You ain't a woofing.

It ain't what it's stacked up to be. It ain't what it used to be.

That there sawbones ain't no MD, he's a horse doctor. He sets folks broken bones and gave Hadacol to Grandma for the rheumatiz.

VERNACULAR SHORT SAYINGS

He went lickety-split.	It chapped me.
Don't be so touchous.	Keep on plugging.
I'll sweat it out.	He's a pain in the ass.
I figured he was teed off at me.	Don't lose your grip on it.
He was prickly about it.	Dofunnies.
His nose is out of joint.	I'm buffaloed.
Make yourself scarce.	It's a cull.
He didn't show hisself.	Hightail it.
He commenced to carrying on.	Hot foot it.
He had a little age on him.	Kiss it goodbye.
Don't be too hard on him.	It's enough already.

She's got a mean streak in her.	Keep this between us.
He unloaded both barrels on me.	He outdid himself.
She swept it under the rug.	Keep kicking.
What's on your mind?	Pull in your horns.
Don't stick your neck out.	Two-faced
This news is hard to swallow.	Bury the hatchet.
I didn't mean you no harm.	Don't preach to me.
He shot his wad.	Don't push me around.
I'm sick of hearing about it.	It blows your mind.
It's high time.	Take a listen.
It's as easy as pie.	I've washed my hands of it.
I'm a sucker for it.	I'll wrastle you for it.
Uppity	She did him in.
Nip it in the bud.	You take the cake.
You can't beat it.	He plunged in to help.
Buck up; never give in.	I'd like to give it a go again.
It boggles the mind.	Do it this very minute.
Give him the boot.	Dodging the bullet.
Knocked his socks off.	Smack dab in the middle.
He snookered me.	He's on the ball.
A cool cat	Don't screw it up.
I gave him the business.	He blew his top.
You just gotta face it.	In the middle of nowhere.
Go fetch it.	Get at it.
Well, I reckon.	Get the job done.
Hold your horses.	Soft peddle it.
God bless you.	Cozy up to.
Piss on you.	That's the stuff.
It worked just right.	A flat-assed girl.
It ain't what it used to be.	Playing nice.
Cut him off at the pass.	A slap on the wrist.
Put the kibosh on it.	Make yourself at home.
She had it bad.	Don't be a piker.
Don't fiddle with it.	The buck stops here.
I take back what I said.	Rolling with the punches.

Mavis Kelsey, high school graduate. 1929.

Smoke 'em out.	Taking it on the chin.
Out with the dry cattle.	Full of piss and vinegar
A stogie (cigar)	He missed the boat.
Vamoose.	Get out of my hair.
A southpaw	He took to worrying.
He had to eat crow.	I got clobbered.
They split the blanket.	Turn the other cheek.
Don't run it in the ground.	Pull up a chair and sit down.
Meet it head on.	It rained cats and dogs.
The love bug has got you.	He's going against the grain.
Don't fib me.	The tail is wagging the dog.
He has it backwards.	Got the draw (or drop) on him.
Y'all come.	The folks on his mother's side.
He squared off (for a fight).	You can't sell me that stuff.
I reckon (I believe).	Shoot Luke or give up the gun.
Toe the line.	Loud mouth schoolyard bully
His ramblings	You ought not a' said that.
The icing on the cake	I'm minding my own business.
You little devil	Without as much as goodbye.
Get it right.	He's a good-hearted guy.
Dive into it (eat).	Getting in the swing of things.
Can't you take a hint.	I talked him in to it.
Keeping them on their toes.	The fact of the matter.
Rootin', tooting', high falutin'	Don't get your britches in a twist.
As common as chicken tracks.	A one-track mind.
Feathering his own nest.	I'm a good mind to do it.
Busting out at the seams.	I bit off more than I could chew.
Don't get your hackles up.	I've had my fill.
Don't make a fuss about it.	I ran out of juice.
He came right out and said it.	He got boxed in.
He's slow to learn.	Now, what have you got to say?
Chick Sales	In spitting distance
He paid me no mind.	Tickled pink
God was ready for him.	Dumb as a door post
I paid five coppers (cents) for it.	I'm gonna coldcock him.

Old age has got me.	Cold as a witch's tit
I ain't going nowhere no more.	It don't look so good.
He took a hit right in the chops.	You old goat
He was an ornery old bastard.	Spilled the beans
They're as alike as two peas in a pod.	Poot, fart, pass wind
The last of the Mohicans (his kind)	I'm as happy as a pig in the mud.
The last of pea time	Cracked under the strain
I've got to hand it to him.	He's done it again.
He just got off on the wrong foot.	He's toting the load.
He played it up to beat the band.	It's ain't worth a plugged nickel.
Gabbers and non-gabbers	She's got pots full of money.
What's a body to do?	It's up the road a little ways.
Quit yammering.	It ain't as easy as it might look.
I'm burnt out on beans.	They are a good match.
Get to the point.	He's throwing his weight around.
Plunk down your money.	I don't give a hoot.
He makes a thousand plunks a day.	I'll bust a gut trying.
He thought he hung the moon.	Put the lid on it.
A bang up good job	That's no bull.
A rawboned codger	Hog tied
He's gant (gaunt).	Chomp down on it.
She's right peart.	I fritted the day away.
He flew off the handle.	You old reprobate
You hadn't oughta' done that.	You broke it, you fix it.
The way I recall it.	I'm wasting my time on you.
A colored gal	I've got bad news for you.
Whoever heard of such a thing?	We've got the goods on him.
What goes around comes around.	What's going on around here?
Money talks louder than words.	Like a coon eating persimmons
It don't make no sense a'tall.	It's worse than pulling teeth.
You get the drift of it.	He's raring to go.
There's no rest for the weary.	He's got money to burn.
You go to the Devil.	I'm in the right frame of mind.
That's for sure.	They fight like cats and dogs.
Thrown for a loop	Cats have nine lives.

Those were the good old days.	Ladybug, ladybug, fly away home.
She cracks the whip.	Large ears mean you are smart.
Has the cat got your tongue?	It's a kick in the ass.
They're making a big to-do about it.	It come a rain.
I got knocked on my butt (or ear).	He went whole hog.
Roll up your sleeves and get at it.	Grease the skids.
Who killed Cock Robin?	I got the jump on him.
Storks deliver babies.	I beat him to the draw.
He loves me, he loves me not.	Well, hush my mouth.
My teeth almost fell out of my mouth.	He's stirring up trouble.
She pulled her hair out about it.	Give 'em hell.
Put up or shut up.	I'll teach you a thing or two.
Stubborn as a mule—an iron will	He's off on a wild goose chase.
In the time it takes to pluck a chicken	She's no spring chicken.
Don't hog it all.	She don't pay me no mind.
He's always bitching.	He got it backwards.
He split his britches.	I don't give a hoot.
He's too big for his britches.	It fizzled out.
He jumped the gun.	He's frying bigger fish.
It tastes awful.	It's snake oil.
Come daylight	He's got a lot of learning to do.
It's dog eat dog.	She taken him to raise.
He got his ass in a sling.	You old so and so.
She will or she won't.	He was buffaloed.
Stay put.	He mooched off his neighbors.
Since old Hector was a pup	Make hay while the sun shines.
I put a half-nelson on him.	He skipped out on us.
What in thunderation?	Quit dickering.
Don't get your ass in a sling.	Don't get riled up.
Quit belly-aching.	I'm give out.
I'm aiming to do it.	Don't cause a ruckus.
Come in and wash up.	Gimme a second.
I might could have.	I reasoned this way.
I allowed that.	I oughta not 'a done it.
I'm ruint.	He done himself proud.

Sure nuff; how come?	I'm gonna call it quits.
The cook totes.	I sat there like a knot on a log.
He's touched in the head.	He don't look too good.
It weighed on his mind.	They ganged up on me.
What in heaven's name?	He's up to snuff.
A grass widow	He got hisself into this mess.
Thank the Lord.	He came up empty-handed.
Another day, another dollar	He stirred up a hornet's nest.
She didn't mince words.	Oysters make you sexy.
He cooked up a whopper (or fib).	I wanted it something fierce.
Looka' here.	He went ahead and cranked it up.
It galls me.	His bark is worse than his bite.
I'm fed up with you.	It's coming on night.
It runned him ragged.	It's my bounden duty.
Fork over your money.	Like as not, he'd cut me in.
Look what the cats dragged in.	Mind you, I pitched in to help.
It'll cost you an arm and a leg.	My ownself kissed her.
She's mad as a wet hen.	Screech to a halt.
We're not fooling around.	She's might nigh naked.
I tell you what.	Take and learn something.
A body would rather starve.	That there is a sissy boy.
Don't be contrary.	Them's his'n and her'n.
He don't seem to learn.	There's a ketch here.
He learnt hisself a new tune.	Let me relate what he said.
He learnt me to read. I learnt it.	It was love at first sight.
He seen his duty and he done it.	She married up with him.
He taken off his hat.	He's a harum-scarum husband.
Him and her up and got married.	It took some doing.
Him and me swapped horses.	It's just not right.
Him and me, we saw eye to eye.	She's a fallen woman.
I come to my senses.	She's in a family way.
I fell into fixing the harness.	I never said pea turkey about it.
I give it my best thought.	He didn't need no lookin after.
I gotten into cattle raisin'.	He's not crazy a'tall.
He done well.	I don't misdoubt.

I declare, it do beat all.	I learn't to better myself.
I knowed for a certainty.	It didn't hardly take no time a'tall.
I knowed I wouldn't of.	Them giggling, snickering gals.
I scant knowed him.	Wash your own self.
I throwed him the ball.	He could think out solutions.
She took and made a cake.	He cracked down on us.
I don't want no back talk.	He knocked the whey out of me.
It's eating away at me.	He slapped him in the face.
I'm biting back.	He whacked him upside the head.
If I'd knowed then.	He doesn't know up from down.
It come to mind.	He's going to the dogs.
It slipped my mind.	He's not all together.
Just yonder a few steps.	He's sparking her (courting).
My mind went off somewhere.	I couldn't bring myself to do it.
You hit the nail on the head.	I couldn't get by with nothin'.
Let your conscience be your guide.	I hoped (helped) him.
A good man is always prepared.	I poked my nose in.
I double dog dare you.	I vow it's not so.
It's been on my conscience.	I'm still of that mind.
He's a conscientious objector.	Make up your mind.
I'm conscious of it.	I'm calling it quits.
He dropped the ball.	It came down through the ages.
He won't get to first base.	Keep his feet to the fire.
He's a wolf in sheep's clothing.	It's a bald faced lie.
He's not much of a field hand.	He told a whopper.
He's not worth a plug nickel.	My mind drifts back.
He's out in left field.	He lost his mind.
I couldn't hold a candle to him.	I couldn't keep my mind on it.
I'll tell you if you'll tell me.	Proud to meet you folks.
His goose is cooked.	Sitting on the front gallery.
I got fed up with him.	She's a cute filly—heifer.
I kicked the stuffin outa him.	She's pouting and sulking again.
I never saw the like.	She's tacky and he's sissy.
It's a crying shame.	That's all there is to it.
Just look-a-here.	The shanty in the shinnery

My tail is dragging.	The two-hole privy
She carried tales (gossiped).	They gave the groom a shivaree.
She grew up like Topsey.	They sent him to the asylum.
She got her tit in a wringer.	They're going steady.
That was somethin', I tell you.	Whatever do you mean?
They have an indoor toilet.	What do you think about that?
Truth is, she's a hit.	You all come right on in.
We put him up for the night.	You don't know the half of it.
We worked by the day.	You told a fib—a story.
We worked from can till can't.	Don't make a pig of yourself.
A good time was had by all.	Folks commenced to gather.
Come in this house.	He jumped the traces.
Don't work your fool self to death.	He went on a tear.
Don't pin me down.	He wore me out.
He put one over on me.	He's sowing his wild oats.
He raked him over the coals.	He takes after his father.
He let down his guard.	He took off, lit out, beat it.
I'm just tickled pink to see you.	I was thrown for a loop.
In the back of my mind.	It's a right smart of a crowd.
It's a big to-do about nothing.	She fits right in.
With not so much as a by your leave.	She egged him on.
Out of the frying pan, into the fire	The woods are full of them.
Right on up till dark	Why are you singing the blues?
She had her eye on him.	You can take that to the bank!
She let the cat out of the bag.	I'm gonna squirrel it away.
That's what makes horse races.	It's none of your business.
Wringing a chicken's neck.	What business is it to you?
The news gets spread around.	I took a back seat to him.
It went a good way to help.	Don't be sassy.
You think you're smart.	Don't get cold feet.
Working on the chain gang.	Have a snort. I don't mind if I do.
He got the chair (the electric chair).	He blew into town.
Can't say as I blame you.	I felt like a fool.
Come and sit a spell.	Women come in handy.
He whipped him near to death.	Don't say that again.

A horse apple	She unloaded on him.
A bodark apple (Bois d'Arc apple)	We up and moved
It's right from A to Z	Don't sass your mother
She had no sense a'tall.	I sensed it right away.
I smelled a rat.	He's diggin' up dirt on me.
Wonder what the poor folks are eating.	I stays here.
Overalls to overalls in three generations	

VERNACULAR PHRASES

Such nonsense	Good sense
Slim pickin's	Chewing her cud
All tuckered out	Chewing the fat
His belly button	The Sunday pasture
The horse's mouth	Hamstrung
An indoor outhouse	A push over
A cock and bull story	Pointing a finger
A nigger in the wood pile	Full of grit
Full of piss and vinegar	Dirty as a dog
Down at the heels	Weak as a kitten
Green with envy	Happy as a lark
Sucking hind tit	Loud as thunder
Pulling bollies (cotton picking)	Deaf as a post
Frog gigging	Hot as a pistol
Them there hills	Soft as soap
Way back when	Hard as a rock
A regular cat fight	Fussy cry baby
A hoedown	Hornswaggled
Scorching hot	As American as apple pie
Brand spanking new	How it stacks up
Elbow grease	In hot water
Messing around	A do-gooder
Somewhere or other	In high cotton
Blessed by the Almighty	Well-off
Stuffed to the gills	Hooping it up
Bright-eyed and bushy-tailed	Ginning around

Drunker than a goat	Gunny sack
Sashaying all over the place	Hell bent for trouble
As honest as Old Abe	Hell on wheels
I'm tired of being kicked around.	Herd broke
A right smart spell	A hogleg (pistol)
Just being a good girl	Shoots from the hip
Finicky, persnickety	A honky-tonk
Finger lickin' good	Horseplay
A frog in my throat	A hot shot
Right before your very eyes	A Johnny-come-lately
Nobody in their right mind	Mountain oysters
In the middle of nowhere	A nighthawk
Puts me in mind of	On the warpath
My kind of folks.	Mind you
Jewed me down	Truth be told
The rub of it	Trying to figure it out.
Pitching in	Wiggle room
Got all screwed up	Cantankerous old fool
A whole slew	In the thick of it
Dishing it out	Called his bluff.
With eyes wide open	Threw him a curve.
Caught red-handed	Tight as a tick
Picking a fight	Fast as lightning
Foot-dragging	Sour as a pickle
Having a hissy	Bitter as gall
Spouts off at the mouth	Cool as a cucumber
Hits the ground running	Slow as molasses
Caught in a bind	Pretty as a picture
Ruffled feathers	Sharp as a tack
Setting a trap for him	Crazy as a bat
Getting off the hook	Green as a gourd
Hard knocks	Black as the ace of spades
Picky eater	White as a sheet
Ever now and then	Slick as grease
Look up to	Dirty as a dishrag

Where he ended up	Old as the hills
In over his head	Strong as a bull
Pulled up stakes	Mad as a wet hen
Botched the job	Mean as the devil
In cahoots	Poor as a church mouse
Got gyped	His work cut out for him.
Diarrhea of the mouth	Flat-out tough
Cut a rusty	Down and out
Folks on his mother's side	Jumps in feet first
Cow chips	Nit-picking
A pot gut	Plumb wore out
A grass widow	Up and at 'em
Hamming it up	Dead as a door knob
Larrapin' good	Spill the beans
Pleased as punch	Got it wrong
Barreling down the pike	Something to croak about
Eating away at him	Gushing with pride
Took the sap out of me	Throwing a tantrum
Feeling woozy	Thumbed his nose at me
A barrel of love	Riding herd on
Balked at it	Sand in his craw
Raising a stink	A shooting iron
All shook up	Riding shotgun
Ran it into the ground	Heading out
Raising hell	A heap o' folks
Tender as a mother's love	A tear jerker
Not for love nor money	Don't fiddle with it
The fixin's	On the hot seat
Going to a church supper	An old hand
Playing with fire	Lock, stock and barrel
Hit it lucky	Elbowing his way in
Easy pickin's	A church supper
All the time on the go	Dinner on the grounds
Rubbed the wrong way	Hung out to dry
His dander was up	From toe to cowlick

Cold-cocked him	Healthy, wealthy and wise
A bear hug	Acts dead like a possum
A bag of goodies	Backwoods folks
A lead pipe cinch	The front gallery
A long shot	Got paddled
A pure dee fact	Got razor-strapped
A cow's tail full of cockleburs	Got scolded
Bawling out	Harks back
All wore out	Lit a shuck; hightailed it
Bedding down on pallets	Just let her be
Busy as a bee	Lickerish stick
Boiling mad	Making faces
Couldn't care less	Preened like a bird
A sloppy job; dead wrong	Pulley bone (wish bone)
A heap a trouble	Readin', writin' and 'rithmetic
Fiddle with	Squatted on his hunkers
First thing I knew	Squired a girl
Gallery (for front porch)	Store-bought clothes
Grew up on her mother's knee	How about that? Well, I'll be.
I figured	Oodles of —or full of—beans
Knocked him silly	A fur (far) piece
Roughhousing	A cold spell
Like as not	Going steady; necking
Passel of kids	Homefolks; us kids
My wife's folks	Kindlin' wood
A sidekick; a tagalong	Over yonder
Played out	A stud horse
Plumb surprised	Nigger-shooter
Putting up a fight	Old Scratch; a spook
Right shortly now	The sitting room
Settled in	These days
Sweet talk; short and sweet	Goes a long way
That is to say	Hanging out
That sorta thing	All over the place
Traipsed up the hill	A play purty (a toy)
Quit figeting	

VERNACULAR SAYINGS

I reamed him out	Come stay a spell
Stick around for a spell	I'm so thirsty I'm spitting cotton.
I couldn't take it any longer.	Trying their hands at it
He uses lots of words.	I'm not going to take it any longer.
He pulled the wool over our eyes.	I'm going to hell in a hand basket.
Whole hog, don't be a hog, hogtied	A dressing-down; I told him off.
They are not out of the woods yet.	Busy as a one-armed paper hanger
Cold as a well-digger's ass in Alaska	Don't know from doodley squat
Don't get in a stew. Keep the lid on.	Pull in your reins. Come to a halt.
As plain as the nose on your face	What have you got up your sleeve?
I need this like a hole in the head.	It don't make no sense a 'tall.
Locked horns; pull in your horns.	The whole caboodle or shebang
Already saucered and blowed	Got his tail over the dashboard
Only a whoop and a holler from here	Takes a lickin' and keeps on kickin'
Taking a back seat to no one	Opened up a whole can of worms
Separating the wheat from the chaff	Richer than six feet up a hog's ass
Put your John Hancock right here	Get the point, missed the point.
I came across a surprise (Leon Hale) .	Looking at a mule's tail (plowing).
When whites and blacks knew their place	Like ugly on an ape (Rick Carrell)
He knows where his bread is buttered.	He don't have nuthin' to hang on to.
As sure as God made little green apples	He was drummed out of town.
I haven't seen him in a coon's age.	They made mincemeat out of him.
Don't bug out on me. Don't bug me.	Smack dab in the middle of Texas
This coffee is saucered and blowed.	He's so sissy, he has to squat to pee.
I've got a hitch in my getalong.	You ain't doing your duty by me.
I'm going to see a man about a dog.	He doesn't have a pot to piss in.
Hot Rods, flivvers, jalopies, tin lizzies	Swapping and to boot (trading)
Giving your word and keeping it	I knew it backwards and forwards.
My conscience wouldn't let me do that.	He burns the candle at both ends.
He was caught with his pants down.	He didn't get away with nuthing.
She don't eat enough to feed a chigger.	She made the feathers fly.
We worked from sun up til sundown.	It's more than I can shake a stick at.
He's between a rock and a hard place.	He never backed down from a fight.
He came out swinging.	He sets a great store by it.

You can bet your bottom dollar on it.

You ought to be ashamed of yourself

He knowned more'n me.

I allow as to how that's the case

He's nutty as a peach orchard boar.

That there machine is out of kilter

Try your hands at it.

Right smart of a crowd

Don't butter up to me.

It's just around the corner

He carries his feelings on the end of a stick.

Where the Indian shot you (belly button)

Busy as a one-legged man at an ass kicking contest.

Two jumps and a holler from the sheriff

Pretty considerable of a snarl (David Crockett)

Money to burn; money running out of his ears

Ugly as a mud fence—as homemade sin

Give me the old time religion, it's good enough for me.

The sweetest melon I ever put in my mouth (Leon Hale).

He fished out a couple of cans of beer (Leon Hale).

Where you been keeping yourself? (Leon Hale).

I'd as soon talk to a cedar post (Leon Hale).

They all liked never to have got out of the second grade (Leon Hale).

She's the cutest thing that ever walked down a dirt road (Leon Hale).

Quit tinkering (or messing, fiddling, stewing, screwing, fooling)

I haven't heard that in a coon's age (Betty Carrell).

Instead of asking for permission, ask for forgiveness later (Sheldon Ericson).

Grapplers—noodlers (catch their catfish by hand).

He wasn't one to sit around and feel sorry for hisself.

Me and bears don't mix—don't get along (David Crockett).

Get your cotton pickin' hands off of me.

He's meddling in other folks business.

You're tucked away back here (visiting English Priest).

We're not going to drag our feet to get this done (Obama).

A gopher, someone who runs errands, "go-for"

She cried her eyes out; She burst out crying.

That's not fit to eat; I wouldn't feed it to my hogs.

The telephone operator (early 20th Century)

He don't bathe till he gets to smelling bad.

He don't have his mind on his business

He couldn't get as far as you could throw a bull by its tail.

It's raining like a cow pissing on a flat rock.

Jumping the broomstick (getting married).

Throw a pinch of salt over your shoulder to avoid bad luck.

Lightning never strikes twice in the same place.

I'm so mad I could bite iron and spit nails.

It takes spit and vinegar to do this job

Driving a horseless carriage (in 1890s)

Woodseys (people living in the Piney Woods)

How are you? Just tolerable; Fair to middlin'; Still on my feet

He throws money around like a drunken sailor.

He's an accident waiting for a place to happen.

An honest job for an honest day's pay

Don't put off until tomorrow what you can do today.

Clean your feet before you come in this house, and take your hat off.

Every child is supposed to learn The Facts of Life on his own.

It takes a lot of doing to keep things going.

He had money coming out of his ears.

He had a roll of bills that would choke an ox.

He's between the devil and the deep blue sea.

He will be in the pen at twenty if he doesn't get killed first.

Your chickens come home to roost.

Names for jail: the calaboose; jug; clink; cooler; pokey; lock-up; jailhouse

She turned on us as sure as you are born.

He threw a monkey wrench in the works.

Her daughter jumped the traces and eloped.

He don't know from Adam's off ox.

Holler calf rope. Holler uncle (Give up!).

Whittling, chewing, spitting, lying and gossiping

Don't forget to close the door (Get out!).

Be careful or you will rip your drawers.

The booger bear will get you if you don't watch out.

I'll bet you two bits—four bits, six bits, a quarter, a buck

I'm able to be up and take nourishment.

I've got money I haven't even used.

See you later alligator. In a while crocodile.

Don't call me a dirty name—say a dirty word.

He's got book learnin but he ain't got much common sense.

I can read readin' but I can't read writin'.

The teacher leaned back in being strict.

Them critters done killed our rooster.

This here is my wife, them there is my boys, and that there is my girl.

He sashayed around and trifled on her.

It's might nigh on to a quarter of a mile to the store.

That little twerp went and told Mama a bald faced lie.

The woods are so thick a snake would have to back out to turn around.

I growed up enough to need some college learning.

Maybe she don't need all that learning out of books.

I've had my breakfast and I'm ready to start my day (Helen Goggans).

We all pick up a few problems as we go along (Helen Goggans).

You ain't a whistling Dixie (NY Times, Sept. 18, 2011, making fun of the South).

Come mornin', dad right up and went out to the barn, fed Bossy some cotton-seed hulls and meal, while he juiced her, and then throwed her a block of hay.

Dinner: when the main meal comes at noon. Dinner was always at noon in Deport. Lunch was a snack, supper was the night meal.

Don't go out in the cold with your pores wide open or you will catch your death of cold (a nurse at Scott and White Clinic, 1939).

The Kelsey Buggy Wagon and Hardware Company 1908.

Activities During My Youth

BOYS GREW UP FASTER IN THE COUNTRY THOSE DAYS

*B*y far the most important occupation in my rural town of Deport, Texas was cotton farming. Virtually every acre was planted in cotton. Texas raised more cotton than any other state. Our family owned several cotton farms. We leased the land to tenant farmers or share croppers on the half—where the landowner paid all expenses and got half the sales—or on the quarter where the tenants worked the crop and paid the expenses while the owner got one fourth of the sales.

This was before tractors were available and all the cultivating was done row by row by a team of two mules. The farmer first broke (or plowed) the land and made rows. The seeds were then sown by a cottonseed planter. When the seeds came up, the plants were thinned (cotton chopping) by hand with a hoe. While the cotton was growing, the grass and weeds were cut out with a hoe (hoeing cotton). As the cotton got larger the soil was loosened by a

Type of surrey used by Cooke Wilson at Spindletop. From Kelsey Buggy and Hardware catalogue, 1908. Price $60.00.

mule-drawn walking or riding cultivator. When fertilizers and insecticides became available, they were spread by mule teams or airplanes called crop dusters. When the bolls opened the cotton was picked by hand. The cotton pickers stooped over or crawled on their knees with knee pads to place the cotton into long canvas sacks which were strapped over their shoulder and dragged behind. When the sack was full the cotton picker threw it over his shoulder and carried it to the cotton wagon. The wagon had high sideboards so as to contain 1500 pounds of seed cotton. The cotton scales were hung from the wagon tongue which was propped up. Each cotton picker was paid one cent a pound for the cotton he picked. When 1500 pounds of seed cotton had filled the wagon, the farmer brought his pair of mules to haul the wagon to the gin where the lint was separated from the seed to produce a 500 pound bale of lint cotton and 1,000 pounds of cotton seed.

The farmer usually sold the seed to the local oil mill. His cotton bale was loaded in the wagon and hauled to the main street of town where cotton buyers took samples of the cotton to measure the length of the fiber and offered a bid to buy the bale. Cotton buyers could estimate the fibers to 1/32 of an inch. The longer the fiber, the more the price. There was a name for each length. **Fair to middin** was a good length and brought a good price. When you asked someone how he felt and he said "fair to middin", it meant he felt pretty good. When the cotton bale was sold it was tagged and hauled to the elected public cotton weigher who charged twenty-five cents to weigh and record it.

The bale was then hauled to the cotton yard and warehouse located on a railroad siding. It was shipped by train or truck to Galveston. There several hundred bales at a time were loaded on a ship and sent to the cotton mills in New England or Great Britain.

The cotton oil mill separated the cotton seed hulls from the kernels. The kernels were boiled, then crushed, extracting the oil from the cotton seed meal. The oil became cooking oil. The meal became cattle feed. The hulls were put into cattle feed.

When I was about fourteen or fifteen Grandmother Kelsey leased me a two acre plot. I hired a neighbor to plow it and I raised my own cotton crop. For a few years I did all the work of chopping, hoeing, picking the cotton, taking it to the gin and selling it on the main street. In later years raising cotton became highly mechanical. Cotton picking machines replaced the tiresome work of picking cotton by hand.

I have fond memories of the cotton harvesting season during my youth. I remember clearly to this day awakening on a moonlit night to the sound of mockingbirds singing, the cotton gins humming all night, the cotton wagons rumbling on the road in front of our house on their way home form the gin where they had to wait their turn to get their cotton ginned. I would go out in the yard barefoot to pee in the grass. This was in the days before indoor toilets.

However, there were other duties around home and the farm. We had our own vegetable garden and a **fenced-in backyard** containing a **one-car garage**, a **storm cellar**, a **woodpile**, a **wash pot**, a **water tank**, a **chicken house** and a **cow barn**. There was also an **outdoor privy**. **Cord wood** was sawed for firewood for the **wood stove** and split into **stove wood** for the **kitchen range**. There was no electricity, no public water works or sewerage. We **fed the chickens**, **collected the eggs**, **set the hens**, and **raised the chickens**. Mother would catch a chicken, **wring the head off** and fry it. Early each morning Dad would awaken us with, **"Get up, wash your face and comb your hair, and get yourself ready for the Dallas Fair"**. Dad, brother John or I **milked the cow** and **led her to the pasture**. When the **sweet milk clabbered**, we **churned it** in the new **Daisy churn** to make buttermilk and butter.

Our Negro servant Bessie boiled the laundry in the outdoor wash pot and hung it on the clothesline to dry. We wore different clothes or **duds**. Boys wore dresses until they were three or four years old. Then I grew up wearing **knee pants** with **long stockings** and **Buster Brown button-up shoes**. Girls still wore **bloomers**. Women wore dresses down to their ankles and wore tight **corsets** to make their waist small. Later they became **flappers,** wearing dresses that cut off above the knees. They **bobbed** their hair. Women became beauticians and opened **beauty parlors**. Our **Sunday-go-to-meeting clothes** were only worn on Sunday or special occasions when we dressed **fit to kill**. Other clothing items were: **drawers**, **BVD's**, **long handle underwear**, **unionalls**, **overalls**, and **galoshes**. There were also **Stetsons**, **britches**, **umbrellas**, **parasols**, **raincoats** and **slickers**.

We read by **kerosene (coal oil) lamps** and went to an **outdoor privy**. Only later did we have an **indoor water toilet**. We used a **chamber pot**, a **slop jar** or a **piss pot** at night. Before running water was available, most folks had a sort of cabinet called the **wash stand**. On it was placed a large tin or stoneware **wash bowl** and a pitcher of water. On the side was a towel rack. This was placed in the hall or in a **wash room** with the chamber pot. This was a precursor to today's bathroom. On Saturdays my family bathed in a washtub in the kitchen where it was kept warm by the **cook range**. The dishes were washed in the **dish pan** and dried with a **cup towel**. Heating and cooking was done on wood stoves. The iceman put ice in the **icebox** every day. Uncle Russell often hatched our chickens in a **home incubator**. The women used **curling irons** which were heated in the glass chimney of the kerosene lamps. This was before **bobbed hair**. Mother used

Type of buggy owned by Dr. J.B. Kelsey. I rode in this buggy with him in 1915-1920. These buggies sold for less than $50.00.

her own **hair clippers** to cut our hair at home. Dad used a **shaving mug** and a **straight-edge razor** which he sharpened on a **razor strap** that he also used to whip me. I never got a whipping I didn't need, and I needed many I didn't get.

On Saturdays I joined my friends with my dog Stranger and my **single shot shotgun** for a **rabbit hunt** or a **dove shoot**. Uncle Tom Parrott raised Russian Wolfhounds for hunting coyotes in Throckmorton. He gave me one of his hounds. That dog had trouble catching rabbits. The rabbits always dodged and got into a briar patch as the dog raced by it. The dog just couldn't smell or trail the rabbit. At night we went **coon or possum hunting**. All our men had guns and hunted. Dad hunted and fished all over from Mexico to Canada. My friends had **.22 targets (rifles)**. Dad said a **good sportsman** would not shoot a duck in the water or a bird on the ground. My friends and I were **bum sports**. We would shoot at anything. We weren't good shots; we were **bum shots**. Game didn't suffer much from our shooting.

When we grew up we became **good sportsmen** and **better shots** and knew more about hunting. For example, we got to the woods before daylight and sat still waiting for the squirrels to come out and then we shot. We sat by a **water-hole** in the late afternoon when the doves flew in to get a drink and get shot. Many years later I hunted ducks and geese on the Gulf Coast and hunted white wing doves in the Rio Grande Valley. I never became a **good shot**.

There was much less auto travel in the early 1900s. The auto was just becoming widely owned and there were no highways. My wife Mary's father, Cooke Wilson, and Reverend Peter Gray Sears drove to California in the early 1900s. For most of the 1500 mile trip there were no road maps. They worked their way west on dirt roads by finding the way from one town to the next. They no sooner arrived than an earthquake hit so they quickly got on a train and returned to Texas.

There were people in Deport who had never left Lamar and Red River Counties their entire life. Most of the road to Dallas was dirt or gravel. Near Greenville was the first paved country road in Texas. It consisted of two strips of concrete, one for the right wheels and one for the left. Some city streets were paved with **cobblestones** or **wood blocks**.

When my parents began traveling, I thought they were old mature people but when we first drove to the Arkansas Ozarks and Hot Springs, Dad was only twenty-seven and Mother twenty-five years old. Dad and Mother told this story many times. We were in a large Detroit Abbott Touring Car made by John Deere Implement Company. Each night we camped out. We pitched a tent, slept on cots under mosquito nets, and cooked by campfire. Each night we tried to find a spring for water. We bought chickens, eggs and vegetables from farmers along the way. There were few bridges, just crossings, so we were held up several times when the creeks got up. We camped in a park near Hot Springs while Dad and Mother took baths on Bathhouse Row. After I was in college, I once drove up to Hot Springs with several friends and also camped out.

Frequently we had flat tires and occasional blowouts, even a broken spring or axle. We would jack up the wheel, take off the tire, find the leak in the inner tube and patch it. When it rained we installed the **isinglass curtains**.

We usually went to Throckmorton by train and slept in a **Pullman car**. When we drove we camped on the way. Three hundred and fifty miles was a two-day trip. After some highways were paved, we began to see Burma Shave signs along the road.

An oil well was drilled on our Deport farm but it was a **dry hole**. However they **struck oil** on the Parrott ranch in Throckmorton County and Mother got royalty payments and helped send us to college.

During my boyhood I witnessed the end of the horse and buggy age and the beginning of the automobile age. Both horse-drawn vehicles and automobiles crowded Main Street on Saturdays when the farmers came to town. Grandfather Kelsey still had a horse pasture and a barn with horse stalls and a big corncrib. There are still many sayings about horses such as **he's got horse sense** and **that's a horse of a different color**. When an automobile broke down the owner was told, **"Get a horse"**. **That's horse and buggy** became a saying for anything old fashioned.

In 1908 before there were many automobiles my grandfather Dr. J. B. Kelsey opened a buggy, wagon and hardware store for my dad and his two brothers to operate and begin careers. The business, called the Deport Hardware Company, stayed in business for more than fifty years. When the buggies became obsolete, the brothers started selling automobiles. They organized the Kelsey Motor Company and spent the rest of their business lives as automobile dealers. They first had a Brush Delivery Truck. They sold **Dorts** and **Maxwells** and then they operated **Ford** and **Chevrolet** dealerships. They put a car on nearly every farm in the area. Dad provided me with automobiles even when I was in medical practice in Houston.

Grandfather Kelsey still had a buggy when I was a small boy. I remember riding in it with him. I still have the 1908 catalogue of buggies sold by the Kelseys 'buggy store which illustrates one like the one I rode in with my grandfather and a surrey like the one my future father-in-law rode in while drilling oil wells at Spindletop about 1908.

Dad bought a ranch in Red River County and we **raised cattle**. We also **killed hogs**. The hog killing story has been told so often by others I will omit it here.

The following list provides a sample of the activities of my boyhood before I left for Texas A&M College at age sixteen. We grew up faster in the country those days.

POPULAR ENTERTAINMENT, BANDS & PRODUCTS OF THE 1920S

I heard some of the music played by the Light Crust Doughboys Band out of Fort Worth. This band was sponsored by Pappy W. Lee O'Daniel who used the band for publicity in his election campaign for Governor of Texas and in his campaign for United States Senator. Will Rogers had a Sunday radio talk show. Our family sat around the radio and listened.

Some of the big time twentieth-century dance bands were Benny Goodman, Tommy Dorsey, Tex Berneke and Woody Herman. While in medical school I danced to Phil Harris in Galveston when the Maceos brought him to the Hollywood Club and Sui Jen. I watched Cab Calloway at the Dallas World's Fair in 1936.

My favorite radio entertainer in the 1920s was Bob Burns of Ft. Smith, Arkansas. Bob always told jokes about Arkansas rural life. He said reading material was so scarce that he would spend hours reading the label on a tomato can. On the way to town he always visited a guy fishing in a waterhole. The guy never caught any fish. When asked why he kept fishing there, the guy replied, "It's such a convenient place to fish." He used to see a guy who, instead of staying on the road, took a shortcut through a pasture and was chased by a bull and narrowly escaped by crawling under the fence. Bob said that was a close call. The man replied, "Yeah, it happens every day."

Popular movie stars included Al Jolson who sang "Sunny Boy"; Tom Mix; Gene Autry; The Lone Ranger; Stepin Fetchit; Rudolph Valentino; Matt Dillon and Festus; and Mae West. Roy Rogers and Rock Hudson later became my patients for several years in the Kelsey Seybold Clinic. Sometimes Dad would give me a quarter to go to the picture show. I never had an allowance and never carried money until I went to college. There wasn't much money around. Most of our fun didn't cost money.

Ford or Chevrolet coupes with **rumble seats** and **Cabriolets** were the rage in the 1920s and 1930s. Other automobiles that were produced then were: **Essex**, **Nash**, **Morman**, **Edsel**, **Franklin Electric**, **Cord** and **Dusenberg.** One-seat cars were called **roadsters** and held two passengers. Touring cars had two seats, while large cars also had jump seats. All the cars had **running boards** on the sides where people could **catch a ride** to town. Automobiles that had two jump seats in front of the back seat were called **seven passenger limousines**. The three limousines I remember were **Cadillacs**, **Lincolns** and **Packards.**

The first pickups could haul a ton, and some were built as dump trucks. The Deport Hardware Company had a two-cylinder **Brush delivery car**. Punctures and flat tires were very common; blowouts with a loud popping noise often happened. While working at Kelsey Motors, I restored several old **Model T Fords** that were about to be junked.

I remember some of the popular companies of that era. The **Sears and Roebuck** and **Montgomery Ward** catalogues ended up in the privy. The **Watkins** man came to our door selling products. We went to the **J. C. Penny Store, Kress** and **Woolworth's 5 & 10 Cent** stores in Paris, Texas, the county seat.

Some of the popular products were **Crayola**, **Big Chief tablets** and the **O.N.T. thread** my mother used to make and patch our clothes. Many men and women dipped **Garrett's snuff** and **Devoes snuff**. The men smoked **corncob pipes** and **Bull Durham** and **Prince Albert** roll your own cigarettes. They chewed **Thick (and Thin) Tinsley plugs** of tobacco. **Hadacol** was a popular **tonic** made of sherry wine. **Black Draught** and **I.Q.S.** (iron, quinine and strychnine) were other tonics. **Vicks** and **Vapo-Rub** were useful ointments. **Burma Shave** had roadside ads all over the country.

Browning, Remington, Winchester, Colt and **Smith and Wesson** made most of the guns for hunters.

The Kelsey families subscribed to the *Saturday Evening Post, Field and Stream, Hollands Magazine, Literary Digest, Cosmopolitan Magazine, Ladies Home Journal, the National Geographic Magazine, Harper's Magazine,* and *Atlantic Monthly.* When *Time* and *Life* magazines came out we signed up because our Deport friend Maurice Moore married Elizabeth Luce, the sister of publisher Henry Luce. The Deport Presbyterian Church and the Moore and Read families of Deport helped finance Henry Luce's father when he was a missionary in China. I met him and the Luce family at Maurice Moore's apartment in New York while I interned at Bellevue Hospital.

We subscribed to the *Deport Times* which has been going for a hundred years as well as the *Paris* (Texas) *News,* the *Dallas News* and often the *Fort Worth Star Telegram.* The Kelseys were voracious readers.

The Deport Public School had a small library on a wall shelf in the superintendent's office. I checked out books by Mark Twain, Jack London and B. M. Bower.

GAMES & SPORTS

There was no TV and very little radio in my youth. Uncle Russell Kelsey made our family a **three tube radio** which could only get WFAA in Dallas, WBAP in Fort Worth, and Dr. Brinkly, the goat gland doctor in Del Rio. So we had plenty of time for the wholesome entertainment of a country town. At school we had the usual games of baseball, basketball, football, volleyball and **crack the whip**. We also played **hide and seek, kick the can** and **anny over; see-sawed, walked on stilts, shinny, kick the can, pitched washers and horseshoes, spun tops and yoyos,** and **shot marbles** while the girls **played jacks**.

We had **mud ball fights** on the unpaved streets and **corn cob fights** at the barn.

There was much music at church and **fiddling at square dances** in the country. Everyone had a **Jew's harp** and **harmonica**. A few could play a guitar, banjo or ukulele. We played **dominoes, Forty-Two, Mah Jong,** card games and checkers.

There was the **swimming hole** and the gin ponds for fishing and **swimming nude**—no one had a bathing suit.

On Halloween we nearly wrecked the town with mischief—**putting horses in the superintendent's office at night, mounting a Ford car on top of a store, letting people's livestock out, scaring the chickens off their roost**. It was all trick and no treat.

There were always **wrestling matches** and **fist fights, calf riding and roping, whittling, frog gigging, possum and coon hunts, raising pigeons, having your own dog, robbing a bee hive, attending a circus** (Sells-Floto Circus came to Paris), **traveling carnivals, medicine shows**, and **rodeos**. We attended **Chatauqua lectures** in Paris, played baseball against neighboring towns and went to **Boy Scout camp where I learned to shoot dice**. We watched **Juneteenth celebrations**, the **Holy Rollers entranced** and **Baptist immersion baptisms** in the gin pool.

An exciting event was **shooting off anvils** on holiday nights. This was something I heard but never saw. There is a small hole on the bottom of an anvil and two of them were filled with gunpowder. The bottom of one anvil was placed on the upturned bottom of the other so the gunpowder-loaded holes were opposite each other. A streak of gunpowder to the outside of the anvils acted as a fuse. The fuse was lit by a flame on the end of a pole which a person touched to the gunpowder fuse. When the gunpowder in the holes exploded, it pitched one anvil up in the air, made a noise heard for miles and shook the earth. One night a boy was badly injured by shooting off anvils. In spite of being crippled, the boy, Tom De Berry grew to become a prominent Texas senator in the 1930s.

Finally by age sixteen I became interested in girls—**necking girls** and **trying to have sex**. I had a car, **drank home brew, chewed tobacco, dipped snuff, spit** and **smoked**—all the things which changed me completely and drove my parents mad.

This is just part of the games and sports we enjoyed so you can see we had plenty to entertain us in those days before TV.

ACTIVITIES BEFORE I WENT TO MEDICAL COLLEGE

Robbing a melon patch

Tying a can to a dog's tail

Mowing lawns

Gunning up an old hoopy tin lizzy, flivver, jalopy, rattletrap

Taking stock to breed, horseback riding, calf roping and riding

Catching squirrels, coons, possums or birds and keeping them in a cage

Work on road building; labor in house building; painting country schools

Grease monkey in Kelsey Motor Company

Clothing salesman in dry goods store during Christmas season

Making homemade ice cream in a hand-cranked freezer

Milking the cow and leading her to pasture, slopping the hogs

Making blackberry wine; picking blackberries

Raising pigeons; gigging bull frogs

Rabbit hunting on Saturdays, coon hunting at night, running trot lines

Hunting for arrowheads on our farm

Fishing trips in Oklahoma; horseback riding in Throckmorton

Catching butterflies, grasshoppers, July flies, stink bugs and daddy longlegs

Riding freight trains and hitching rides

Interscholastic league debating; Sunday School; Epworth League

Raising a two-acre cotton crop; riding the cultivator

Shucking corn and taking it to the grist mill; shocking oats

Mischief on Halloween night: Making ghost sounds by rubbing resin on a string attached to a window screen (see *Making of a Doctor*)

The carnival: Ferris wheel, a flying jinny, nigh half-naked girls, a bearded lady, a high dive, a merry-go-round and a shooting range for prizes

Gathering pecans, black walnuts, hickory nuts, persimmons and mustang grapes in Sulphur Red River Bottoms

*Bonita Kelsey holds her newborn grandson
Thomas Kelsey with Mavis and Mary Kelsey
and with sons John and Cooke, Dayton, Ohio, July 1944.*

Descriptions *of* People

❖

IT TAKES ALL KINDS OF PEOPLE.

I*have divided descriptions of people into groups according to their place in society, their physical traits and their personal qualities. These are the words and sayings that help us identify and stratify our acquaintances.*

OUR FAMILY AND ACQUAINTANCES

I called my parents Mother and Dad but most of my Deport friends called their parents Mama and Papa or Ma and Pa. My parents called their parents Mama and Papa. I called my grandparents Nanny and Papa and Granny and Paw. Aunts were often called Aunty. The unmarried were called **old bachelors** *and* **old maids.** *Pregnant wives were described* **as being in a family way.** *I didn't know any couples* **living in sin** *in Deport; however, there were some bastards (children born* **out of wedlock)** *when there had been* **some hanky panky going on.** *There were several* **widders, grass widows,** *and* **widdowers** *in town. The head of the household was often called* **the old man.**

So's your old man was a derogatory expression. The wife was called **the old lady.**

Some older couples **kept company,** but unmarried couples living together was unheard of; they could have been **run out of town**.

Most families referred to their children as a **chile, chillum, brats, kids, tots, young sprouts, young 'uns, little tykes** and **little squirts**. They soon got **too big to nurse** but still could be a **crybaby** or **not dry behind the ears**.

A person was sometimes referred to as **a body**. Country people were known in many ways: **tacky, hicks, from the sticks, hayseeds, country cousins, greenhorns, green as a gourd, seedy** and **ignoramuses**. On the other hand there were **city slickers, high-society folks, the well-to-do, the old guard, high brows** and **low brows**.

In my youth we were still **Rebels** and **Proud Southerners** in contrast to **Damn Yankees** and **Nawtherners**. Our great-grandparents had slaves and plantations which were wiped out by the Civil War, otherwise known as the **War of Northern Aggression**. My **great, great grandfather** Thomas Gill Kelsey, father of eighteen children, had seven sons who fought in the Confederate Army. There were still Confederate veterans in Deport who celebrated with **squirrel stews** at the Deport Methodist Church. I remember Uncles Steve and Nate Grant and Till Woodard to this day. Everyone called them "uncle". Many counties had statues of Confederate soldiers on the courthouse grounds.

There were many World War I veterans in town including my Uncle Russell Kelsey who had been wounded in France. The Infantry veterans were called **grunts**, the **Marines** were **leathernecks** and sailors were **old salts**. These veterans built the American Legion Hall where community gatherings were held. They had a **croquet court** on the lawn where I often played. On the north side of the hall was the **volunteer fire truck station** and the **telephone central operator** was next. Central operated the **telephone exchange** from her house. She kept up with the goings on in Deport and knew how to locate anyone you wished to talk to. On foreign duty during World War II we called the portable phone **the horn**. Veterans got in the habit of calling the phone the horn. An example: **"You're wanted on the horn."**

There were some businesses in Deport during the early 1900s which no longer exist. J. R. Westbrook opened a general merchandise store in the late 1800s. Before the Paris and Mount Pleasant Railroad came through about 1905, Westbrook supplied his store by hauling in his stock by **oxen-drawn wagons**. He picked up his stock at Jefferson, Texas, the inland port on Red River, and hauled it over the Chocktaw Trail to Deport. Albert Singleton operated a large blacksmith shop where he shod horses and mules and repaired farm implements. I liked to watch him heat the metal to red-hot in his forge and hammer it into useful articles on his anvil. He and Dad and Dr. Steve Grant often went fishing on Glover River in Southeastern Oklahoma and deer hunting in the Texas Hill Country.

George Porterfield ran a **cobbler and leather shop**. He made fine leather harnesses for the hundreds of mules used in growing cotton. He made a leather case for Dad's Browning shotgun which I kept for more than fifty years.

Mr. Ferguson ran the **gristmill** where he made our cornmeal from the shelled corn we brought him. There was a picture show, open on Saturday afternoon and night, where I saw my first movie, "The Battle of the Alamo". The Shumans operated a two-story wooden hotel which was patronized by **traveling salesmen**. Later young Tom Ferguson opened an icehouse. He married the Shuman girl and became an auto mechanic at Kelsey Motor Company where he remained for many years.

The Kelseys operated the Deport Hardware Company and Kelsey Motor Company on Main Street. In my teens I worked there as a **grease monkey** and **car washer**. Before filling stations, the Kelseys sold gasoline from a pump in front of the store. Soon after this a filling station opened. We hung out there when I starting driving and **chasing girls**. The automobile **took holt awful fast** (became popular very rapidly). It changed our lifestyle completely. For me it provided a place to **neck the girls** when we **parked on a lonesome road**.

There were three **gins** and a **cotton seed oil mill**. They stayed open twenty-four hours a day during cotton-picking time.

The Barretts had a **cleaning and pressing shop** and sold me a custom-made suit for $15 while I was in medical school. Their son Pete Jack Barrett became a very wealthy man living in Harrison, Arkansas. He flew his own plane until recently. We visited by phone every few months before he died in the summer of 2011.

Mack Grant had a furniture store and funeral home where you could go right in and pick out a bed or a casket. His son James ran the business until recently.

Doctor Steve Grant had a two-story hospital called the Deport Sanitarium. Miss Rhoda Oliver was the nurse-anesthetist. Although many farmers were driving Ford cars (**Flivvers** or **Tin Lizzies**), there was still a **livery stable** in Deport. A few people rode into town on horseback and hitched their horses to posts or left them in the livery stable to be fed, bred, or seen by the horse doctor (or vet) or to do a little **horse trading** or buy a gentle old mare for the kids to ride to school. The kids hitched their horses in the city tabernacle next door to the school. Many towns had a tabernacle. This was years before school buses. Some kids rode on horseback four miles to school. Some rural mail carriers were still **carrying the mail** on horseback.

Albert Singleton, the only one of the **blacksmiths** I knew, kept the horses and mules shod. Horses were always dropping their horseshoes. We picked them up to pitch horseshoes and nailed one on the barn door for good luck.

Even little Deport had a jewelry store. I still remember well when Dad took me in there in 1929 to buy a watch for my high school graduation present. It was an Elgin watch in a white-gold case that had elaborate engraved designs on it. Eighty-five years later it still runs if I wind it up. I wore it in my vest pocket. In 1936 when I became an AOA honor graduate at the University of Texas Medical Branch Medical College in Galveston, I wore the AOA medal on my **watch chain**. Wesley West gave me a gold wristwatch in 1949 when I came to Houston to practice medicine, so I put my **pocket watch** away.

Another Deport facility was the **calaboose** (jail). It was a small one-room wooden building with no facilities except a bunk and a **piss pot**. It was right on Main Street in plain sight in the business district. If the constable (the local law officer and sometimes **bootlegger**) who jailed you didn't release you the next morning, he hauled you up to the county jail in Paris for the sheriff to take over. I was put in the calaboose one night for being rowdy in the pool hall of the Masonic Lodge. The next time I was taken to jail was in 1942 in Anchorage, Alaska. I was a 29-year-old flight surgeon medical officer. I was flown up from the Aleutian Islands with a group of fighter pilots for a brief furlough. That night we all went to town, got drunk and started a fistfight with some infantry officers in front of the saloon. The cops hauled us in to the local jail to sober us up before they released us to the air base the next morning.

We had three churches in Deport, the Baptist church, the Presbyterian church and the Methodist church which my grandfather helped build when he moved to Deport in 1908. We called the pastor or minister of the gospel **preacher** and he addressed us as **Brother** or **Sister**. I attended church and the **Epworth League** regularly as well as the **outdoor revival meetings** each summer. Dancing wasn't allowed in Deport but the **Antones** invited us young people over to their house to dance by **Victrola music**.

Most every white person in Deport was a southern Anglo-Saxon Protestant. There was one prominent family of French origin, the Antones, from Louisiana I believe, but we never called them Cajun. They liked frog legs which I **gigged** in the **gin ponds** and sold to them. A Jewish family moved in and opened a dry goods store. The store had a going-out-of-business sale every year.

There was an old ex-slave who lived near the railroad bridge. He liked to talk about his slave days where he had been happy and well treated. I visited him several times. A large Negro population lived in Deport. They did labor and farm work, especially the handling of the mules. The women did housework. I remember Bess who often helped Mother. The blacks (**colored folks, niggers**) had their own church and school. Unfortunately they were strictly segregated and couldn't come on Main Street. They drank out of a different **dipper** at the water cooler in our store, even though they cooked and served our food.

There have always been folk words, vernacular and slang words to describe people's physical appearance. People are frequently nicknamed for their physical appearance.

I was never aware of racism until I attended Texas A&M. There they called Italians **Wops**; Jews, **J-folks**; Mexicans, **Greasers**; Germans, **Krauts** or **Dutch**; Cajuns, **Coonasses**; Poles, **Bohunks**; Middle Eastern students, **Camel-herders**; Chinese, **Chinks**; and Japanese, **Japs**. These appellations were used in jest and meant no offense or racial slur. Racial equality prevailed at A&M except for the blacks who were discriminated against nationwide. Since that segregated time, I have lived to see a black president of the United States.

There was also stratification among the **white folks**. We had nothing to do with **white trash**; **pore folks**, **sharecroppers**, or **migrant cotton pickers**. **Farm hands** and even people who didn't go to church (**backsliders**) were looked down on.

There was only one Republican with a family in town. He was the postmaster and had to bcomee a Republican to hold his job when a Republican was elected president.

Mavis and Mary Kelsey with son John, Beaumont, Texas, 1942.

SAYINGS ABOUT CHILDREN

Parents who are afraid to put their foot down have children who will step on their toes.

Children evoke many well-known expressions. Many are vernacular sayings passed down from parents to children. Most sayings about children are meant to train them to take care of themselves and are meant to be affectionate and loving.

In spite of the present methods of teaching, I believe **rote memory** is still the best way to learn some subjects. Outside the school room we learn by rote memory all our lives. It is a part of normal brain function. Repetition establishes lasting circuitry of brain cells.

Another way to impress on our memory is by exciting or traumatic experiences, events we will never forget. That's why we say, "**Burned once, never again**." It's why corporal punishment or **tough love** judiciously applied by parents can teach us to behave. I will never forget when my mother applied a **peach tree switch** to me for using **bad words**. To this day that switching still makes me watch my speech, even in this book. I can remember a **paddling** given me by the Deport school superintendent for **cutting up** in class. I still try to behave and **not be a jerk** in gatherings. I deserved a lot more **lickings** than I received.

In my time punishment came in several forms: a spanking on a bare butt; a switching with a peach tree switch; a whipping with a razor strap by my dad; and paddling with a wooden paddle by the school superintendent. I gave and I received paddlings during hazing while I attended Texas A&M College.

Corporal punishment so often leads to child abuse that it is now prohibited in schools and is no longer accepted in most homes. Unfortunately, some of the meanest of all sayings are directed to children, even to the smallest of them. This is harassment, the same as physical abuse. Thousands of children die from physical abuse every year. The situation does not seem to improve. More and more children are born out of wedlock, often to drunken or drug-impaired parents. These children are the most vulnerable.

Under the best circumstances, raising children can be a trying experience, both for parents and the grandparents who are often obliged to raise them. One grandparent said it all, **"Stay away from kids."** (Barbara Bush quoted in Laura Bush's autobiography).

The teacher's pet	She's a keeper
Wash behind your ears.	The tooth fairy
Don't say or do that again.	Peck's bad boy
Big girls don't cry.	Look here, look at me
Don't spill your milk.	Be quiet; don't talk back.
Chew your food good.	Give me a kiss.
Don't take big bites.	No means no.
Clean your plate.	Do your lessons.
Make up your bed.	Pay attention to me.
Now, that's better.	Clean up your mess.
I didn't mean to do it.	Stop making excuses.
I won't do it again.	Look, Mom, no hands!
Sleep tight.	He twisted my arm.
Be quiet.	Just look at you.
Playing house	He punched me in the belly.
Little Miss Goody Too Good	Just wait till I get you home.
Miss Prissy	You'll wish you had never seen me.
Say your prayers.	Take back what you said.

DISCIPLINE AND ABUSE

Drop your drawers and bend over.	Go sit still till I tell you to get up.
I'm gonna paddle your little hiney.	Don't tease her.
I'll give you what for.	Mother knows best.
Slap him in the face.	Go stand in the corner.
Blister his butt.	Give him a licking.
I'm gonna knock your ass off.	Take a razor strap to him.
He whacked him over the head.	Quit crying.
Stand still, stand up, stand straight.	The kids are going after each other.
Don't pinch me, don't pull my ear.	I'm gonna beat the devil out of you.
Get a switching with a peach tree switch.	Cross your heart and hope to die.

You know as well as I do that you did it.

A tween (between childhood and teenhood).

Go stand in the corner with your face to the wall.

If you don't behave I'm gonna skin you alive.

Don't let me catch you doing that again.

Sit still, don't say a word, don't move a muscle.

Say "I'm sorry, I did it" a hundred times.

I'll send you to bed without your supper.

I don't know what I'm going to do with you.

Now I lay me down to sleep, I pray the Lord my soul to keep.

Let your child's first lesson be obedience and the second will be what you wish.

SLEEP: Sweet dreams, sleep tight, snooze away, sleepyhead, bedwetting, sweet bye-and-bye.

Mavis and Mary Kelsey, Charlotte Wilson, John Kelsey, Mr. and Mrs. Cooke Wilson and Fay Wilson, Beaumont, Texas, 1942.

SAYINGS ABOUT GIRLS AND WOMEN

There were many names for **female girls** (to point out she was not a **tomboy**): **gal**, **girlie**, **filly**, **heifer**, **doll** and **dish**. As they grew up they **titted** or **sprouted tits**. When full grown, girls were known as **skirts**. Yankees called them **broads**.

There were many allusions to a woman's beauty. She could be **good looking**, **easy looking**, **take your breath away**, **pretty as a picture** or **a peach**, **peachy**, **a plum**, **apple pie**, **the apple of my eye**, or **a real dish**. She might be **kind as an angel**, **a jewel**, **cute as a tater** or **cute as a pussy cat**. Women could also be **a piece of work**, **curvy** or **attractively packaged**. She could have a **nice figure** or a **cute ass**. She could have **ample breasts (a tit bit)**, a **nice ass**, **flat belly**, or **shapely legs**. Or today she may have **big boobs** or be **portly, stocky, stout, rotund, well-upholstered, buxom** or **hefty**. She may be **queen size**, **pleasingly plump, well-proportioned, voluptuous** or even **formidable** and **Amazonian**. She could be **slender**, petite, **skinny, willowy, svelte, dapper, natty, spry** or **scrappy**.

If she had a **fat ass**, she had **a lot of junk in her trunk**. She could be **sweet sixteen**, a **social butterfly, loaded with personality**, a **glamour girl**, a **cool cat**, a **joy to the eye**, a **beauty queen**, a **sweetheart**, a **knock out**, a **doozy**, or a **honey of a girl**. She could be **drop-dead gorgeous**, a **showcase of talent**, a **pretty girl**, a **good-looking girl**, a **sweet little baby girl, clean as a whistle, clean as the driven snow, easy to like**, a **three-ring circus all in herself**, have **a lot of personality**, be a **one-of-a-kind**, or a **woman of many talents**. She's **got everything it takes and then some**. She is **somebody else** or **something special**. She **has it all**. She's **the bell cow**, a **hot potato**, a **hot tamale**, a **hot mama**, a **sweet mama, sweet as sugar**, or a **petite blond**. She's the **it girl** or **she navigates her own course**.

On the other hand, a woman could be **a mess, a bitch, ugly as homemade sin, a cat** or **bear cat** or **a sweet vicious old lady**. Some folks said there were two kinds of girls: **nice girls** or **girls who put out**. Unfortunately, some old women were and still are called **old crones, old hags, old biddies** and **old crocks.**

Not so bad girls could be described as a **babe in the woods**, a **wallflower**, the **weaker sex**, a **made-over girl, fancy pants**, a **mama's baby, set in her ways**, a **tacky country girl**, just a **plain Jane, being a good girl**, a **stay-at-home mom**, a **funny girl**, a **surrogate mother**, a **single mother**, a **daffy wacky woman** or a **hot mama**.

Bad girls could be described as a **push-over**, a **brazen hussy**, a **floozy**, **someone who puts out**, a **shady lady**, a **sporting girl**, a **hooker**, a **street walker**, a **madam, in the oldest profession, hot** or a **flapper**. She could have a **mean streak** or be **an uppity woman**. She could be **flat-assed**, have **big tits** or be **ugly as a mud fence**.

SAYINGS ABOUT BOYS AND MEN

Boys were referred to as **young colts, young sprouts, toddlers, a brat, a mama's baby** and sometimes as **the new kid on the block**. A male could **talk tough, be brash and bellowing, shoot from the hip, think big** or be **full of grit**. You could **depend on him**. He could be a **heavy hitter** or a **thin wisp of a man**, be a **stuffed shirt, sly as a fox**, a **high-class man**, or **full of piss and vinegar**. He could be a **feather merchant**, a **power player**, a **pillar of strength**, on his toes, a **strong man**, a **manly man** or a **big gun**. He might be the **big cheese**, a **hot shot**, **brave as a lion**, **big time**, a **regular guy** or a **right-hand man**.

Some were referred to as a **dude**, a **big buddy**, a **big daddy**, a **playboy**, a **shavetail**, a **fat cat**, a **whiz kid**, a **daredevil**, a **high roller**, or a **wheeler-dealer**. Others were described as a **big wig**, a **powerhouse**, **one of God's gentlemen**, **Mr. Nice**, **you can depend on him**, a **straw boss**, **top gun**, a **big gun**, a **stem-winder**, or **hard-nosed**. Some had plenty of **spunk**, **guts** or **grit**, were **hard as a rock**, **rough-hewn**, **the last of his tribe**, a **wisp of a man**, a **big fish in a little pond**, or a **BMOC (big man on campus)**. Some were just an **ordinary guy**, a **go, go guy**, an **average Joe**, **Joe six-pack**, a **nice guy**, a **nice kid**, a **self-made man**, a **clean-cut man**, a **man about town**, a **jolly good man**, a **man of his own**, a **man of his word** or **a man who has a lot of get up and go**.

There was **Slim** and **High Pockets** for a tall guy. He could have been **skinny as a rail**. A short guy might have been called **Squatty** or even **Dusty** since his butt got dusty because it was close to the ground. A classmate at A&M was called **Whale** (Terry) because he was so large. A longtime friend at medical school was called **Jumbo** (Blocker). Both these men became prominent physicians. One of my nicknames was **Lefty**, obviously because I was left-handed.

Other common words defining physical appearance: **fat as a pig**, **hairy as an ape**, **strong as a bull**, **big as a barn**; a **hulk**; a **hunk** and a **gentle giant**; **rawboned** or **muscle-bound**; **scrawny**, **scraggy** or **lanky**; **stocky** or **chubby**; or **bald as a cueball**; **wrinkled as a prune**, **baby-faced**, **double ugly** and **magnificently ugly** (an oxymoron). I am **deaf as a post** and **can't hear it thunder**, and I am **as clumsy as a bull in a china closet**.

My best friend was Dr. Red Butt, a **redhead** who died recently at 98 years. A Deport redhead was called **Pinky** all his life and a Texas humorist is **Kinky Friedman**. My partner Bill Seybold became **silvery grey**, then **white-headed**.

Favorable comments include the following: **sharp as a tack**, **rapier-witted**, **bright as a penny**, **a deep thinker**; **the real McCoy**, **a Jim Dandy**; **a smart cookie**, **cool as a cucumber**; **a Renaissance man**; **squeaky clean**, **straight as an arrow**, **a cut above**; **plugged in**; **hard as a rock**, **hot as a pistol**, **his head is screwed on right heads up**, **a good egg**, **the top dog**, **a big daddy**, **a right hand man**; **a high brow** or **high caliber**.

Some descriptive sayings about personalities include: he's a **big shot**, he's **rich as Croesus**, **has the Midas touch**, **born with a silver spoon in his mouth**; **tight as Dick's hat band**, **Indian giver**, **a spendthrift**, **stingy**, **chinchy**, **close-fisted**, **skin flint**, **a penny pincher**, **tight wad**, **poor as Job's turkey**, **penny wise and pound foolish**; **tight as Scrooge** or **tight as a tick**; or **he's busted**.

He's the **cock of the walk**, **puts on airs**, a **clothes horse**, has a **cowboy**

image, is a great **ladies' man, struts his stuff, a stuffed shirt, struts like a peacock, a real dude, a big show off, a real stinker, a smart aleck, a loud mouth, stubborn as a mule, headstrong**, an **ornery cuss, good-for-nothing, no good, shiftless, trifling, bad egg, a stud, hot as a pepper, puffed up like a toad, full of himself**, got the **bighead, proud as a peacock**, and **thinks he can walk on water.**

He's **hale and hardy, frisky, spry, peart, clumsy, feisty, hard-boiled, street smart, tightly wound, fit as a fiddle, tough as a boot, a tough customer, fast as a deer**, has **plenty of spunk, hungry as a bear, a speed demon, more bark than bite, rough around the edges**, and **cusses like a sailor.**

He's **slow as molasses, sloppy and slouchy, sleeps like a log, happy-go-lucky, lazy bum, full of monkey shines, a put-on, a born musician, a slow poke, quirky, middle brow**, an **egghead, a maverick, wacky, a crackpot, screwball, nutty as a fruitcake, goofy, a geek, crazy as a bat, slipshod, funky, fruity, good-natured**, and **puts his foot in his mouth (foot-in-mouth disease).**

A lot of guys are **lowdown stinkers, a snake in the grass, a skunk, a pissant, crooked as a barrel of snakes, a dirty dog, a dog in the manger, a horse's ass, a Trojan horse, a lowdown dirty villain, as slick as owl grease, a sneak, mean as the devil, a wolf in sheep's clothing**, and **no earthly good.**

Some people are **full of baloney, full of malarkey, full of hot air, a bag of wind**, or **a real feather merchant.** There are **apple polishers, ass-kissers, stuck up, genuinely bogus, perfectly rotten, a gutless so-and-so, a sad sack,** an **abomination, a jackleg, not worth two bits, a sleazeball, a jerk, a good for nuthing rascal**, an **SOB, a thorn in my side, a burr under the saddle, an albatross around my neck**, or a **PMB** (poor miserable bastard).

Some people aren't so bad. They are just: **cranky, crabby, fussy, stubborn as a mule**, have a **short fuse, downright creepy, cold as a fish, a light weight, a milk toast, afraid of his shadow, hardheaded, a pill, a pig, set in their ways, sour as a pickle, a crybaby, gossipy, a rumor mill, a goof ball, fat head, mule head, bull-headed, a sore head, a sorry cuss, a sore ass**, or a **well-meaning pain-in-the-ass.**

One of the worst insults is to impugn someone's intelligence. It's a **dirty trick**, not often done to a person's face but often to his back. He's **dumb as an ox, a dumbbell, has a small mind, dumb as dirt**, or **dull as dishwater.** He's **clear as mud, thick-headed, knuckle-headed, a fathead** or, worst of all, **a pinhead.** He's **brainless, a birdbrain, green as a gourd, a greenhorn, a nitwit**, has no **gumption** and **won't get to first base.** His mind is a **blank slate.** He **can't cut the mustard.**

Major Mavis Kelsey, Adak, Aleutian Islands, Alaska, World War II, 1942.

Lt. Col. Mavis P. Kelsey at a party, Wright Patterson Field, Dayton, Ohio, 1945.

Spouts off at the mouth	An ass-kisser
Has diarrhea of the mouth	Underdog
Talks a blue streak	Snake-bit
Has his foot in his mouth	A queer duck
Flannel mouth	Out of money
A naysayer	Tight-fisted
A tattletale	Penny-pincher
A gossip; a wag	A stiff
Rapier-tongued	A back-slapper
Blabbermouth	A tree-hugger
Bad mouth	A crockpot
A know-it-all	High-handed
A rabble-rouser	A hen-pecked husband
A drudge	Quirky
A sad iron	Scapegoat
A sucker	A hog
A clod-hopper	A wet blanket
Sponger	Slick as grease
Baby-kisser	Scatterbrained
Icky	A creep
A real pill	A drag
Gloomy Gus	A bluff
A goof-off	A nobody
All screwed-up	Kooky
A shine ass	A flake
A flop	The unwashed
A gold brick	Harebrained
Screwball	A blow-hard
A sad sack	A short fuse
A blabbermouth	A nit-wit
A cheapskate	He just wants to get by.
A fly-by-night	Mealy-mouthed
A gone gander	A top water; a small fry
A miser	He's spooky.
Mooches off his neighbors	A weak link

A person of interest	Riff-raff
A party-pooper	A little devil
Slow as molasses	Flat out tough
Easy pickings	Out of hand
A nervous wreck	Big spender
Not playing with a full deck	A thorn in my side
Wacky	Not worth a tinkers damn
A hopeless case	Hot-blooded
A deadpan	Dirt-poor
The undivorced	Deaf as a post
A Johnny-come-lately	A scalawag
Conservative to the core	Is bad news
Too hot to handle	A piker
A busy body	A public nuisance
A do-gooder	Crazy as a bat
A glutton for punishment	A tin horn
Carries his feelings on his shoulder	Such a bother
Doesn't fit the mold	A pain in the ass
Weak as a kitten	A downer
A spin doctor	Allergic to work
A bar fly	A glad hander
A spoiled brat	A straggler
A social climber	A nerd
A high flyer	A gadabout
Ham actor	A screwball
A dark horse	A feather merchant
A dimwit	A grind
A rooky	A has-been
Slap-happy	A throw-back
He's full of hot air.	A crackpot
A wimp	A weirdo
A pipsqueak	A joke
A laughingstock	A scapegoat
A bighead	A quirk
Goofy	Gawky

A flat tire	Sloppy
Lounge lizard	Has an ugly side
Half-pint	Funky
A piece of work	A duffer
A square	Nerd
A cup-cake	A straggler
A heel	A wild card
A creep	A drip
Ignoramus	A couch slouch
Has bats in his belfry	A wimp
A worry-wart	Crappy
Snobby Cheesy	Tipsy
Hacker	A sponger
Hunk	Tightwad
Dirtball	A loud mouth
A queer	Sour-puss
A pop-off	Two-faced
A dumbbell	A scatterbrain
Too big for his britches	Lazybones
Always looking for a fight	Stuck up
Busted out at the seams	Rawboned
Hell on wheels	An upstart
A windy	A goofy
From the wrong side of the tracks	

BAD PEOPLE

A Frankenstein	Free-loader
A real stinker	A mad man
Hustler	Bogus
Deadbeat	A brawler
A drug czar	A jerk
A pure-dee bum	Raunchy
A real flake	No account
A rotten egg	Trash mouth
Sleezeball	The guy in the black hat

Schoolyard bully	A gun-slinger
Four flusher	A jihadist
Scam	A phony
Two-timer	A double cross
A hustler	A mobster
A liar and a cheat	A trouble-maker
A scoundrel	A jackass
A snake in the grass	A horse's ass
A fagin	A no good
A villain	A worm
A goon	A hooligan
A grafter	A voracious predator
A con man	The lowest of the low
A sneak thief	Rotten to the core
A fraud	Rotten egg
A dead head	Out for blood
A hit man	No earthly good
Pick-pocket	A slob
Cold-blooded killer	At the best unreliable
A big time crook	At the worst fraudulent
Raging, ranting and raving	A no account
Backbiting; backstabbing	Hooligans
Slippery as an eel	A punk
Was caught red-handed	She's knocked up.
A dog in the manger	She's gone astray.
A dead-beat dad	Genuinely bogus
A crook; A loser	Perfectly rotten
A loan shark	A Peeping Tom
A card sharp shark	A stool pigeon
A Dr. Jekyll & Mr. Hyde	Mean as the Devil
Out-of-control train-wreck of a person	Highjacks and stick 'em up artists

CHAPTER FOUR

The Kelsey boys:
John, Cooke, Tom and Mavis, Jr.,
Beaumont, Texas, summer 1948.

The Good & The Bad

BAD AND GOOD ARE ENTWINED WITH ROPE. *(Chinese proverb)*

Many folk expressions register pleasure or displeasure with people or situations. There are many more complaints than positive remarks. Perhaps folks take the good for granted and offer few compliments, but when they are unhappy they are quick to complain or criticize.

We live by omens for the good and bad. An omen is an occurrence or phenomenon supposed to portend some future event or to foretell by signs or portends.

Mary Randolph Wilson at rehearsal dinner. 1939

GOOD AND BAD

The good news first, then the bad.

The best of times and the worst of times.

You are either a hero or a zero in the end.

They are falling into one camp or another.

What went right and what went wrong?

Keep 10 yards from a horse, 100 yards from an elephant but the distance you keep from a wicked man can never be measured. (Asian proverb)

FAVORABLE COMMENTS

Man, that's livin'	A smash hit
Mouthwatering good	Going full throttle
Good luck	Right down my alley
Feeling my oats	Love one another
Belle of the ball	A true believer
Sweet talk	Home folks
You lucky dog	A bright spot
Life's a bowl of cherries	He goes the distance.
Bread on the waters	The power of prayer
Ahed and Ohed	A standout
Made a good meal outta nothing	Dressed to a fare-thee-well
Might nigh as nice	Too good to be true
On the sunny side	Hitting his stride
Apple pie order	A brand new world
Had it in spades	The gift of life
Saddle a winner	Nice going
Got it down pat	Clinched the victory
Smooth sailing ahead	Three cheers
A good time was had by all.	A win for the home team.
Right from the start	Cutting a rug
Lots of know-how	Stroke of good fortune
Free for the asking	Happy hunting grounds
Stepping stone to success	Being sexy
Easy as shooting fish in a barrel	The joy of giving
Clean as a whistle	She's straight as an arrow.

Snug as a bug in a rug	The sunny side
Tender as a mother's love	How sweet it is
Crystal clear	Life on the upswing
I'm having a ball	A place of honor
Window of opportunity	Family friendly
A glimmer of hope	Neat and tidy
Starts the ball rolling	In high spirits
A blessing in disguise	Playing it cool
Easy as pie	Lucky or just plain good
A good try	Warm relationships
Free as the wind	Thumbs up
Dodged the bullet	Just me, myself and I
Packs a wallop	Squeaky clean
Fit as a fiddle	Golden opportunity
Just right	The gift of thanks
Never looked so good	No problema
Houston will percolate right along.	Have a good day
Over the top	A step in the right direction
Without a care	Down lover's lane
Getting better all the time.	On easy street
A barrel of fun	We'll be there with bells on.
In high cotton	Down memory lane
In La-La Land	Delighted to be here
It's a larkShe's a sweetheart.	
The stamp of approval	Mother was right.
A howling success	Winning ways
The pick of the litter	Reaping rewards
A good eye and a steady hand	A token of friendship
It's a breeze	A glamorous girl
Work is my blessing.	Embracing the underdog
Attaboy	I'll drink to that.
He makes the grade.	Unconditional love
You did good.	As good as it gets
Living the good life	A winning streak
Friendly as a pup	Passing muster

Full of piss and vinegar	Like a breath of fresh air
As easy as 1, 2, 3.	Through thick and thin
Manna from Heaven	Doing a good job
A green thumb	Good will
An act of God	The seal of approval
The milk of human kindness	Joy in your heart
Lands a winner	Loved ones
On cloud nine	A pillar of strength
The good old days	The welcome mat
A man of his word.	Sets his sights high
Hit the jackpot	A friendly word
Sexy dress	The good stuff
Getting a green light	Picture perfect
A lot of get up-and-go	A feather in his cap
Some good eating; finger lickin' good	Cooking with gas
A jolly good fellow	We got off lucky.
The love bug has got you.	A joy to the eyes
Happy as a lark	Getting ahead
Live a happy, healthy life.	Alive and kicking
Hit it lucky	A kinder, gentler world
Blowing kisses	Earning brownie points
A window of opportunity	Kid-friendly
A job well done	Easy as falling of a log
Loaded with dough	Fare-thee-well
There's not a lazy bone in his body.	On the gravy train
We've got it made in the shade.	A lead pipe cinch
I'm back in the saddle.	Right as rain
He came out smelling like a rose.	In seventh heaven
He's a big small town hero.	Spunky; full of spirit
In the lap of luxury	The time of my life
True to his word	Full of vim and vinegar
Forgive and forget	Full steam ahead
A social butterfly	Running on all four
A breath of fresh air	A cup of kindness
A barrel of love	It makes mom smile.

He's a man after my own heart.	Putting on the Ritz
We've got 'em on the run.	A win-win situation
That sounds like music to my ear.	Keep the good times rolling.
Pure as the driven snow	Happy days are here again.
Spit and polish	The best days of my life.
I'm in the know	This will make you laugh.
Giving back to your country	It makes life worth living.
Busy as a beaver	I never had it so good.
The more the merrier	Thank God for small favors.
We're on the right track.	Let the good times roll.
My heart jumped with joy.	Shipshape
I'll go to bat for you.	A world of fun
She kept her cool.	Red carpet treatment
She holds the cards.	Everlasting love
It's right up my alley.	Made in Heaven
We're just rolling and rolling.	Home sweet home
A person of boundless energy	Sealed with a kiss
The land of milk and honey	Smiling eyes
He hit the jackpot.	Flush with success
He's running with the big dogs.	A man of his own
Hitting on all the right notes	We pulled it off.
We hit it off.	The comeback kid
The comfort zone	The go-to guy
A few good men	I can make it.
A small amount of glee	In a fine fettle
A storybook ending	Doing God's work
Good clean fun	The silver bullet
An upbeat view	The good life
Don your comfies.	My cup runneth over.
Do the right thing.	Stars in their eyes
I like your looks.	Buoyed up
Ain't she sweet.	A bed of roses
A spring in his step	He has it all.
In a blaze of glory	Higher purpose
Sweet sixteen	Takes the cake

A honey of a deal	Mi casa es su casa.
Riding high	Walked away winning
A healthy marriage	A labor of love
Happy ever after	Gets an "A" for effort
Holding his head high	Proud as a peacock
I'm in the pink.	Sales sizzled
Buckets full of love	Sitting on a big pile of dough
Old Glory	Road map to success
A cute package	Saved by the bell
He hit a home run.	He made a killing.
Put on a happy face	
Viewing the world through rose colored glasses	
Good friends, good food and comforts of home	

UNFAVORABLE COMMENTS

No good end	Messed up
Behind the eight ball	Cracking up
Jumped ship	Lazy bones
Kicked in the rear	A Pollyanna
Asleep at the switch	Wild and woody
A necessary evil	Falling through the crack
Next to nothing	Flew the coop
Wrought up	Thrown a curve
Damn the consequences.	The blame game
You unlucky bum.	It's rubbish.
Fallen on hard times	Counted him out
Can't cut the mustard	In the dust bowl
A kettle of fish	The tornado belt
Out of the frying pan, into the fire	Came away empty-handed
A heap of trouble	Screaming bloody murder
Knocked from his pedestal	Dead wrong
Touched a sore spot or a nerve	I ain't got nobody.
Rubbing salt in the wound	Hotter than Hades
Eating me out of house and home	He got out of hand.
Gave me a hard time	A big to-do about nothing

Leaves a bad taste	He's nuts.
The end of the line	Dead-beat dads
Hit rock bottom	He wound up dead.
Taking him down a peg or two	A string of bad luck
In the doghouse	Gone to pot
It's no picnic.	Madder than a wet hen
Too much on his plate	Dragging his feet
Taken to the woodshed	A dim outlook
Stung by bad news	Losing face
Up against it	Shot himself in the foot.
Blew his top	She was jilted.
Dropped the ball	Living in a fool's paradise
Won't get to first base	He got the axe.
He struck out.	Getting nowhere fast
Pulling the rug out from under him	A kick in the pants
Took a shellacking	Coming unglued
A bitter pill to swallow	Going to pot, to the devil
Adding insult to injury	He's licked.
From bad to worse	The worst of times
He got himself into this mess.	From honeymoon to heartbreak
A poison pill	Lost some of his marbles
Cheating on his wife	Missed the boat
Road rage	Heads to roll
Griping	Living on borrowed time
Time is not on our side.	I could do without you.
A shady business	Caught off guard
Bad loans	Sour grapes
Freezing your butt off	A helluva mess
A tantrum	An albatross around my neck
He went busted.	Lost his edge
Wipe Israel off the map (Iran)	Under fire
Chug holes	Choked off
Fueling fears	He smells.
On the wrong track	Takes a bite out
Running out of gas	He's bad news, a fluke.

Going nowhere fast	Let down
A back seat driver	Pie in the sky
Cheesy; tacky	Quaking in their boots
Pulled the plug on him	Being cowed
Hatred begets hatred	Life's a drag
A sinking feeling	Ran for the hills (gave up)
A shake down	A slap in the face
A bunch of goons	On the ropes
Hurling insults	Up to your ass in debt
A lousy year	A wolf in sheep's clothing
Asleep on the job	A house of cards
A bum rap	Stir crazy; cabin fever
A road block to justice	Going to the dogs
He fled the scene.	Going downhill
It doesn't add up.	He overdid
A fat chance	A half-ass job
Habitual lateness	Shame on you.
White-washing it	It's a nightmare.
He got soaked.	Rigged from the beginning
A fender bender	Wagging tongues
Gut-wrenching	It smells of trickery.
A house divided	The runt of the litter
A fly in the ointment	Left behind
A false alarm	Give me a break.
Played out	Truth is not in him.
Bank heists	A raw deal
Running out of steam	Double-crossed me
Laid up	I hate your guts.
Montezuma's revenge	He don't get it.
No lead in his pencil	Grin and bear it.
Had his way	Hard times
Living in sin	Thrown to the wolves
He made bad choices.	A throwback
Damning with faint praise	Empty promises
Verbal garbage	A stab in the back

Mealy-mouthed	A snow job
Hair pulling	Bad mouth it
Rabble rousers	Real stinker
Flat broke	Boiling mad
Left holding the bag	It doesn't set well.
In a blue funk	Plenty to be ashamed of
A dog in the manger	His thinker is puny.
Frying in your own grease	A wet blanket
Belching smoke stacks	A scalawag
A dead beat; a crook; a fraud	Considerable whiff: a stinker
A hustler; pickpocket	Pissed off
A scoundrel; a two-timer	Crop failure
A sponger; stool pigeon	Rotten spoiled
A scam, four flusher	Mean spirited
A sorehead	Friendship soured
Taken to the cleaners	A dirty trick
Way off base	Dirty work
He's a dead duck.	Cold blooded killers
Binge eaters-drinkers	A job-killing tax
Blindsided him	The lowest of the low
The bitter end	Knee-deep in trouble
Tarred and feathered	An inside job
Dark and bloody ground	Rotten to the core
A gone gander or goose	A bad- or rotten-egg
Getting his goat	DOA-dead on arrival
It gummed up the works.	Getting blackballed
He gets in my hair.	Set on him like a wild cat
High-handed	The very picture of hard times
Gone haywire	Going to hell in a hand basket
Hit below the belt	Caught in a bind
Left in the lurch	In over his head
Mad enough to bite nails	Botched the job
To rack and ruin	Coldcocked him
Sucking hind tit	Sour as a pickle
A tempest in a teapot	Poor as a church mouse

Lead poisoning (got shot)	Mud slinging
Teetering on the brink	He's gone to pot.
Playing the race card	A peeping Tom
Stone cold with no soul	Got his tail kicked
He didn't have a prayer.	He put his foot in it.
He spoils what he touches.	Hung out to dry
He can't win for loosing.	The empty saddle
They blew his cover.	He was lead to slaughter.
He needs to sharpen his pencil.	It blew up in his face.
The night was a downer.	Thrown for a curve
It's a kick in the ass.	She's got a mean streak.
They turned against him.	Caught red-handed
The bad news blew me away.	He spouts off at the mouth.
Getting out of hand	Thin-skinned
I ran out of juice—steam.	Two-faced
He lost his grip on it.	A pain in the ass
Oops, we've got a problem.	He's allergic to work.
He's out looking for trouble.	He was pink-slipped.
He's a liar and a cheat.	All downhill
He's ranting and raving.	You ain't getting nowhere.
He can't get to square one.	A fight to the finish
A whole string of problems	A moral cesspool
Sailing under false colors	Foul play
I lost my shirt on it.	Dry gulch him
He got the short end of the stick.	Dust him off.
He's running out of answers.	A necktie party
His money ran out.	The road to ruin
Sick and tired of it	Filled with hate
The well blew out, a dry hole.	This dog-eat-dog world
A firetrap	Kicking butts
He mooched off his neighbors.	A web of lies
You snooze, you lose.	He screwed things up.
Loose talk	Sowing seeds of fear
Overrated	He dropped the ball.
Digging up the dirt on him	Scorched earth

A lame excuse	I'm snake-bit.
A sleezeball	Wallowing in red ink
A gone gosling	The bottom fell out
Breeding mistrust	The road to corruption
A no-brainer	Worse than pulling teeth
A turncoat	He cracked under strain.
He got his ass in a sling.	I got knocked on my butt.
Something's rotten in Denmark.	He couldn't take it any longer
The blues; the dumps	Just a pure D bum
A top water	Getting hijacked
A dog's life	His mind was in the gutter.
A personality I can't handle	I'm in a pickle.
Getting ugly	The evil within us
A pip-squeak	Trumped-up charges
A brawler	A bitter backlash
A stool pigeon	A rude awakening
Slim pickings	Obscene gestures
I can't win for losing.	Out for blood
I'm give out.	A major blow
Bogged down; case of the droops	A cover up
Singing the blues	Not a chance in hell
A sour reception	Verbal dodges
Down in the dumps	Pseudo-speak
A rotten mood	White lies
A reject from the soap factory	Less than honest
Stupid in love	Screwed up
A shell game	Swimming upstream
A stinky mess	Foul output
Went busted	Anti-American
Muddying the water	The decline of civilization
Left out in the cold	The fox in the hen house
The fat is in the fire.	A cold reception
Sold down the river	His dark side
Taken for a ride	A mean streak
Up the creek without a paddle	Always griping

In a rut	Faced with problems
He's on the road to ruin.	Death claims him.
He fell by the wayside.	Less than cordial
Opening old wounds	Playing chicken
Hooked on drugs	The butt of a joke
In hot water	Bad mouth; loose mouth
Reigniting controversy	Dirty mouth, flannel mouth
He flunked out.	He's meaner than the Devil.
Drop dead!	Stuck up
They crammed it down our throats.	Too big for his britches
Getting a taste of his own medicine	
Damned if you do and damned if you don't	
The most out-of-control train-wreck of a person	

Mary and Mavis P. Kelsey on day of wedding, September 17, 1939, Beaumont, Texas.

OMENS

There are good omens and bad omens. There are many omens that give us warnings to keep us out of trouble. We confront omens all our lives. Some are universally known. Most omens are superstitions while some are founded in fact. Before you are born your mother was confronted with good omens which would lead to a healthy birth or bad omens which might lead to birthmarks, maybe big or little ears, or even deformities.

Some people think all omens are pure superstitions but, in spite of this, they can't keep from observing them. They still **avoid stepping on cracks in the pavement**. They fear **bad luck when a black cat crosses their path at night**. Or they **feel a little uneasy on Friday the 13th**. Some **pitch a coin in a fountain for good luck**. Others **cross their fingers to avoid a loss**. It's amazing how many people **carry luck pieces**. When I was a boy **we carried a rabbit's foot or a buckeye**. Most men's wallets contain a picture or a **special good luck coin**. I still carry the Social Security card that I was issued in 1937 when Social Security was enacted.

I believed that storks brought babies until I was nine years old when my brother John was born. I believed **Santa Claus lived at the North Pole** and **on Christmas Eve night he flew through space in a sleigh pulled by reindeer and went down our chimney with a sack full of presents to fill our stockings which were hung from the mantle**. I believed my mother when she told me that **Santa wouldn't bring me any presents if I had been a bad boy**. I was one of the children whose letter to Santa Claus was published in the Deport Times. Santa read it and brought me the present I requested.

SOME OMENS WE HAVE BELIEVED OR LIVED BY

Horses anticipate earthquakes.	Knock on wood.
Always bless your food.	Say "God bless you" after sneezing.
An apple a day keeps the doctor away.	A four leaf clover brings luck.
A horse shoe nailed over the door brings good luck.	
There's a pot of gold at the end of the rainbow.	
I cross my fingers to bring good luck.	
I "grabbed my left one" to help A&M win.	
At Christmas we hung up mistletoe so we could kiss the girls.	
Women wore new dresses on Easter Sunday.	
Throwing a coin in a fountain brings good luck.	
Being awakened by roosters crowing was good luck.	
Seeing a ladybug or a doodlebug brought good luck.	

Putting a lost tooth under your pillow so the tooth fairy would leave a coin.

I carried my bride over the threshold of our apartment for a happy home.

"Christmas Eve gift"—greeting to everyone you meet on Christmas Eve.

It's good luck to win the larger half when you break a wishbone.

Wherever you travel, pick up a rock for good luck (I still have a box of rocks that my wife Mary collected during our world travels).

A girl will soon get married if she finds a ring in her slice of a wedding cake or catches the bride's bouquet.

Some good luck pieces to carry: a rabbit's foot, a horse chestnut, a lucky coin or stone, a photo of a loved one

SOME BAD OMENS

Thirteen is an unlucky number.   The evil eye

Walking under a ladder brings bad luck.

A black cat crossing your path is a bad sign.

Wearing a hat in the house or opening an umbrella in the house is bad luck.

You got warts if you handled a toad.

Stormy weather on a wedding day brought a stormy marriage.

Getting up on the wrong side of the bed brings bad luck.

Lending salt will break up a friendship.

If someone thumbed his nose at you it meant you were a son-of-a-bitch. This was a serious accusation and you had to fight back to save your family honor. If you didn't fight back you were a coward.

OMENS WHICH WARN

It's bad luck to give a knife. Always get a coin as payment.

Don't eat fish on Friday.

Don't eat fish and drink milk at the same meal.

A rainbow in the morning, sailors' warning; a rainbow at night, sailors' delight

Carry a St. Christopher medal while traveling.

Never point your finger at someone.

Throw salt over your left shoulder to prevent bad luck.

Unpleasant experiences in pregnancy may cause birthmarks, big ears, even deformities such as club feet.

If you pick up a coin, it's good luck for you but it's bad luck for the person who lost it.

Don't go out in the rain with your pores wide open or you will catch a death of a cold (Mrs. D., Scott and White Clinic, 1930).

Dehorn calves when there's a full moon or they will bleed (Carl Paben at Live Oaks Ranch, 1970s). I didn't believe him and instructed Paben to dehorn when the moon was not full. Many of the calves bled profusely.

Plant all crops when the moon is right (Carl Paben). Carl and my wife Mary planted our ranch garden only during the full moon. We had a wonderful garden. Mary's mother, Mary Wilson, Sr. was a strong believer in planting according to the moon.

MORE OMENS

When your ears twitch, someone is talking about you.

Every good side has it's bad side.

A cat has nine lives.

Big ears mean you are smart.

Trick or treat on Halloween. If you didn't treat it was bad luck.

April Fool's Day was an unlucky day. Someone would trick you.

Oysters are aphrodisiacs.

You can make a girl want sex by giving her Spanish Fly.

Cats wail during a burial wake (I have actually witnessed this).

The bride should wear something borrowed and something blue at her wedding.

You can tell whether he loves you by taking off the petals of a daisy.

The groom should not see the bride on the wedding day until the wedding.

Lightning never strikes twice in the same place.

Rain, rain, go away; come again another day (effort to stop the rain).

Never awaken a sleeping baby or sleeping dog.

It's okay for a girl to propose marriage on February 29th on leap year (every fourth year).

Eating scrambled eggs will prevent a hangover (we lived by this omen when I was in medical school).

Being left-handed is bad luck and should be corrected by being taught to use your right hand. I was born left-handed and was forced to write with my right hand, but I still throw with my left arm.

Mary Randolph Wilson at about eighteen months old.

CHAPTER FIVE

Sayings About Your Body

WHEREVER THE HEAD GOES THE TAIL FOLLOWS.

"*Why do you behold the mote in your neighbor's eye but do not consider the beam in your own eye?" from Matthew 7:3 may be the best known Biblical metaphor about the human body. People are very aware of seeing and being alive. There are more sayings about the eyes and the heart than about all other members of the body.*

WORDS OF THE HEART
Folk language and everyday sayings contain many references to the heart, the seat of our affections. Most folks think of a kind, loving, warm *and* generous *heart but occasionally there are* cold-hearted, heartless, hardhearted *people who do bad things to other people. There can be* heartache, broken hearts, heart-wrenching *events, a* merry heart *and a* sad heart.

Black heart	I lost my heart.
Angry heart	The Devil's in your heart.
An envious heart	Within beats a heart of drama.
A fickle heart	My heart isn't in it.
A hard heart	Cold hands, warm heart
The heart of love: marriage	If you lose heart, all is gone.
Open up your heart.	Home is where the heart is.
The greatest of all, sweetheart	A heart-to-heart talk
Bless your heart	Playing hearts
Dear hearts and gentle people	A sickness in my heart
A place, or room, in my heart	Taking up space in my heart
An open heart	The heart of the matter
A loving heart	Change of heart
My heart's desire	A heartbeat away
Dear heart	The heartland
Purity of heart	Pulling at heart strings
Close to my heart	Heartless
Heart and soul	Heartbreak
From the heart	Heartthrob
Hearty	Half-hearted
Heartfelt	Faint of heart
Warm heart	A heart of gold
A noble heart	My heart jumped with joy.
Brave heart	A man after my own heart.
A youthful heart	Take heart.
Whole-hearted	It breaks my heart.
A generous heart	A heart full of love
A tender heart	A heart stopped.
A stout heart	Take it to heart.
A soft heart	Young at heart
Set your heart on it.	A heavy heart
The heart wants what it wants.	To steal the hearts of youth
She broke my heart.	It heartened us to great effort.
She bares her heart.	It's straight from the heart.
A big heart and a massive ego	Spoken from the heart.

I don't have the heart to do it.	A good-hearted guy
Faint heart never won fair lady.	My heart swells with thankfulness.
From honeymoon to heartbreak	I cross my heart and hope to die.
Thank you from the bottom of my heart.	It warms the cockles of my heart.

Absence makes the heart grow fonder (for somebody else).

Two souls with a single thought: two hearts that beat as one.

The heart of the wise man is like still water.

Where your treasure is there will be your heart.

What the world needs is more warm hearts and less hot heads.

Skinny knees are easier to fix than broken hearts.

The Mavis P. Kelsey, Sr. family,1958. From left: Thomas, Mavis, Sr., Cooke, Mary, John and Mavis Jr.

THE HEAD

Butting heads	He's got the big head.
I'll bash his head in.	Head hunters. Heads up.
A stiff upper lip. Keep your chin up.	By cheek and jowl
Long on tooth	From tooth to toenail
What a mug.	I was all ears.
An ear for an ear and a tooth for a tooth.	Play it by ear. Lend an ear.
The sage has large ears and a small mouth.	Your dome, noggin, puss, blinkers
You put words in my mouth.	They crammed it down our throats.
Put your money where your mouth is.	Keep your mouth shut.
Born with a silver spoon in his mouth	A hard nose, a schnozola
Don't get your nose bent out of joint.	Poked his nose in. Nosing around.
His nose is up in the air.	We were nosed out by a landslide.
Don't turn up your nose at me.	I thumbed my nose at him.
Don't cut your nose off to spite your face.	Don't stick your nose up in the air.
It's plain as the nose on your face.	It's no skin off my nose.
Nose to nose	Nosing out the competition
Paying through the nose	Talking through his nose
I smell a rat.	It doesn't pass the smell test.
By the skin of his teeth	He holds his head high.
Don't waste your breath.	She led him around by the nose.
Give lip service.	Zip your lip.
Tongue in cheek	

Let's get our heads together; Two heads are better than one.

The third ear hears what the others don't.

In one ear and out the other. He got an ear full.

Lips that touch liquor shall never touch mine.

That's one thing you're not going to hear out of my mouth

Don't stick your nose in other people's business.

STOMACH

Belly up, belly laugh, belly flop

That's hard to swallow.

I can't stomach that. I'll bust a gut trying.

Had the guts to do it. He had the spleen to say it.

The belly, craw, crop, gizzard, paunch, tummy, bay window, breadbasket

A belly laugh. A beer belly. Pot gut. Belly fat.

The way to the heart is through the stomach.

A full belly makes a dull brain. (Benjamin Franklin)

Let the guts be full, it's they that carry the legs. (Cervantes)

TAIL

My tail is dragging.

Kiss my ass. He's a pain in the ass.

Coon ass, bad ass, half ass, a cute ass

Up to my ass in alligators

I butted in. Butt out. Kicked in the rear.

Get off your ass and go to work.

Get your ass (or your behind) up here.

Cover up your privates; you're so gross.

If he doesn't keep his nose out of my business, I'll knock his rear off (*Wall Street Journal*, 29 April 2010).

LIMBS

I'm keeping my fingers crossed.	Footloose and fancy-free
I got my foot in it. I stepped in cow do.	Cool your heels. Close on his heels.
Foot-in-mouth disease	Fleet of foot. Light on his feet.
Getting cold feet	Caught flat-footed
Getting off on the right foot	Going toe to toe
Stay on your toes.	Kicking up your heels
Cold shoulder	Don't lift a finger.
I got a foothold.	I got a leg up on him.
Hot foot it home.	Landing on his feet.
One foot in the grave.	Rule of thumb.
A free hand.	A lefty.
Right-handed.	I elbowed my way in.
I rubbed elbows with him.	I muscled in.
I breasted it.	I strong-armed him.
Slue-footed	Knock-kneed
Double-jointed	

You better take care of your body. It's the only place you have to live.

CHAPTER SIX

Mavis P. Kelsey, at graduation, University of Texas Medical Branch Galveston, 1936.

Health, Sickness, Old Age & Death

I GUESS I'M GOING TO KEEP ON LIVING AND CAUSING EVERYBODY A LOT OF TROUBLE.

Folk medicine started thousands of years ago before there were medical doctors, and continues today alongside science and organized medicine. Folk medicine is now enjoying a revival. Since people have now learned a little about medicine, they are questioning doctors and promoting their own remedies. Quackery is thriving today.

For several generations there have been doctors in my family. I spent much of my childhood with my grandfather, Dr. Joseph Benson Kelsey, who lived next door. He had retired from practice and spent his time in his garden and orchard and in the barnyard with the horses and mules, the pigs, the cow and his feathered friends. We built a pigeon cote together and nailed it on the side of the barn.

Dr. Kelsey built a house next door for each of his four children when they grew up and married, thus forming a family compound. He and my grandmother were products of the old plantations of Mississippi which existed before the Civil War.

Although retired, Dr. Kelsey still treated us. In the Spring he gave us kids a **round of Calomel** followed by a **purge of castor oil** or **Epsom Salts**. He vaccinated us for **smallpox**. He gave us **IQ&S** (**iron, quinine** and **strychnine tonic**) each hot summer. He cured our **chills and fever** (malaria) with **quinine**. He treated me for **yellow jaundice** when I was so weak I **couldn't break the skim on a chocolate pudding**. Dr. Kelsey said **smoking tobacco was like driving nails in your coffin**. He opposed alcohol and my grandmother Parrott said "**Lips that touch liquor shall never touch mine**." Dr. Kelsey died of **acute indigestion** (heart attack) one night when I was eleven years old.

Consumption (tuberculosis) was killing twenty percent of the people. They were sent for treatment to the State Tuberculosis Hospital in San Angelo. The **crazies** were sent to the Wichita Falls State Hospital. The **deaf, dumb and blind** were sent to the **asylum** in Austin. Many children died of **diphtheria** or **summer diarrhea**. There were lots of bugs: **lice, chiggers, tapeworms, pinworms, hookworms**, even **horse flies** which inflicted very painful bites. This was before **Hadacol** (Dr. LeBlanc's tonic) or **antibiotics**.

People suffered from **the shakes, cricks in the neck, locked bowels, Cory morbus, the squirts** and **rheumatiz**.

Bellevue Hospital in New York City where I interned in 1936-1937.

Life expectancy was fifty to sixty years. There are many expressions for death: **went to see his Maker** or **was called by the Lord**. There are many crude sayings for death: **bit the dust**, **conked out** and **six feet under**, to mention a few.

My path to becoming a doctor began with my grandfather, Dr. Joseph Benson (J. B.) Kelsey, who inspired me to become a doctor. He still kept his **horse and buggy** and I remember riding in the buggy with him. After retirement, Dr. Steve Grant had become our family doctor. When my mother went into labor Dr. Grant didn't get there in time, so my grandfather Kelsey who lived next door came out of retirement and delivered me. He must have done a good job because I arrived as a healthy baby boy and my mother delivered three more babies without difficulty.

I started hanging around Dr. Grant's office in my teens. He gave me chores to do in his **laboratory** and I learned to use a microscope. He even took me on some house calls. Dr. Grant talked about his days in the medical school at the University of Texas in Galveston. He also interned there for a year, mostly under Dr. Thompson who was recruited from Edinburgh to be the first chief of surgery. Dr. Grant admired Dr. Thompson. He said Dr. Thompson advised him that there were two things a doctor should never admit: drinking and pissing in the office sink. We thought that was really funny.

During my medical school days I spent much time in the Deport Sanitarium where Dr. Grant practiced. It was a two-story wooden structure. The ground floor had a doctor's office, an operating room, x-ray room and a clinical laboratory. Upstairs were rooms for patients. I saw patients with Dr. Grant. One day we drove out to a house in the country and Dr. Grant performed a hysterectomy on a woman who had fibroid tumors. All the sterilized linens and instruments were brought out in a large container. The operation was performed on a table. Miss Rhoda Oliver, Dr. Grant's registered nurse, anesthetized the patient with ether. The uterus with a large fibroid was removed and was examined closely, appeared benign and was buried in the farmyard. We left when the patient regained consciousness. She recovered nicely and I saw her on Main Street a few weeks later.

I agreed to join Dr. Grant in general practice after medical school and training, but I specialized and decided to become an internist. After two years on the Mayo Clinic staff, I came to Houston on January 15, 1949, to practice and started a general clinic and practiced medicine until I retired in 1986.

The sayings which I have collected are of and by people who are patients, not doctors. There is no scientific medical terminology here.

SOME SAYINGS ABOUT HEALTH AND MEDICINE

Laughter is the best medicine.	I'm laid up.
Abstinence is the best medicine.	He couldn't hear it thunder.
Listen to your symptoms.	He's bald as a cue ball.
Always answer nature's call.	I am still on my feet.
It's a bitter pill.	I am as happy as a hog on ice.
A dose of his own medicine	Time heals.
The laying on of hands	I've got a new lease on life.
I'm bent out of shape.	My tail is dragging the ground.
I'm all wore out.	The hospitals are on the sick list.
He's holed up sick.	My old ticker will not behave.
He's having a bad spell.	I'm a bit off.
He's gone to pot.	The cure is worse than the disease.
I'm all stove up with the rheumatiz.	It's a cure for whatever ails you.
He couldn't stand the sight of blood.	He's swelled up like a poisoned pup.
I'm played out.	I've had it.
I'm dog tired.	I'm coughing up a storm.

I coughed my head off.

The spirit is willing but the flesh is weak.

My get up and go has got up and went.

I am able to sit up and take nourishment.

I'm under the weather, as weak as a kitten.

He had chills and fever. A congestive chill

Good morning. I'm ready to get going again.

I'm still picking 'em up and putting 'em down.

An ounce of prevention is worth a pound of cure.

We all have forgotten more than we remember.

Medicine is a jealous master and a hard taskmaster.

I'm pooped out; tuckered out; I need to limber up.

A doctor who treats himself has a fool for a patient.

God heals and the doctor takes the fee (Benjamin Franklin).

The only way for a rich man to be healthy is to live like a poor man.

Nature, time and patience are the three great physicians (Chinese).

The art of medicine is usually a matter of time (Ovid, 43 BC-18 AD).

Smoking is driving nails in your coffin (a frequent saying of Dr. J. B. Kelsey).

Let the guts be full; it is they who carry the legs (Miguel de Cervantes, 1547-1616).

Wherever the art of medicine is loved, there is also a love of humanity (Hippocrates, 460-357 BC).

In writing a medical article: tell them what you are going to tell them; tell them, then tell them what you told them (Dr. Mandred Comfort, Mayo Clinic).

SOME MENTAL SYMPTOMS

Crazy as a loon.	Kinda slow.
Touched in the head.	Loco
Playing with half a deck.	Worried sick.
He's playing with his belly button.	He doesn't seem right.
He's out of his head.	He became childish.
He's a little nutty.	He stutters.
He's got water on the brain.	He has fits.
He's fit to be tied.	He had nightmares.
Bad dreams.	Delusions
The blues.	Walks in his sleep.
He passed out.	He was knocked out.

His brain is fried with marijuana—cooked.

COMPLAINTS AND MEDICAL CONDITIONS

Belly ache	Colic
Cramps	Croup
Constipation	Acute indigestion
Throwing up	Belching
Hiccups	Heaves
Cory (cholera) morbus	Bilious
Yellow jaundice	Piles
Locked bowels	The trots or squirts
The quick step	He wet his pants
Wet the bed	Had wet dreams
The clap	Syphs
Crabs	Lice
Itch	Athlete's foot
Ringworm	Earache
Toothache	Stye on the eye

Fever blisters	Snaggle-toothed
Cross-eyed	Colorblind
A crick in the neck	A black eye
Poison oak	A sprained ankle
A stumped toe	Hang nails
Gout	Knock-kneed
Bowlegged	Double-jointed
Flat-footed	Slue-footed
Humpbacked	A shin splint
Stiff as a board	Sciatica
Hamstrung	Dropsy (edema)
Night sweats	A splitting headache
A hard on	A piss hard
Strismus	Stone ache

Sprouting tits (or beginning to tit)

Short winded—can't catch his breath

He's had hives, boils, risins, carbuncles

All twisted up inside; chills, fever, the shakes

She hasn't had the curse. She's in a family way.

A freckled-faced, snotty nosed, pimply faced kid

Bitten by skeeters—horse flies, chiggers or bed bugs

SOME MEDICINES AND TREATMENTS

Syrup of figs—casara	Opium; morphine; codeine

This medicine cleans out your insides.

Vicks VapoRub®; mercurochrome; iodine

Hadacol, a tonic of sherry; quinine for malaria

Epsom salts; castor oil; bismuth and paragoric

Vermicides (for tapeworm, hookworm, pinworms)

A round of calomel; IQ&S tonic (iron, quinine and strychnine)

SAYINGS ABOUT OLD AGE

I've run out of juice—or steam.	When life hands you a lemon
I've closed up shop.	I've cashed in my chips.
Old age is not for sissies.	Wishing you a ripe old age.

After seventy it's a bonus.

There's not much left of me.

Too soon old, too late smart.

There's little room for error.

Age is a matter of feeling, not years.

Age is nothing but a number.

Age is like love; it cannot be hid.

I'm getting weaker by the day.

I have seen my best days.

In old age once again you are a child.

You're as old as you feel—as your heart.

I'm too busy staying alive to take a nap.

Well done thy good and faithful servant.

I'm pretty good for the condition I'm in.

When I feel good I stay awake to enjoy it.

Wiping the cobwebs out of the aged brain

Old age has got me; they took my car keys.

Snow on the roof (white-haired old geezer)

I'm glad some of the good old days are over.

As the years roll by; I ain't what I used to be.

A gray thatched old timer. A crusty old timer.

When you get to my age you will understand.

I'm bent out of shape; I'm three-fourths plastic.

I'm like an old coat that's all tattered and torn.

The old gray mare, she ain't what she used to be.

It takes a second to get hurt and a year to recover.

I really like you old guys; he had a little age on him.

Age is an incurable disease. (Seneca 54 BC-39 AD)

When you get old everything leaks or is stopped up.

To grow old is to grow remorseful (Samuel Johnson).

The best classroom is at the feet of an elderly person.

Age needs the company of youth (Eleanor Roosevelt).

He's a shell of his former self; the shady side of prime.

He's getting on with life; he's lived his life to the fullest.

Meeting a challenge inspires the aged man to live longer.

I can never jump up and run to the icebox or I get tipsy.

If age gets written on your face, you can erase a little off.

Time engraves our faces with all the tears we have not shed.

Don't let old age get you down; it's too hard to get back up.

Old age and the wear and tear of time teaches many lessons.

To extend life a year, take one less bite at each meal (Chinese).

You can live without sex but you can't live without your glasses.

It's just live from day to day; after sixty it's patch, patch, patch.

Exercise does me a lot of good; it keeps me from getting worse.

Old rocking chair's got me; when things you buy won't wear out.

Disability makes you appreciate what you once took for granted.

I just live from day to day (from a one-hundred-year-old woman).

Centurions dodge heart disease and sidestep cancer and accidents.

Amiable friendly people appreciate charity and inspire you to do it.

I'm trying to do something worthwhile to be chalked up on my ledger.

Pleasant memories are a wonderful asset for the old and handicapped.

Your joints are more accurate meteorologists than the weather service.

Your secrets are safe with your friends because they can't remember them.

Life is more delightful when it's on the downward slope. (Seneca 54 BC-39 AD)

Don't say money can't bring happiness. (How about servants, nurses, doctors and comfort? MPK, Sr.)

The tender with the young; compassionate with the aged; tolerant with the weak and wrong; sometime in life you have been all of these (A Word a Day).

Many people, just by nature, are charitable and generous. You learn this when you become handicapped.

Do not resent growing old; many are denied that privilege. At one hundred years, I know about getting old and what people think of when they are ninety. There's always something wrong. You grow old in stages.

An old geezer; old goat; old fart; old gruffy; old codger; old nester; old friend; old pal; old grouch; a crusty old curmudgeon; a cantankerous old fool; old reprobate; old battle ax; a grumpy old man; a kind and gentle old man

PHRASES AND SHORT SAYINGS ABOUT OLD AGE

What's left of me	Way beyond his years
The over fifty-five set	The rest of life's journey
The old lady; the old man	The good old days
As the years roll by	Back on my feet again
Triple-digit age	Getting weaker by the day
Aging gracefully	Still alive, if not well
A stolen life	Getting on with life
Plumb wore out	Live life to the fullest.

Age before beauty	Living from day to day
She's no spring chicken.	Going downhill
Old folks at home	Not getting out anymore
Age is relative.	All bent over
Ripe old age	

EXPRESSIONS ABOUT DEATH, SOME TO AVOID THE WORD DEATH

In the sweet bye and bye	He has gone to his Maker.
He's gone forever	There's not much left of me.
The kiss of death	Time is running out on me.
Paid the ultimate price	He was laid to rest.
Facing his hereafter	My days are numbered .
His last hold on life	No one gets to stay.
On death's doorstep	The rest of life's journey
Until death do us part.	Drop dead
As sure as death	I'm a goner.
Life itself is the end.	I'm about played out.
Death is the only way out.	It's time to say farewell.
He off and died-up and died.	He didn't make it home.
Shot his wad; bit the dust	I'm still alive but unwell.
He's finished-licked, had it.	He's flirting with death.
He nailed himself to the coffin.	The walking dead
He turned up his toes.	At the end of life's highway
They took him out feet first.	Don't cry for me; celebrate
DOA (dead on arrival).	A race with time
Man can die but once.	As death approaches
Nobody gets out of here alive.	Death is as sure as sunset.
Dead men tell no tales.	The art of dying
Asleep in the deep	I'm cheating death.
Life is a gift.	He refuses to die.
In the jaws of death	I'm living on borrowed time.
Death-the debt we all must pay.	He curled up and died.
Crossing the bar	Davy Jones' locker
The downward path	You can't take it with you.
The Grim Reaper	Until my dying day

Never say die.	Until death do us part
The Day of the Dead	I no longer fear death.
The death rattle	He wound up dead.
A brush with death	Back from the grave
Life after death	Is gone forever
Looking death in the eye	He kicked the bucket.
As death approaches	He died dead, right here.
The empty saddle	Bit the dust
Gone before his time	Cashed in his chips
His swan song	Had it
It's a matter of life and death.	Finished life
It's curtains for him.	On his last legs
It was his last curtain call.	Not long for this world
He takes his final bow.	Facing his hereafter
His life drew to a close.	His last hold on life
His worries are over.	Staring down death
He lived a good life.	Life is but a dream.
The walking dead	My days are numbered.
A race with death	The merchant of death
Passed away	Not long for this world
Met his maker	Conked out
He kicked the bucket.	Croaked
He died right there.	He met a violent death.
Rolled over	He passed away peacefully.
It's curtains	Pushing up daisies
Six feet under	The quick and the dead
He died in his sleep at home.	The valley of the shadow of death
The way of all flesh	I have counted my life in days.
The doomed to hang hangs on	I have a rendezvous with death.
He's on boot hill.	He's in the marble yard.
Six feet under, pushing up daisies	All men are equalized by death.
Life itself is the end.	As we gathered to say goodbye
To die is only to be as we were.	The kiss of death
On death's doorstep	As sure as death
Looking death in the eye	Death claims her.

I'm playing out, one thing at a time.   The dead have few claims to privacy.

Life has a beginning as well as an end   It's a done deal

The last words of a dying cop

Life has a beginning as well as an end. To die is only to be as we were before.

He was laid to rest; He has gone to a better place.

Is it worth living? It depends on the liver.

Life is a fatal complaint and an extremely contagious one.

We owe God a death (Shakespeare).

For dust thou are and unto dust shall thou return (Bible).

Oh, death, where is thy sting? Oh, grave, where is thy victory (Bible).

He'd make a lovely corpse (Dickens).

We all gathered to say goodbye (at the funeral).

Helping people into their afterlife

Be careful of reading health books; you might die of a misprint (Mark Twain).

He's on boot hill—in the marble yard.

Shuffling off this mortal coil

The happy hunting ground (Indian for Heaven)

I never worry about my life; never worry about my death.

If you die on Friday you go straight to Heaven (an omen).

It's pleasant to die if there be gods and sad to live if there are none.

I'm waiting for the good Lord to take me home.

He has shed the shackles of this world.

He's living with one foot in the casket—in the grave.

When there's no option but to plan for your funeral.

The killer got death; two accomplices got life (*Houston Chronicle*, May 10, 2010).

Live as if you were to die tomorrow, as if you were to live forever.

Life is like a roll of toilet paper. The closer you get to the end of time, the faster it goes.

I'm just going to keep on living and cause everybody a lot of trouble. (Dorothy Sloan)

He's enjoying what the rest of us are waiting for (*Houston Chronicle* obituary).

I hope there's a place at the table when I make it there.

I don't mind dying; I just don't want to be there when it happens.

I don't mind dying, but I'd like to hang around a month to hear what people say about me.

I don't mind dying, but I hate to miss what is going on.

Death must be so beautiful. To lie in the soft brown earth with the grass waving above one's head and listening to silence. To have no yesterday and no tomorrow. To forget time, to forgive life, to be at peace. (Oscar Wilde)

We leave as we came and, God willing, we shall return with peace and hope for the entire world. (Astronaut Gene Cernan on returning from the Moon)

Death the leveler entered my cottage and tore from my children and me an affectionate mother. (David Crockett)

They don't have a death penalty in Mexico. The don't have a trial. They pick you up and you are never seen again. (Keith Tyler)

FROM THE COLLECTION OF TOMBSTONE INSCRIPTIONS BY GERVAIS BELL ENTITLED" NEVER SAY DIE"

An angel of the Lord came for him.	He broke through to the other side.
The final chapter of his earthly life	Concluded his long life on earth
Departed this world for a better one	Ended his journey
Drew his final breath	Ended his life for an even better one
He fought the good fight.	Is now walking with angels
Lost his battle with cancer	Passed away quietly
Passed on to another life	Played his last gig on this earth
Slipped his earthly bounds	Took his own life
Was called home	Was granted his wings
Went from labor to reward	Went on his final voyage
Went to the dance with the stars	

Bayou Club March 26, 2009

CHAPTER SEVEN

*Mavis P. Kelsey, Sr.,
Tom and Ann Kelsey celebrate in 2010.*

Food & Drink

EAT THY FOOD WITH JOY, AND DRINK THY WINE WITH A MERRY HEART. *(Eccl. 9:7)*

There are probably more folk words about food than any other subject. Since the onset of humanity, nothing has been more pressing than obtaining food. I remember the food customs of rural America in the early 1900s. There were no supermarkets and little refrigeration and much food poisoning. Many children died of infectious diarrhea. There were no giant feedlots or fish farms. We ate what we and our neighbors raised, slaughtered or caught. There was legal prohibition against drinking alcohol so we drank what we and our neighbors brewed or the moonshine and white lightning our bootleggers provided.

I believe I can remember more about the food I ate than about any other activity of my boyhood. Our **vittles** *were varied: mustard greens,* **collards**, *and turnips cooked with salt pork;* **snap beans, speckled butter beans**, *black-eyed peas, okra and tomatoes from home gardens;* **roastin' ears** *from the field;* **sweet taters** *fried and baked; fried catfish from*

Sulphur Bottom; home-cured sausage, sause (**head cheese**) and ham with red-eye gravy; fried chickens and baked hens with cornbread stuffing; hot tamales made from the old rooster when he quit performing; **Blue Ribbon syrup** and sorghum molasses; sweet milk, **clabber** and buttermilk, homemade lightbread and cinnamon rolls. We put chopped onions and cornbread in the **pot likker** from beans or mustard greens. We had **muskmelons** (cantaloupes) and watermelons; **homemade ice cream, peach and blackberry cobblers**; and **fried pies**, **jams** and **jellies**.

The grocery store had canned goods such as **hominy, tomatoes, Gebhardt's chili, Boston baked beans**, sardines and salmon. There was a **large hoop of cheese** and boxes of apples and oranges in season and a stalk of bananas occasionally. Staples included rice and flour as well as potatoes and onions. My favorite was the **candy counter**. We ground our own **cornmeal**. On some Saturdays I went to the **corncrib, shelled some ears of corn**, put them in a **tow sack** and carried it to the **gristmill** for **grinding our cornmeal**.

The **ice man** came every day and put twenty-five pounds of ice in the **ice box**. If the cow ate **bitterweeds,** the milk was too bitter to drink. I witnessed **molasses being made, catching catfish on a trot line, hog killing, curing hams in our smokehouse**, and **peaches being dried**; **wringing a chicken's head off, making lye soap**; **Confederate veterans' squirrel stews, dinner on the grounds, a moonshine whiskey still** in operation; **squirrel hunting**; **gathering pecans, walnuts, hickory nuts, persimmons** and **mustang grapes** in the woods; **a robin's roost** in Sulphur Bottom where people killed thousands of the birds for food; **ginning cotton** and **making cottonseed oil** (**Wesson® oil**) for cooking at the **oil mill**; **breeding pigs, cows and horses**; and **frog-gigging.**

All in all, we had it pretty good. There were plenty of **eats**, but few **eateries**. We rarely went to a restaurant but Rankin Bell had a **hamburger joint** to serve the **new-fangled hamburger**, and his brother Stanley ran a café. Hamburgers were invented in Athens, Texas. They were made popular when sold at the World's Fair in St. Louis in 1903. **Chile Con Carne** was sold on the streets of San Antonio. According to my friend Albert Maverick, if you found a dog's tooth in a bowl, you got another bowl free. Gebhardt was the first to can chili or **wrap it into loaves** to sell and make it popular.

The drugstore had a **soda fountain** where you could get a lime coke, a milkshake, a malted milk or even a banana split which cost twenty-five cents.

When I married Mary Randolph Wilson from Beaumont, I became a fan of **Cajun food.** The best restaurant in Beaumont was **The Black Cat**. It was located in **Hotel Beaumont** which was owned by Mary's father, Cooke Wilson. Another popular restaurant in Beaumont was **Fuller's** which advertised

"**Where the Elite Meet to Eat**." When we moved to Houston the finest place was **Maxim's**. The owner was very proud when we took Bishop and Mrs. Clinton Quin there to eat. A Mr. Hebert ran a Cajun restaurant in an old house and called it "**A-Bear's**"; it had a bear on the sign. **Swazey's Restaurant** advertised "**The Best Barbeque in the World or Anywhere Else**". The **San Jacinto Inn** was a huge seafood restaurant near the San Jacinto Monument. **Mad Tony's** (now La Colombe D'Or) was named after the owners, Madeline and Antonio. **The College Inn** was near the Medical Center. Actually, most people ate at home and there were not many restaurants. This was before the days of restaurant chains. **Kentucky Fried Chicken** was the first restaurant chain to open in Houston. Then came **McDonald's** and hundreds of other restaurant chains. Now there are over 14,000 restaurants in Houston.

Gaye and John Kelsey.

SOME SAYINGS ABOUT FOOD

So rich he ate hummingbird tongues	Old time, country style fixin's
I just want a taste.	Too many cooks spoil the broth.
Fish and milk don't mix.	Feed a cold and starve a fever.
It's better than ham (a Jewish expression).	I'm hungry as a wolf —bear.
I grew up on collard greens.	Chomping and chowing down
The old pot still cooks good broth.	You are what you eat.

Eat, drink and be merry, for tomorrow we die.

Soup's on! Come and get it! Get it while it's hot! Let's eat!

There's no better food this side of paradise.

Concerning a too rare steak: A good vet could get this steer back on his feet in no time.

Is this milk fresh? Yes, an hour ago it was grass.

It looks good enough to eat. It was good to the last drop.

If you don't eat your vegetables, you will never grow up.

All day preaching and dinner on the grounds

The way to a man's heart is through his stomach.

If you don't drink, don't start (Denton Cooley).

Good food, good friends and the comforts of home

Some like it hot, some like it cold, some like it in the pot nine days old.

Food fans find fresh fare (tongue twister).

*The family of
Tom and Ann Kelsey.*

Some prefer carrots and others cabbage.

The only way to keep your health is to eat what you don't want, drink what you don't like and do what you'd rather not (Mark Twain).

Taking the pledge will not make bad liquor good, but it will improve it (Mark Twain).

Jack Sprat could eat no fat, his wife could eat no lean; yet, together they licked the platter clean.

In the winter on Sunday afternoons our family went to the woods and gathered our own pecans, black walnuts, hickory nuts and persimmons. The nuts were shelled at night by ever-busy hands and went into cakes and candy made for festive events.

The cadets at the **Sbisa Mess Hall** at A& M had nicknames for foods. Instead of saying "**Please pass the bread**," they said, "**Shoot me the gunwadding**." **Milk** was **cow**; **salad** was **rabbit**; **coffee**, **dope**; **meat**, **bull neck**; **potatoes**, **spuds**; **butter**, **grease**; and **dessert**, **cush**. Dad learned the same many years before when he was a boy at Texas Military Academy. He teased my mother by calling the lightbread she made gunwadding.

There were certain foods that made up the majority of our food and were typical of our time and place. For example, we had our own corn ground into cornmeal at the local grist mill. I was very fond of cornmeal mush when cooked as a cereal for breakfast and served with cream and butter. Fish was fried in cornmeal batter. Pancakes (and sorghum molasses), **corn bread**, **corn pone**, **corn dodgers**, and **hushpuppies** were made from cornmeal.

Our milk supply lived right on the place with us. In my boyhood I milked our own cow twice a day, and the kids drank the milk while it was still warm right out of the cow. The fresh milk was called **sweet milk**. Skim milk was called **blue john**. **Cream** was skimmed off the top of the milk to put into cereal, coffee, homemade ice cream and cream puffs. When the milk **soured** and **curdled**, we ate the **clabber** with a spoon. Today it is **doctored up** with sugar and flavoring and sold as **yogurt**. We churned some of the cream to make our own **butter** and **buttermilk**. My grandfather was the last one in the family to drink the **whey**; otherwise we fed the whey to the chickens. Mother made **milk custard** and **puddings** while many people made **cottage cheese** of the milk. This was before **junk food**.

Mother stored her canned goods underground in the **storm cellar** where it was cool. One of mother's favorites was pineapple upside down cake. People started from scratch with flour to make all kinds of breads, cakes, pies, dumplings and puddings. Mother made several loaves of **lightbread** once a week.

I remember Grandfather Kelsey killing his own hogs. He had a **smokehouse** where he **cured** hams, bacon and sausage. We ate the fat on beef, pork and chickens, and we put cream on just about everything. We cooked with **hog lard**. It was many years later that we learned that animal fat caused arteriosclerosis. There was a high incidence of coronary heart disease for many years.

My mother **stopped at nothing**. She even made **fruitcakes**, **mincemeat**, **chili and tamales**, **homemade pickles** and **pulled taffy**, not to mention making all our clothes.

We made **squirrel stew** and cooked doves, quail, venison and fish, but Mother wouldn't cook a coon, possum or **crawdads**.

For some reason I have a vivid memory of making **homemade lye soap** by cooking leftover grease with lye. My Grandfather Kelsey made lye by pouring water through stove ashes in a stone pot made for the purpose. You could also buy lye in a can at the grocery. We saved all the leftover cooking grease or **hog fat**, mixed it with the lye and cooked it outdoors in a wash pot over a wood fire. When it was done, it became lye soap. It was cut into hunks or bars and used for laundry or even washing dishes. It was way too strong to bathe with.

This **wash pot** was a large twenty-to-thirty gallon cast iron pot kept outdoors where water was boiled in it over a wood fire. Dirty clothes were pitched in the water with a bar of lye soap, boiled thoroughly, and rinsed in a wash tub full of water with **bluing** in it. They were then rinsed ("**wrenched**") and put through a **clothes wringer** before **hanging on the line** to dry. The clothes were ironed in the kitchen with a **flat iron** which had been heated on the kitchen stove.

DRINKING AND DRUNKENNESS:

Since our family for generations were **teetotalers**, we had no drinks at home, with the exception of a little **peach nectar** at Christmas. They let the boys make and drink a little **blackberry wine**. I was bad. I parted from family principles in many ways. I took my first drink while at A&M. It was a custom to **hitchhike** (you couldn't own a car) to Navasota and buy a pint **of moonshine whiskey**, delivered in the restroom where the **bootlegger** left it for you to pick up. You never saw him. Then you hitchhiked back to College Station and joined in a party in the dorm and **made a fool of yourself**.

My eight great, grandchildren. Top row, from left: Wilson Kelsey, Robert Riser, Patrick Connor, Carter Kelsey, Clara Connor. Bottom row: Thomas Connor, Carleton Riser, and McClelland Riser. May 8, 2012, Crested Butte, Colorado.

Archeologists have found evidence that wine was being made 7,000 years ago, long before recorded history. Alcohol is **a sword that cuts both ways** and **a boon and a bust for humanity**. The Baptists fought liquor while some members were bootleggers or made moonshine. In our community the principal bootlegger was the constable and a prominent Baptist. He was pretty much above the law but he was a good constable and a respected citizen.

Prohibition didn't deter me from starting drinking at Texas A&M, patronizing the local **home brew makers** in Deport and Galveston and buying **rot gut likker**, **moonshine** or **white lightning** from the local **bootlegger.** Bootleggers provided **moonshine** (liquor made in the shine of the moon), **white lightning** (moonshine that hadn't been colored with caramel). Much of it was loaded with fused oil and called **rot gut likker**. Most of our **smart juice** was made in the hills of Southeastern Oklahoma. That at A&M and Galveston was made near **Fairfield,** the seat of Freestone County, then often called the Free State of Freestone because it made illegal whiskey during Prohibition. Mrs. Beebe was the bootlegger for our AKK Fraternity in medical school in Galveston. We called her whiskey "**Mrs. Bee's Honey.**" We ordered it by phone and it was delivered to the house. We also drank **bathtub gin** and alcohol in grapefruit juice. During Prohibition grocery and drug stores sold packages of yeast and hops with directions for making home brews. We made our own at the AKK Fraternity and kept it in mason jars or bottles which we capped.

While camping in the mountains of southeastern Oklahoma, a friend and I accidentally hiked into a moonshine whiskey still which was in full operation. There was no one there to be seen but we knew the moonshiners were hiding and watching us with their shotguns cocked so we hiked out of there in a hurry.

Some people were not **strangers to alcohol**; others were **hard drinkers** or **boozers**. Even though little wine was available, there were **winos.** A few drank bad Jamaican rum and ended up with **Jakeleg** (Neuritis).

If you offered a friend a drink from your bottle, you said, "**Have a snort**."

The friend replied "**Don't mind if I do**." And "**Here's to you; bottoms up**." Then he **swigged down** most of your pint.

I got **high, tipsy, loaded, under the influence, drunk as a skunk, couldn't walk a straight line, got on a toot**, and sometimes even **passed out**. One night the constable put me in the **calaboose** for being rowdy at the Deport Masonic pool hall. We often got **tanked up**, got **a glow on**, and **loop-legged**. We **got smashed** and **drunker than a coot**. Some of us even **conked out** or **passed out** and had to be **carried home** and put to bed. One of our group became a **chronic alcoholic** and **died from it**. **Old sots** had an **eye-opener** in the morning, a **pick-me-up** at noon and a **nightcap** at bedtime.

Family of Mavis Kelsey, Jr.
Top from left: son Cooke, daughter Winifred Riser, Mavis Jr.
Bottom: Carleton Riser holding little Carleton, Robert Riser, Wendy Kelsey and Mac Riser.

We **loaded up or suited up** for fraternity dances and sang "**Let's Get Stinking Said Old Abe Linkin Cause a Little Bit of Drinking Will Do a Lot of Good**" and "**I'd Rather Get Drunk With an AKK and Everyone Else I Know**." We **lifted an elbow**, had a **thimble-full**, a **wee drop**, a **dram** or a **squidgen**. We got on a **tear** (or a **toot**), **got woozy, couldn't walk straight**, and were **three sheets in the wind. It was good to the last drop**. The next morning we had a **hangover** and tried to relieve it with **the hair of the dog that bit us**. We said **I'll never drink again, yeah**? Mark Twain said "Whiskey is for drinking—water is for fighting for." It was also said that **what whiskey can't cure there is no cure for** or **drown your sorrow with drink**.

While I was interning at Bellevue, I learned about **mixed drinks** and **highballs**: a **Manhattan**, an **Old Fashioned**, a **Martini**, a **Sazerac**, and **rum** and **coke**. There was a White Russian nurse at Bellevue whose family had been run out by the Communists. She taught me about drinking vodka. For a party one nurse took a bucket to a saloon and got it filled with beer. This was called **rushing the growler**. We called beer **suds** or a **cool one**. I never tasted tequila until I came to Houston in 1949.

CHAPTER EIGHT

Deport Methodist Church, where Mavis Parrott Kelsey was baptized.

Old Time Religion

GOD PREPARES FOOD FOR EVERY BIRD BUT DOES NOT DELIVER IT TO THE NEST.
(Chinese Proverb)

A hundred years ago the vast majority of Americans held Judeo-Christian beliefs and practiced their religion. Congress opened with a prayer and it still does in spite of widespread opposition. The chaplain of the Congress was a highly honored man. Our coins are imprinted with In God We Trust. God bless America was widely proclaimed.

I believe that faith in God kept us more honest, and I believe the present decline in ethics and morality results from forsaking religion.

The widespread belief in God resulted in many supplications to God: **Thanks to God, Praise to God** *as well as the knowledge and quotations of Proverbs and other scripture of the Bible.*

All my family were very religious, never missed a service, contributed generously to the church, entertained the preacher, prayed regularly, read the Holy Bible, lived by the Ten Commandments, believed in Heaven and Hell and were strict with their children. I didn't live up to their expectations.

I attended Sunday School and then the church service at the Deport Methodist Church every Sunday until I went off to college. Grandfather Kelsey's name was on the marble cornerstone of the little church. The grounds were large enough to hold the annual outdoor **summer revival**. Occasionally I mowed the church lawn and was paid a dollar for it. On Sundays between Sunday school and preaching, the men and boys stood around under a big pecan tree and talked about the weather and the crops. After preaching we tarried outside the front entrance and visited among the members. There were always visitors and relatives to be introduced.

Grandfather Kelsey had a Sunday school class for young adults called **The Young Peoples' Class**. This class continued under the same name for many years. The original members continued going to this class as long as they lived, some having children and grandchildren to become members. It may still be going on.

My family, being musical, provided the music. Aunt Lucille had a degree in music from Kidd-Key College in Sherman. She played the piano, led the choir and sang solos. She married Dean Oliver and he played the violin. Dad played the trumpet or cornet; Uncle Russell, the saxophone; and Uncle Joe, the cornet. They had many musicals in the Dr. Kelsey home. Sadly I was never able to play an instrument and neither do members of my family. We are missing a lot.

The pastor was called **Brother** and he called members **Brothers** and **Sisters**. In Deport we had **Wednesday prayer meetings**, **Sunday night preaching**, **Sunday dinners on the grounds** at noon, and **outdoor summer revivals** held by a **visiting evangelist**. There were revivals in the **City Tabernacle** held by the combined churches of Deport (the Methodist, Presbyterian and Baptist). We had **Cemetery Day** when we **pitched in** and cleaned the cemetery. We wore our **Sunday go to meeting clothes.** I remember we sang "Onward Christian Soldiers," "Amazing Grace," "Rock of Ages," "I Love to Tell the Story," "Washed in the Blood of the Lamb," "Jesus Loves Me, This I Know," and "The Old Rugged Cross."

I believe it was the Nazarene Church which we called **Holy Rollers** because they sang in **unknown tongues** and **rolled on the floor**. They had a country church and held a **tent revival** each summer which we kids watched from the sidelines. You could hear loud calls of "Amen," "Hallelujah," and "Praise God" at these revivals.

The Lord's name was taken in vain by many people, including myself (**God**

dammit, Hellfire, By Jesus). I heard many proverbs from the Bible and will list some along with other expressions about religion. There are many expressions referring to Heaven (**for Heaven's sake**), Hell (**It's hell on women**), or biblical figures (**Holy Moses**).

SOME SAYINGS ABOUT GOD AND RELIGION:

There are many sayings about religion and morality. Many have their origin in the Holy Bible while some are comments of the people about their religion.

We have dozens of proverbs and other quotes from the Holy Bible. I am familiar with them since I heard them repeatedly by listening to a sermon in church on Sunday since I was a child. I've read the Bible from cover to cover twice. I've also read two different translations of the Quran. There is much repetition in the Bible. In my opinion, the Quran is about eighty percent repetition. Much of the Quran is taken from both the Old and New Testaments of the Bible.

Put away childish things.	Confession is good for the soul.
These are God's people.	God moves in mysterious ways.
We're all God's children.	Love your neighbor as yourself.
You reap what you sow.	Heaven, I don't know what all
Judge not lest you be judged.	It's God's wonder.
It's a crime against humanity.	Give the devil his due.
Thank God for small favors.	Lord, have mercy on us.
Preaching hellfire and damnation	Here but for the grace of God go I.
To err is human, to forgive divine.	Love is a many splendored thing.
In God we trust. God save us.	You cannot live by bread alone.
God bless America. God bless you.	Idleness is the devil's workshop.
If there is no God, life is pointless.	Woe to those who call evil good.
Marriage: a match made in Heaven.	Cleanliness is next to godliness.
I once was lost but now I'm found.	
Heaven is for real. There is a Santa Claus.	
God is a presence to be sensed but not seen.	
God is the only Being who, to exist, need not even exist.	
Final proof of God's omnipotence is that He may not exist at all to save.	

How the West was won: Bible, fist and gun.

A scientific study is a revelation of God.

Not everyone's a saint who goes to church.

Any man's religion is his own business.

It's an act of God. That's the gospel truth.

Thank the Lord. Peace be with you. The love of God.

Praise the Lord and pass the ammunition.

I have studied the Holy Word. It's God's word.

Don't be so heavenly good that you are no earthly good.

There are 252 examples of humor in the Bible.

We will be there if the Lord be willing and the creek don't rise.

Lord, keep your arm around my shoulder and your hand over my mouth.

We thank Thee for these and all other blessings.

God tests children for reasons of His own.

His eye is on the sparrow and I know He watches me.

The Lord helps those who help themselves.

The Lord provides our daily bread but He expects us to do the baking.

Cast your bread upon the water and it will float back buttered and toasted.

Now I lay me down to sleep, I pray the Lord my soul to keep.

The sins of the father are visited on the son.

Those who live by the sword must die by the sword.

You cannot serve God and mammon—no man can serve two masters.

The road to Hell is paved with good intentions.

Don't have your head in the clouds and your feet in a brothel.

My cup runneth over; Count your many blessings.

Hell has no fury like a woman scorned.

If you talk to God you are praying. If God talks to you, you are a schizophrenic.

An atheist is showing the greatest of conceit, saying that he is smarter than 99% of all kings and queens.

Serving God is doing good to man, but praying is an easier service and therefore more generally chosen. (Benjamin Franklin)

Think of these things, whence you came, where you are going and to whom you must account (Benjamin Franklin).

The Bible: There's no reason why God could not write a book in different voices. No amount of research is going to resolve this.

SOME FREQUENT SAYINGS FROM THE BIBLE

God is love.	Pride goeth before a fall.
The just shall live by faith.	Be thou faithful to the end.
The wages of sin are death.	Not my will but thine be done.
Be sure your sin will find you out.	Blessed are the peacemakers.
Thou shalt love thy neighbor as thyself.	By their fruits you shall know them.

Blessed are the meek for they shall inherit the earth.

Blessed are the poor for theirs is the kingdom of God.

Blessed are the pure in heart for they shall see God.

Whatever a man soweth, that shall he reap.

They have sown the wind and reaped a whirlwind.

A prophet is without honor in his own hometown.

The Lord giveth and the Lord taketh away.

God said, Let there be light and there was light.

Greater love hath no man than to lay down his life for another.

He that is without sin among you, let him cast the first stone.

It is more blessed to give than to receive.

Fear God and keep His commandments.

It is not good that man should live alone.

Out of the abundance of the heart the mouth speaketh.

Seek and you shall find, knock and it shall be opened to you.

Why beholdest thou the mote in thy brother's eye, but considerest not the beam in thine own eye? Matt. 7:3

Render unto Caesar the things that are Caesar's, and to God the things that are God's.

THE BEST KNOWN PHRASES OF THE KING JAMES BIBLE

The root of the matter (Job 19:28)	Suffer little children (Luke 18:16).
East of Eden (Gen. 4:16)	Get thee behind me (Luke 4:8).
Fell flat on his face (Num. 22:31)	A thorn in the flesh (2 Cor. 12:7).
A man after his own heart (1 Sam. 13:14)	No small stir (Acts 12:18)
The skin of my teeth (Job 19:20)	Be horribly afraid (Jer. 2:12).
Put words in his mouth (Exod. 4:15).	Set thine house in order (Is. 38:8).
A still small voice (1 Kings 19:12)	Pour out your heart (Ps. 62:8).

Save up for yourself shares in heaven (Matt. 6:20).

Beat their swords into plowshares (Is. 2:4).

How the mighty have fallen (2 Sam. 1:19).

A lamb led to the slaughter (Is. 53:7).

Known for a certainty (Joshua 2:23-13)

Let us now praise famous men (Eccl. 44:1).

Turned the world upside down (Acts 17:6)

Unto the pure, all things are pure (Titus 1:15).

To everything there is a season (Eccl. 3:1).

Stand in awe (Psalms 4:4).

Much study is a weariness of the flesh (Eccl. 12:12).

From time to time (Ezek. 4:10) – This one is the best known of all

Twenty-six of the 258 most classic phrases from the King James Bible, published in *The National Geographic Magazine*, "The King James Bible; Making a Masterpiece," December 2011, p. 36-61

Mavis P. Kelsey, Sr., on his 90th birthday with his granddaughters, Winifred Kelsey Riser, Kelly Elizabeth Kelsey and Margaret Connor Kelsey.

QUOTES TAKEN DIRECTLY FROM THE BIBLE

Flee youthful lusts. (2 Tim. 2:22)

Be patient toward all men. (1 Thess. 3:5)

The wages of sin is death. (Rom. 6:23)

God loves a cheerful giver. (2 Cor. 9:7)

Two are better than one. (Eccl. 4:9)

Am I my brother's keeper? (Gen. 4:9)

Be sober, be vigilant. (1 Peter 5:8)

Speak evil of no man. (Titus 3:2)

Eyes have they but see not. (Ps. 82:5)

How are the mighty fallen? (2 Sam. 1:19)

Jealousy is the rage of a man. (Prov. 6:34)

Through faith we understand. (Heb. 11:3)

Wise men lay up knowledge. (Prov. 13:14)

Do not weary in well doing. (2 Thess. 3:13)

Whosoever hath shall be given. (Matt. 6:21)

Wisdom is better than strength. (Eccl. 9:16)

The light of the body is the eye. (Luke 11:34)

Be strong and of good courage. (Deut. 31:6)

Taste and see that the Lord is good. (Ps. 34:8)

Make a joyful noise unto the Lord. (Ps. 100:1)

All we, like sheep, have gone astray. (Isa 53:6)

Be sure your sins will find you out. (Num. 32:23)

Thou shall not raise a false report. (Exod.. 23:1)

There is no man who sinneth not. (1 Kings 8:46)

A soft answer turneth away wrath. (Prov. 15:18)

You shall know them by their fruits. (Matt. 7:16)

I am fearfully and wonderfully made. (Ps. 139.14)

New wine must be put in new bottles. (Mark 2:22)

If it were not so, I would have told you. (John 1:14)

Wisdom is better than weapons of war. (Eccl. 9:18)

Thy shalt love thy neighbor as thyself. (Matt. 22:39)

Even in laughter the heart is sorrowful. (Prov. 14:13)

It is more blessed to give than to receive. (Acts 20:30)

Turn not to the right hand nor to the left. (Prov. 4:27)

Whatsoever a man soweth, that shall he reap. (Gal. 6:7)

I am undone because I am a man of unclean lips. (Is. 6:5)

No violence to no man, neither accuse him falsely. (Luke 3:1)

He who soweth bountifully shall reap bountifully. (2 Cor. 9:6)

Happy is the man who findeth wisdom. (Prov. 3:13)

In my Father's house are many mansions. (John 14:2)

The heart of the wise teacheth his mouth. (Prov. 16:23)

Let us eat and drink for tomorrow we died. (Isa. 22:13)

Get wisdom, get understanding, forget it not. (Prov. 4:5)

Follow me and I will make you fishers of men. (Mark 5:14)

Dust thou art, and unto dust shall thou return. (Gen. 3:19)

The love of money is the root of all kinds of evil. (Tim. 6:10)

A house divided against itself shall not stand. (Matt. 12:25)

The very hairs on your head are all numbered. (Matt. 10:20)

I have fought a good fight. I have kept the faith. (2 Tim. 4:7)

Can two walk together, except they be disagreed? (Amos 3:3)

The last enemy that will be destroyed is death. (1 Cor. 15:26)

Hear ye deft and look you blind that you may see. (Isa. 42:18)

A hypocrite with his mouth destroyeth his neighbor. (Prov. 11:9)

Let us run with patience the race that is set before us. (Heb. 12:1)

The race is not to the swift or the battle to the strong. (Eccl. 9:11)

The drunkard and the glutton shall come to poverty. (Prov. 23:21)

Do unto others as you would have them do unto you. (Luke 6:31)

Let not your heart be troubled, neither let it be afraid. (John 14:2)

Swear not...but let your yea be yea and your nay, nay. (James 5:12)

In the beginning God created the heavens and the earth. (Gen. 1:1)

Walk worthy of the vocation wherewith you are called. (Eph. 4:12)

You shall know the truth and the truth shall set you free. (John 8:32)

What God hath joined together let no man pull asunder. (Mark 10:9)

None of us liveth to himself and no man dieth to himself. (Rom. 14:7)

As you would that man should do, do you also unto them. (Luke 6:3)

Man that is born of woman is of few days and full of trouble. (Job 14: 1)

God so loved the world that He gave His only begotten son... (John 3:16)

Old things are passed away; behold all things are made new. (2 Cor. 5:17)

Do not be carried about with diverse and strange doctrines. (Heb. 13:9)

A good man leaveth an inheritance to his children's children. (Prov. 13:22)

Let every man be swift to hear, slow to speak, slow to wrath. (James 1:19)

Incline thy ear to wisdom and apply thy heart to understanding. (Prov. 2:2)

In the lips of him that hath understanding, wisdom is found. (Prov. 9:16)

They that be whole need not a physician but they that are sick. (Matt. 9:12)

Come to me, all you who are weary and burdened,
and I will give you rest. (Matt. 11:28)

What is a man profited, if he shall gain the whole world
and lose his soul. (Matt. 16:26)

A man hath under the sun nothing better than to eat,
drink and be merry. (Eccl. 8:15)

Teach us to number our days, that we may apply
our hearts unto wisdom. (Prov. 90:12)

If thou has nothing, why should he take away
the bed from under thee? (Prov. 21:27)

Whosoever shall smite thee on the right check,
turn to him the other cheek. (Matt. 5:39)

A time to weep, and a time to laugh, a time to mourn
and a time to dance. (Eccl. 3:6)

A merry heart doeth good like a medicine, but a broken
spirit drieth the bones. (Prov. 17:22)

Let us not love in the word, neither in the tongue
but in deed and in truth. (1 John 3:18)

The tongue can no man tame, it is an unruly evil,
full of deadly poison. (James 3:8)

Aged men be sober, grave, temperate, sound in faith, in charity,
in temperance. (Titus 2:2)

Everything comes from You and we have given You only what comes
from Your hand. (1 Chron. 29:14)

Consider the lilies in the field; they toil not...yet even Solomon in all his glory
was not arranged like one of these. (Rom 6:38)

Train up a child in the way he should grow, and when he is old he will not
depart from it. (Prov. 22:1)

He maketh the sun to shine on the evil and the good, and sendeth rain to the
just and unjust. (Matt. 5:25)

If thine enemy thirst, give him water...for in doing so thou shall heap coals of
fire on his head. (Rom. 12:2)

The floods came and the winds blew and hit upon that house, and it fell not
because it was founded upon a rock. (Matt. 7:20)

There shall be no more death, neither sorrow, nor crying, neither shall there be
anymore pain. (Deut. 21:4)

Unto one He gave five talents, to another two, and to another one, to every
man according to his ability. (Matt. 25:15)

Let us come before his presence with thanksgiving and make a joyful noise
unto him with poems. (Isa. 95:2)

Oh, death, where is thy sting? Oh, grave, where is thy victory? (1 Cor. 15:55)

Let none of you suffer as a busybody in other people's matters. (1 Peter 4:10)

From the beginning of creation God made them male and female. (Mark 10:67)

Fear not them which kill the body, but are not able to kill the soul. (Matt. 10:28)

If the right hand offends thee cut it off and cast it away from thee. (Matt. 5:13)

CHAPTER NINE

Dr. Mavis P. Kelsey at time of opening the Kelsey-Seybold Clinic on Holcombe Blvd.

Politics

ANGER IS THE CURRENCY OF POLITICS TODAY.

*Political statements tend to exaggerate.
Politicians are torn between extreme views.*

Big money has corrupted Congress.	A whirlpool of politics
Lawmakers' words disguise the truth.	A political football
Enemies are useful in politics.	Political arm-twisting
Timing is everything in politics.	Dirty politics
Playing the race card	A bloated government
A budget brawl looms in Congress.	A landslide; a tug of war
He ramrodded it through Congress.	Dems do soul searching.
Charging Capitol Hill	Working the levers of power
Flexing political muscle	Liberal attack dogs
Keeping the masses confused	Obama lets fly at GOP.
Cringing at the liberal media	Obamacare guts Medicare.
Congress staves off Medicare attack.	Squandered the lead
Rooting out dirty police	Obama has a listening problem.
Vitriolic political rhetoric	Trying to rule instead of govern
Making a dent in the budget	The presidential horse race
Throw the bums out.	Congress slashed the aid.
The gloves are off in this race.	The U.S. dithers; A GOP confab.
He walks out on the panel.	Congress shoots down a bill.
Moving toward the center	Military quashed the rally.
We aired our feelings.	Governmental flab
Palin takes Houston by storm.	Clashing in the Capitol
We hold any politician suspect.	Green lighting bills
He opened the floodgates.	Torn between extreme views
His record serves as a blueprint.	A political backlash
A red state/blue state issue	Liberals are stepping on the gas.
Taking steps for another run	Not tied to a party
We the people; Now it's our time.	Raising political heat
The Fed targets the plan.	Will he or won't he run?
Handcuffing democracy	A bitter political climate
Pork barrel politics	Politics casts its shadow.
The candidates get a ho-hum.	Show me the money (graft, bribery).
A stab-in-the-back type	A bridge-builder
The pendulum swings right.	Partisan gridlock
Dirty politics	Healthy debate; hotly debated
Seeking a middle ground	Approval rating north of 60%

He's geared up for it	He shifts into high gear
His long march to leadership	They bulldozed their opponents
Timing is everything in politics	The blame game; find a scapegoat
Voting on emotion instead of fact	He trails the leader; Political brawls
The candidate put on her running shoes	Headlines that saturate the media
We hold these truths to be self-evident	The GOP won't need any hankies
Those who lean to the right or left	He threw his hat in the ring—or GOP
Something smells in the AG's office	There's rebellion in the voting booths
It's about time for Obama to bite back	Racism; racial profiling; colorblind
Practical politics comes in ignoring facts	A tree hugger; an environmentalist

Giving breaks to the rich will add to the deficit (Democrats)

A modern politician is a creature with very modest literacy and wit

The choice is not the right or left, it's up or down. (Ronald Reagan)

The liberals have a stranglehold on American campuses

A good political compromise gives something for everyone to hate

The powers that be and how to control them

Obama gives it a rubber stamp; Obama is tone deaf to issues.

Today's infatuation with statistics tends to crowd out finesse

Lame duck Congress is a golden goose for Obama

Obama Care starts to unravel; Obama recaptures lost ground.

The Moral Majority; The Christian Coalition.

The voiceless middle; The silent majority.

The unwitting generation of group-speak

Immigration bill reignites fight and fear

The Tea Party is short-lived (says a Democrat)

The right party and the what's left party

The sands are shifting in the Middle East

Instead of mounting a dung hill and crowing

The foul output of sneering anti-Americanism

Bitten by the political bug (Oveta Hobby)

Taking a leaf from the Republican playbook

Republicans are flexing their muscles; Republicans recapture the House

Cranking up the campaign for the GOP Whip

Congress and White House headed for a collision over taxes

A dyed-in-the-wool Republican; A right wing, radical Republican.

A left-leaning liberal; A yellow or blue dog Democrat.

A Libertarian; an Independent; Middle of the Roader, Tea Party

Riding the wave of discontent; Approval rating north of 60%.

The political pendulum is swinging

His record serves as a blueprint. He opened the floodgates.

It's a political bombshell (*Houston Chronicle* about Rick Perry)

There's nothing so permanent as a job in Washington

The Tea Party is riding the waves of discontent

Big talk, little action, by lame ducks

Republicans tighten their grip in Texas; Texas has spoken

The people have spoken, the bastards (Peggy Noonan)

Personality conflicts could be thrown completely into the air

Republican storm created too much headwind; GOP wields the broom

Obama's dealt a tough hand; Democrats crumble

An unvarnished look at backroom politics

The judge cut him a slice of cake and let him go

They are digging up dirt on their opponents

They are bad-mouthing the opponent; He ripped his political opponent apart

The workhorse instead of the showhorse

Acts like he's running for President, says he's not

The further you steer to the right or the left; the more likely you are
to run in the ditch

We don't get good laws to restrain bad people; we get good people to restrain
bad laws

The Senate is the saucer to cool the drink before it becomes a law.
(George Washington)

The democracy will cease to exist when you take away from those who work
and give it to those who don't. (Thomas Jefferson)

If you have a weak candidate and a weak platform, wrap yourself up in the
American flag and talk about the Constitution

Islamists are heaping praise on Bin Laden while his followers are backstabbing
each other and working the system

We're going to have peace, even if we have to fight for it.
(President Dwight Eisenhower)

Diapers and politicians should be changed often, for the same reason

CHAPTER TEN

Kelsey Seybold Clinic

The Business World

IF YOU WORSHIP MONEY YOU WILL ALWAYS FEEL POOR.

There are many old sayings about money and wealth. Benjamin Franklin, in Poor Richard's Almanac, made reference to saving and frugality. Many of his maxims are widely used today.

The economy is also described by many metaphors which are formed by giving action to inanimate subjects. Wall Street is a metaphor for the New York stock markets. The Bulls and the Bears categorize the traders. The ups and downs of business are described by a well-established vernacular. The November 11, 2010 issue of the Wall Street Journal *says the market is sour; tensions still fester; Iraq's oil patch opens the spigot; mergers are drying up; Campbell shaves its outlook; the Dow fights its way; Macy's is in the black again; and taxes bite.*

The business world has its jargon or vernacular called financial literacy. All you have to do to find it is to read the headlines and columns of the *Wall Street Journal*. The business channel on TV calls it "squawk on the street." You better learn the language if you take care of your own personal finances.

SOME AXIOMS, ADAGES AND MAXIMS ABOUT BUSINESS

Hang on to what you've got	Convenience trumps everything
Strike while the iron is hot	It is necessary to risk something
Every little bit helps	Take baby steps toward savings
It's easy to get but hard to keep	Live according to your income
Let the buyer beware	Money burns a hole in the pocket
Nothing succeeds like success	Easy come, easy go
Nothing ventured, nothing gained	Look out for number one
Demand cash on the barrelhead	There's always room at the top
Just breaking even won't cut it	Stay within your budget
The rally has legs	Money often costs too much
Cranking up productivity	Dow's wild ride
Don't throw good money after bad	Put by for a rainy day; Pay as you go.
A fool and his money are soon parted	The more we have the more we want
There's no remedy for death and taxes	We don't know when we are well off

Pay what you owe, and what you're worth you will know (Benjamin Franklin)

Sock or squirrel away money; stash cash

Speak little, speak the truth, spend little, pay cash (German saying)

Live within your means; two can live as cheaply as one

Beware of little expenses. A small leak will sink a ship (Benjamin Franklin)

A penny saved is a penny earned (Benjamin Franklin)

If you would be wealthy, think of saving as well as getting

Save the cost of anything before you buy it

Where your treasure is, there will be your home

The Bulls make money, the Bears make money, the Hogs go broke

It's easier to make money than to keep it

Love, pain and money cannot be kept secret

Every job requires an entrepreneur

A debt can be a millstone round your neck

Don't bite off more than you can chew

Money talks, history walks (destroying historic sites)

The straw that breaks the camel's back

Get your money's worth; Hold on to your wallet.

To know the value of money, go and borrow some (Benjamin Franklin)

Spare and have is better than spend and crave (Benjamin Franklin)

The love of money corrupts (the Bible)

There's no such thing as smart money, only smart people;
the money goes where they go

Corrupt is corrupt, fraud is fraud, Wall Street is Wall Street

Wall Street calling it legal doesn't make it less corrupt

Beauty is as beauty does, business is as business does

The scarcer the commodity, the more valuable it is (Peggy Noonan)

A temporary tax increase is always a permanent tax

No price is too great for works of beauty with known authenticity

A shady business shuts down one day and opens up the next day
under a new name

The problem is not the lack of freedom but corruption

The faster the rise, the faster the fall

The higher the rise, the bigger the fall

In a blow to the economy the market hits the skids

The company takes bold steps forward

Wealth is hard to come by but poverty is always
with us. (Sumerian, 5000-3000 B.C.)

It's not what you earn but what you keep that counts

Money may unmake the man who made it

If you pursue what you don't need you will soon be selling what you do need

Fowl language: Companies are squawking; a flap over Twitter: Early bird gets
the term. (*Wall Street Journal*, September 24, 2011)

There is pain in acquiring wealth, pain in keeping it, pain in spending it, pain in
losing it—why have so much sorrow? (Sanskrit, 3000 BC)

SAYINGS ABOUT BUSINESS

$100 billion is $100 billion	Harvest failure rattles Wall Street
The economy is smiling	Signed, sealed and delivered
Made a killing; made a mint	The market didn't go my way
Too much of a good thing	Living paycheck to paycheck
Probate adds a new twist	The tax deal is within reach
Prices take a wild ride	Time is money, money talks
Heads I win, tails you lose	It costs an arm and a leg
He hoards his money	A rise in prices is afoot
Killed by low interest rates	This guy means business
Locked in negotiations	Sales screech downward
Money-eyed special interests	Power grids grid for chill
Breathtaking dishonesty	Are you finding work?
The financial landscape	Inflation is on the horizon
Battling over the budget	Sticker shock. A wakening call.
Draining the US coffers	An antidote for the poison pill
Runaway costs	The budget: a mess to clean up
They're stealing us blind	Falling into financial chasm
Business is at a crawl	Traders are riding volatility
Business is picking up	Hogs at the public trough
He has a stable of lawyers	Skimming funds off the top
I'm banking on you	Seeing red (losing money)
The bears turned bullish	Unveiling a huge oil find
It's business as usual	The bill is on the fast track
Buy one, get one free	Funds slide on slippery slope
Americans sour on trade	The U. S. sparked a selloff
Sweeping back the losses	Tend to your own business
Boosting the bottom line	Calming the market's nerves
Taking on the big boys	See-saw stocks dive again
Wringing out a profit	Demand cools
Propping up sales	A mom and pop business
Nowhere to go but up	Making a low end push
Seniors tighten their belts	The market sags
The banks opened the spigot	The rally hit the wall
It's the biggest game in town	On the ropes (about to go broke)

We must stop the bleeding

The banks got gun shy

She put on her make up

A whole bunch of money

The greedy financial crowd

Keeping the business afloat

CEO faces stormy times

Hedge funds were raided

It's worth its weight in gold

Doing a land office business

He rides herd on oil prices

Keep the good times rolling

The ruling was shot down

A tough sell, a hard sell, sell out

Walked away from the mortgage

People inside the boiler room

His M.O. (modus operandi)

Your check is in the mail

Soak the rich

More bang for the buck

Chasing fraud, stamp out fraud

Treasure hunting in the market

Hold on tight to your wallet

Another day, another dollar

Pay hard cold cash, no credit

Advertising is legal lying

Business is showing signs of life

Law of unintended consequences

Voters slam the brakes on spending

Struggling to make both ends meet

Oil is fueling the rise of the market

He racked up big bucks

We got soaked on that deal

That's where the smart money is

There's money still left on the table

If you believe in the money fairy

The boss; the brass; the top cop

Taking a bite out of the fund

The U. S. slams Pakistan's efforts

The bottom fell out (of banks)

The market isn't going my way

He walks away from a job offer

People are opening their wallets

The economy is in the toilet

The report muddies the outlook

He likes to get in on the action

The boom bypassed the poor

High prices are a speed bump

The dollar is in a down draft

Rising prices sap recovery

The principle of least effort

Sorting the real from the phony

Sorting the wheat from the chaff

The budget is snarled by a feud

The market goes on a wild ride

Low spending spells trouble

He's drained of cash

A way to your wallet

There's lots of money to be made

Stock scandals are breeding fear

The recession creates new rich

The sweet smell of success

He's out for the money in it

He blew the whistle on the fraud

A leg up on a limping economy

Terror financing flows unfettered

The market sends a warning

The economy is trapped

"A" company ingests "B" company

A cutthroat capitalist (J. P. Morgan)

Dr. Spencer Berthelsen, Chief of Kelsey-Seybold Clinic, and Dr. Mavis P. Kelsey, Sr., at age 97 in 2009.

He's out gunning to stop inflation

The depression was going full blast

Sowing the seeds for a new venture

Breathing new life into Lincoln cars

Spending spree (reckless spending)

He laughed all the way to the bank

He only got a sliver of the winnings

Borrowing on someone else's dime

Scraping the bottom of the barrel

A whistle blower, a tipster, a turncoat

He walked away from the mortgage

He's casting his fortunes to the winds

The government is wallowing in red ink

It begins to pinch; feeling the squeeze

Nothing down and nothing to pay

The market is showing signs of life

Get off the stock market roller coaster

Taking the chill off a weak economy

To leapfrog ahead of the competition

Business restored, comes back to life

Born of power and steeped in privilege

Flirting with an all-time high (market)

A cat and mouse game (with criminals)

U.S. squared off against Chinese Yuan

Beauty is as beauty does, business is as business does

I had him (a congressman) in my pocket for years

Enters new territory (starts a new project)

Breathes new life (reviving a failing business)

The insider was singing (admitting the crime)

HISD takes red pen to summer school

Congress tiptoes through energy issues

Our annual going-out-of-business sale

I sold him the idea, he bought in on it, he took the bait

The business is beginning to hemorrhage.

Investors' forecast: sunny with chance of overheating

Trading is hushed by a blanket of snow

Sitting on a big pile of money (or dough)

Making a living at other people's expense

The oil industry is in shreds (Chávez in Venezuela)

Reach in your back pocket and pull out the money (the dough)

Marketers want to get inside your brain

Pizza chain seeks slice of bicultural pie

Is capitalism at odds with the Golden Rule?

The silver market comes loose of its moorings

They closed the books (on the computer guru)

An economic bottleneck; the cola wars

Is that a bull or a bear in the cornfield?

Gains in income aren't lifting all boats

We dip into our savings; we sponged on friends.

Lawsuit aimed at comptroller; lawsuit dropped

Energy shares pull the plug on the Dow

The rich relax a little but stay on guard

Commodities collapse while we plunge into a recession

Company jumps into the fray; company steps into the spotlight

Companies are always eyeing opportunities for profit

Washington's haggling left Wall Street dangling

The White House wooed the Congress

As the economy tries to find a footing, the investors spooked

The money funds hop off the French franc

Toyota comeback hinges on Camry

The gold price is taking a bath—is sky high

As Ireland flails, Europe lurches across the Rubicon (*Wall Street Journal*)

If you don't have a heart for this business, it will eat you alive

Our economy is doing a double dip with a back flip (*Wall Street Journal*)

Underwater on mortgage (the debt is greater than the house is worth – MPK, Jr.)

Upside down on your car (your debt is greater than the car is worth – MPK, Jr.)

Hanging out to dry; dropped him in the grease; cool your jets. (MPK, Jr.)

Will investors trip in a double dip? (when Dow goes up and down)

Words for money: dough, bread, moola, scratch, shekels

A Benjamin Franklin (a Benjy) – $100; A ten spot ($10); six bits (75¢); four bits, half buck (50¢); two bits, quarter (25¢)

You wouldn't buy an investment from a stranger, so why buy one wrapped in strange words?

The luck of the draw, the roll of the dice, the wheel of fortune, riding the waves of chance

Hot money, cheap money, folding money, walking around money, hard money, dumb money, soft money, easy money, trolled for money

Corruption has become a cultural trend (Peggy Noonan, October 8, 2010)

You get yours and I'll get mine (Peggy Noonan)

You don't know who to trust (Peggy Noonan)

A blizzard of forms and regulations has brought us to a nation of accountants (Peggy Noonan)

Giving the government the right to reap revenue from the public's desire to gamble, then government promoting gambling. (The Road to Corruption, Peggy Noonan, October 8, 2010)

Sayings about wealth: Well off, well to do, rich folks, in the dough, loaded with dough, in high cotton, high class, upper crust, con mucho dinero, highfaluting, filthy rich, hog rich, upscale, had money to burn, money running out his ears, millionaire, zillionaire, richer than six feet up a hog's ass

Sayings about deals: The word deal comes from a game of chance played with cards. Backroom deal, hashing out a deal, landing a deal, cooking up a deal, making a sweet deal, a big deal, raw deal, a dirty deal, a bad deal, a secret deal, a sweetheart deal, they are in bed together

METAPHORS ABOUT BUSINESS

Money flies	Financial bedrock
Fraud exploded	Laundering money
Funny money (counterfeit)	Toxic assets
The glass ceiling	Drowning in oil
At the top of the ladder	Shaving off expenses
Frozen assets	Unlocking the cash hoard
Frozen economy	You could lose your shirt on it
Liquid assets	Market is ripening for a rally
In the red (or black)	Debt ceiling
Hospitals are put on the sick list	Prices tumble
Business is soaring	The banks' bad behavior
Cash on the barrelhead	Strip search airs it's dirty linen
He's casting his fortunes to the winds	Ten percent is a nice round number
The bulls and bears are in a tug of war	Realtor picks up a 10 story building
Throwing the company a lifeline and an anchor	

METAPHORS FORMED BY GIVING ACTION TO INANIMATE SUBJECTS

We look on the market as a living thing.
  (David Brooks in the *Wall Street Journal*, 2011)

The market fights its way up	Banks open the spigot
Goosing the market	The economy grows
Sending stocks diving	A cash cow
Sales stay in the basement	Money talks
Profits sapped	The dollar treads water
A roaring economy	The rally or economy sputters

Profits soar	The bloom is off of some funds
Bonds take cover	Business is showing signs of life
Pork bellies sizzle	Bonds soar to new heights
Prices tip-toe higher	Sent the market scrambling
Gold skyrockets	A bumpy climb for stocks
Business perks up	Goes dark (out of business)
Stocks creep up	Stocks erase last week's losses
Stocks hit the bonkers	Fertile ground for investments
Sales sizzled.	Sales climbed.
Sales are climbing out of the cellar	Stocks slide
Lose steam	Face headwinds
The Dow claws back—inches higher	The Dow leaps
Heading into the red	Stocks lag
Spook the market	Funding fades
The dollar slides	Banks retreat
The battered dollar	The dollar falters
The dollar falls	The market heats
A hot market.	The market gets a lift
The market jumps	The market awakens
The market skids	The market gets a shakeup
The market is stunned	The market wilts
The market awakens	The market plunges
The market stumbles	The market swoons
The market says no	The market comes to life
The market is yo-yoing	The market loses steam
Trading is thin.	An anemic recovery.
The market halts a losing streak	

PHRASES ABOUT BUSINESS

A bloated government	Going busted
A weakened dollar	Sliding debt
A moving target	A price hawk
As good as gone	Driving a bargain
The business world	A hard sell
Blue chips	Losing control

Tricks of the trade	Rigging up profits
Filthy rich	Slaps down a bid
Landed a job	Unlock the economy
Scooped up assets	Pay to play
Cooked the books	Healthy building
Worst-case scenarios	A power player
Takes center stage	Another scam
Weighing the options	Unveils earnings
Battled to a draw	Bashing business
Weighs his authority	U-turn in business
Starts on an off note	Pumping in money
The comeback trail	A sell out
The war of inflation	Get rich quickisms
Paid back, paid up	The horn of plenty
Bad credit	Scooping up data
Jobs on the line	Window shopping
Moonlighting	Trouble-shooter
Cheap as dirt	Ahead of the curve
Crunching the numbers	Identity theft
Pocket bond issues	Group pans taxes
The old boy network	Wrangling for funds
Pooled funds	Placing a big bid
On payday	A price squeeze
Lined his pockets	Tight-fisted
A pay skirmish	A snap back rally
Cash flow	The overqualified
Too hot to handle	A major turnaround
A workaholic	Silver's golden edge
High IQ risk takers	A sucker's play
Rolling in dough	In cahoots with
A hole in the budget	Sleight of hand
Doing bang-up business	Hounded by taxes
Cornering the market	The pulse of the market
Betting on a sure thing	Taking on the big boys
Rescuing the market	Global birth pains

Defanging the unions	A plunge into recession
Roping off bad banks	Voodoo economics
Riding the tech boom	Setting up shop
An unkind market	Shelled out money
Starved by budgets	A win-win situation
A financial rollercoaster	The bottom line
Blueprint for success	Strangled growth
Hunger for quick money	Pumping up profits
Dumb money	Robust profits
Hot money	Charges pared down
Fast money	A target of opportunity
Smart money	Overblown claims
Walking money	Dredging up money
Harvesting rich profits	Dangling discounts
Lifting prices	A buying streak
Slaps down a bid	Easy money; smart money
Rolling the dice for it	Sales booming
Sends stocks diving	Quashed the effort
A hot deal; sizzling hot	Woes fog their hope
Feeling the squeeze	At the helm (the CEO)
Slumping economy	Draining the US coffers
Legal bullying	Scoops up data
Budget crunch	Sweeping back the losses
A wildcat strike	Chockablock market
Hard times	Boosting the bottom line
Bad loans	Wringing out a profit
Sneaky fees	Nowhere to go but up
Employment peaked	Worth its weight in gold
Spilling the beans	The wheel of fortune
Following the money	Doing a land office business
A shell game	Profits jump
Tax breaks	A tough sell
Oil money	People inside the boiler room
A spinoff	Fueling profits
A shady deal; double-crossed.	A clogged network

More bang for the buck	Stanching spending
A nest egg	Junk bonds
Big ticket items	

SHORT SAYINGS ABOUT BUSINESS

Beat the deadline	Shoppers let loose
Charge it to Dad	A budget brawl looms
Follow suit	He clings to his cash
Stake your claim	Traders reverse gear
The new law kicks in	Get a piece of the pie
Rivals are at his feet	China is no easy sale
It comes with a cost	Show me the money
Business is soaring	It spells large gains
It follows the money	A CEO faces a storm
Get it first	He sweetened his bid
Spenders splurge	Options are underwater
The bubble bursts	Reach for the stars
Time is money	Profits are winding down
Keep the change	He's fearing a lawsuit
CEO steps down	The market sags
He's a piker	Fears lift business
Count me out	Buy, sell, fret
Sales climbed	Keep the change
Unlock the economy	Buy one, get one free
Stamp out fraud	Dow inches higher
The rally sputters	The market skids
It begins to pinch	Sales stay in the basement
He's itching for a deal	Hedge funds were raided
Business is keeping him away	I sold him the idea
He's out for the money in it	He bought in on it
The bubble bursts	He took the bait
They're stealing us blind	He rides herd on oil prices
Stay within your budget	It strangled growth
Business is picking up	Bonds roar to rare height
He has a stable of lawyers	Keep the good times rolling
The bears turned bullish	Your check is in the mail

Mavis P. Kelsey, Sr., with sons and daughters-in-law at Live Oaks Ranch Thanksgiving, 2010: John, Gaye, Mavis, Sr., Ann, Tom, Winifred, Mavis, Jr.

The Weather

WITHOUT CLOUDS THERE CAN BE NO RAIN.

Farmers, ranchers and other country people were greatly influenced by the weather when I was a boy ninety years ago. Before the days of scientific meteorology we depended on reading the clouds and other folklore to predict weather from which we had only limited protection. There was no electricity; our houses were heated by wood stoves which required much work in cutting and providing firewood. Severe northers brought freezes, sleet and snow. The only thing between us and the North Pole was a barb wire fence. Admiral Byrd was spending the winter freezing on the South Pole when he said, "God, I'd hate to be in Amarillo tonight."

Each section of the country developed words of their own to describe the weather. It is said that linguists can determine where you are from by asking you about the weather. For example, people in one region may say **sun up** and **sun down**, while people in another area say **sunrise** and **sunset**. Some say **fall** and some say **autumn**; some say

lightning and some say **thunderstorms**. Some say **cleared up**, others say **cleared off**. A freeze is **hog killing weather** in the South. Some say **planting season**, others say **spring planting**.

In Northeast Texas at Deport people rested when the crop was **laid by** until harvest in the fall. We weren't as subject to prolonged **droughts** and **sand storms** as they were in Throckmorton in West Texas. We were in the **cyclone belt**. I heard about a Biblical type seven-year drought in the Great Plains during the 1930s. During cyclone season I saw the results of a cyclone near Paris, Texas, which not only destroyed houses but blew down the **Bodark fence posts**. Soon before I was born a man was killed by a cyclone in our immediate neighborhood. We spent many nights in our **storm cellar**.

I have described the floods of Mustang Creek which **scoured out the dirt** on Main Street of Deport. When we had a prolonged **rainy spell**, the cotton **went to stalk** while during a drought **only a few bolls matured**.

We had **Northers** and occasional **blizzards** or **hard freezes** with snow, sleet, icicles, **busted pipes**. We skated on the **gin pool**.

In the summer on hot nights we slept in the hall, on the porch or in the yard. We often slept under **mosquito nets** to avoid getting malaria. I had malaria several times.

Dust storms were severe in the Texas Panhandle. A driver once stopped to pick up a cowboy hat on the road. When he picked it up, he found a man underneath who was covered up by the dust. When the man was offered help he said he was not worried about himself but he was worried about the horse he was on. People in Amarillo got accustomed to dust. A man fainted on the street and they poured two buckets of sand on him before he came to.

There were frequent sandstorms blowing in off the High Plains during the droughts of the 1920s and 1930s. This caused a great migration of stricken people to California. I encountered them when Mahlon Grant and I rode the freight trains to California during the summer of 1932 (described in my autobiography).

The streets of Deport, all unpaved, were a **quagmire** after heavy rains. **Mule teams** pulled cars out of the mud. In the dry summers the streets were full of dust which settled in our house on all the furniture. The town ran out of water and it had to be hauled in. There was no **underground water** in Deport. We captured all the **rainwater** on our roof with gutters that poured it into a **galvanized iron tank** or a **cistern**. The water in the cistern was cool so people lowered their milk pails into the cistern to keep milk cool. If they spilled the milk in the cistern, it ruined the water and there was hell to pay. A watermelon could be cooled off by lowering it into the cistern.

These conditions prevailed in the towns of Texas and Oklahoma. Living in this environment provoked many comments based on the weather. In 2011 we were going through the worst drought that ever hit Texas. There have been Hundreds of **wildfires**, one near Houston, destroyed dozens of homes. Trees were dying by the thousands, we were running out of water, and there was no end in sight. Meteorologists say this drought may last several years, while it is flooding in New England. These changes are said to be the result of **global warming** caused by widespread use of fossil fuels. If things don't change, we are in for the decline of Global Earth on a grand scale.

EXPRESSIONS ABOUT WEATHER

Come Hell or high water; the creek got up.

I was about to freeze my tits off—balls; butt

It was colder than a well-digger's ass in Alaska.

If you can't stand the heat, stay out of the kitchen

Everyone talks about the weather but no one does anything about it

If you don't like the weather, wait a minute

The only thing between us and the North Pole is a barb wire fence

I'll be there, God willing and if the creek's not up (Dorothy Sloan)

It's hotter than hell. Hot as fire. Hot as a pistol.

March winds and April showers bring the sunshine and the flowers

Lightning never strikes twice in the same place

By the dawn's early light. At the crack of dawn; sun up; daybreak.

The weather cleared up—broke up; moderated

The wind calmed down—let up; died down.

The well went dry.

It came a dry spell—a drought; a sand storm

Tornadoes; hurricanes; storms; cyclones; floods; tempests; twisters; zephyrs

It was too wet to plow; it rained cats and dogs; it was a frog strangler.

It was a real gully washer; it dumped Noah's flood.

The storm clobbered North Carolina and churned to the North

The sunny side   Cold as ice. Cool as a cucumber.

A blue norther blew in; a real blizzard   An ill wind blows no good

Under the weather; three sheets to the wind.

CHAPTER TWELVE

Mavis. P. Kelsey, Sr., was born in this house in 1912. The house was built by Dr. J.B. Kelsey in 1911 as a wedding present for his twenty-year-old son J.R. Kelsey, the father of Mavis P. Kelsey.

Farm Animals & Varmints

BLACK CAT OR WHITE CAT, IF IT CAN CATCH MICE IT'S A GOOD CAT.
(Chinese proverb)

W*e lived closer to animals—especially the horse—before we had autos, so there were many references to them. You were told to get a horse when your horse-less carriage went dead. Later anything old-fashioned caused this remark, "That's horse and buggy." Any true remark was from "the horse's mouth."* People horsed around and chomped at the bit. Something different was a horse of a different color. There were stalking horses and Trojan horses. Horsefly bites were very, very painful.

Out on the ranch there were **cowboys, working cattle and chowing down at the chuck wagon.** Farmers **worked a crop down on the farm.** Some had an **old sow** and fed **her leftovers, swill or slop** in a **hog trough** in the **pigpen.** There were other quotes about pigs: **hogging the road, hogging the headlines, it's whole hog or none, root hog or die, don't hog it, a pig in a poke, like putting lipstick on a pig** and **I hope to kiss a pig.**

We also encountered insects, to name a few: **skeeters, bot flies, hornflies, horse flies, potato bugs, dirt daubers, red ants, piss ants, bumble bees, horse doctors, daddy longlegs, doodle bugs, grasshoppers, leaf worms,** and **boll weevils.**

There were **bullfrogs, horned frogs** and **toad frogs.** There were **water moccasins** in every pool and big **chicken snakes** swallowed eggs.

The creeks and gin pools provided perch, crappie, gar, mud cats, Opelousas catfish, and big old catfish weighing up to forty pounds. We caught a twenty-pound **shovel bill catfish** in Oklahoma. In Sulfur Bottom we caught drum and buffalo. Dad took us on weeklong fishing trips to Little River and Glover River in Southeastern Oklahoma. There we caught bass on lures and by fly-fishing in the clear streams. A couple of fish sayings: **"He's got bigger fish to fry."** and **"A fish doesn't know he's swimming until he's out of the water."**

The **passenger pigeons** were gone before my time but my grandfather Kelsey told me about them clouding the sky in Mississippi and breaking limbs by their weight in their roosts. We had **robin roosts** on Sulfur Bottom where robins roosted by the millions during their winter flights. They were killed by the hundreds with sticks. The breasts were removed, cooked and put in jars or cans for food. We had annual dove hunts near Deport where all our family gathered each year during the Labor Day weekend.

When I was twelve years old, Dad gave me a twenty gauge single-shot shotgun. On Saturdays my friends and I went hunting in the woods along the creeks. Unfortunately, we shot every bird in sight. Woodpeckers were especially good to eat. I have crawled a hundred yards on my belly to get a shot at a dove sitting on a fence wire. The **briar patches** were home to **field mice** and **field rats, skunks, possums, coons** and **cottontail rabbits.** The Deport junk pile was mostly a briar patch with old rusty cans, tools and implements. You could always get a shot at a cottontail there. We had a mutt named Stranger who was a good rabbit dog and my friends had terriers and other dogs for rabbit hunting. Our barns were overrun with mice and rats unless we had one or more house cats to eradicate them. I always had a pigeon cote nailed on the barn wall. I also kept different kinds of pigeons in a cage and tamed some of them. Mother cooked squabs which were a great delicacy. In later years while practicing medicine in Houston, one of my patients often brought me squabs all dressed and ready to cook.

There was a **rare fox** or **bobcat** around Deport. There were no **coyotes** or **wolves** but my relatives in Throckmorton took me wolf and coyote hunting with their hounds. I have mentioned that I went with Dad and his friends **deer hunting** in the Texas Hill Country and Southeastern Oklahoma. There were still **mountain lions** or **cougars** in Oklahoma which tried to steal our game. These mountain lions scared the hell out of me. Dad also hunted **elk** in Colorado. He went fishing in Caddo Lake, Texas; Little River, Oklahoma; White River, Arkansas; and in Mexico and Canada. He was an expert fly fisherman. He often took my brother John and me with him.

Bird watching wasn't a hobby then, but we recognized a few birds. All little birds were **grass birds**. Then there were **peckerwoods, sparrows eating horse manure, sapsuckers, partridges** (for quail), **buzzards, red wing blackbirds, roadrunners, whippoorwills, field (or meadow) larks, mockingbirds, robins, jaybirds, woodpeckers, doves** and **red birds** we could identify. There were very few **quail** but Uncle Dean Oliver took me hunting in the woods of Red River County where there were many. There were **crows, hawks, buzzards** and **owls. Geese, ducks** and **cranes** flew over by the millions in winter migration to the Texas Coastlands.

We shot **water moccasins, chicken snakes, blacksnakes** or any kind of snake that was unlucky enough to cross our path. There were no **rattlesnakes.** As a boy I never knew anyone who got snake bit. My favorite sport in the ponds around Deport was **frog-gigging**. Mother fried **frog legs** for me and I sold others to the Antones. Once I gigged a huge **bullfrog**. When I dressed it I found a whole English sparrow in its stomach, feathers and all, recently caught.

During the summer we picked blackberries which grew on fence lines, roadsides, briar patches and almost everywhere. You could count on coming home, eaten up with chiggers which kept you scratching all night. Rubbing yourself with **coal oil** helped a little. Often you got stung by **hornets, yellow jackets** or **bees**. You could relieve the pain by rubbing **tobacco juice** on the bites.

I was never bitten by a **spider** or a **scorpion**, but I got infested by **lice** and bit by **bedbugs**. We caught **butterflies** and **lightning bugs**. **July flies** could be carried in your pocket alive.

There were **prairie dog towns** on family ranches in Throckmorton County. **Ground owls** and snakes also occupied their holes and underground tunnels. I caught a prairie dog and brought it to Deport but it soon died. I often caught **horned frogs** (lizards).

There are many folk sayings about farm animals that a country boy would recognize. Many of these sayings have left the farm and gone to the city, just like the farm boys have.

When I sent my friend Ben Hulsey a copy of my first book on Texas folklore, he responded to me with these sayings in his letter:

Dear Dr. Kelsey:

Thank you very much for your gift of *Texas Sayings and Folklore*.

As you know, an author leaves himself **out on a limb**, a **sitting duck** for criticism. I am sure there are some that would say that you were just **out on a lark** or **trying to feather your own nest**. Or that the work is full of **bird-brained ideas** or is **for the birds**, and as an author **your goose is cooked**.

These people make me **madder than a wet hen** and should be **watched like a hawk** with an **eagle eye**. I say **what is good for the goose is good for the gander** and that they should follow the **lame duck** congress back home **as the crow flies**. Even though I am no **spring chicken** nor **wise as an owl**, a **little bird told me** before he **flew the coup** that this work is a **real feather in your cap** and that you are **sitting in the catbird seat** with a **bird's eye view**.

I am **proud as a peacock** to know you. Even though I am not a **night owl** nor do I often **eat like a bird** nor feel as **naked as a jaybird**, I do sometimes feel like **the cat that swallowed the canary** when I tell people we have ancestors in common.

I hope you did not **put all of your eggs in one basket** with this work because people like you who are **wise as an owl** are **scarcer than hen's teeth**.

SAYINGS ABOUT ANIMALS AND BIRDS

The empty nest	Cat fur to make kitten britches
It's time to feather your nest	In the dark all cats are gray
Birds of a feather flock together	Hot as a scalded cat
The early bird gets the worm	A cat on a hot tin roof
She's no spring chicken	Fatten the kitty
Talking turkey	Busy as a beaver

Like water off a duck's back	The lion's share
He shot a goose and killed a hen	Pop goes the weasel
Get your ducks in a row	A wolf in sheep's clothing
As bad as a duck on a June bug	Getting his goat
Ducking a blow; he ducked out	Blue dog Democrats
It's duck soup	Yellow dog Democrats
He's a dead duck	Like a whipped dog
A gone gander	Puppy love
His goose is cooked	Putting on the dog
Get a gander (view) of it	It's dog eat dog
Don't goose me	Leading a dog's life
Hogwash!	In the doghouse
That's how the cow bit the cabbage	That dog won't hunt
What's the beef?	The tail wagging the dog
She's the bell cow	He ran like a highlifed dog
Don't get the cart before the horse	The underdog
It's flogging a dead horse	Going to the dogs
Old horses don't forget the way	Barking up the wrong tree
Regular old horse sense	A dog and pony show
A charley horse	Call off the dogs
A dark horse	I double dog dare you
Hold your horses; pull in the reins.	He's going to the dogs
Whoa; gee; haw; giddup	Every dog has his day
Our chickens will come home to roost	It's like putting lipstick on a pig
Don't duck out on me— chicken out	Even a blind hog can find an acorn
Don't look a gift horse in the mouth	That's a horse of a different color
A bird in the hand is worth two in the bush	
He killed the goose that laid the golden egg	
What's sauce for the goose is sauce for the gander	
Don't count your chickens before they hatch	
You can't make a silk purse out of a sow's ear	
I hope to kiss a pig; she's an old sow; a pig in a poke	
You can lead a horse to water but you can't make him drink	
Horse feathers! I got it straight from the horse's mouth.	
Curiosity killed the cat; the cat's got your tongue.	

When the cat's away, the mice will play

It's the cat's whiskers; the cat's paw; the cat's meow; the cat's pajamas

A cool cat; a wampus cat; an alley cat

The sheep separated from the flock becomes prey for the wolf

The first automobile in Throckmorton, Texas, with Uncle Tom and Grandfather Parrott, around 1914.

All About Talk

THEY THAT TALK MOST HAVE THE LEAST TO SAY.

People love to talk, tell secrets, and hear their own voices. Sometimes they say too much and sometimes don't live up to what they say. They give lots of advice as we have shown in the lists of Advice and Admonitions. People also try to stop others from talking.

Mavis Kelsey in full uniform as graduate of Texas A&M College in 1932.

TALK, WORDS, SPEAKING

He talks up a storm	She ate him out
Wash your filthy linen at home	She gave him hell
Practice what you preach	She bared her teeth
Don't tell tales out of school	She bowed her neck
Don't bad mouth me	She scolded the kids
Don't blab on him	She gave them a bawling out
It gave the school a black eye	She turned the tables on him
It rubbed off on me	Zip your lip
I never said pea turkey	He said nary a word
I couldn't get a word in sideways	Saying is not doing
Quit hollering at me	It's easier said than done
She let the cat out of the bag	No sooner said than done
The mouse that roared	He's in hot water
They threw the book at him	He fudged on her
He's a whistle blower; a tipster	It speaks volumes
Don't open up a can of worms	He called a spade a spade
He came out swinging	That's what I said
He cusses like a sailor	He listens to his own drum
It's showdown time	You can say that again
If walls could talk—hear	You get the picture
In one ear and out the other	See what I say
She spilled the beans	Get the jump on him
Because I said so, that's why	Before you could say scat
He likes to hear his voice	I've got it down pat
It's better left unsaid	I knew something was afoot
She flew off the handle	He cast a cloud over it
He drives her crazy	Tell the full story
Listen to the voice of experience	The spell is broken
He's blowing his own horn	Brushing that aside
He's got foot-in-mouth disease	Whistling in the dark
Hard words seldom hurt anyone	Said in jest
She poured out her grief	Cut the flab
Loose lips sink ships	Spit it out
For crying out loud	Idle talk; dry wit

Don't get anxious—worked up	Scandal monger
He warmed up and hit his stride	Turncoat.
It's a tempest in a teapot	Mudslinging
It's a hot potato	A loose tongue; a sharp tongue.
He sidetracked it	A bad mouth; a quick mouth.
He has no clout	A potty mouth; a mealy mouth.
He stretches the truth	Mouthed it
He has my ear	Cusses like a sailor
Put it on the line	On a high note—off note
He's a burr under the saddle	The punch line; the public line.
He had nothing to say and said it	Borrowed a phrase
Silence is more eloquent than words	Chewing the fat
Getting close to the truth	Shooting the breeze
To swear is unbecoming	Insider talk
It goes without saying	Having a spat
He lived to tell the story	Belly laughs
A word to the wise is sufficient	Finger pointing
You can't live on promises	Food for thought
Whatever do you mean?	Go negative
Let justice ring—reign	A cat fight; copycat.
He swallowed every word of it	Overheated rhetoric
He hit the nail on the head	The bully pulpit
It's a political dogfight	Giving voice to it
I heard him loud and clear	He's a blowhard; a windbag.
I'll get my ten cents worth in	He blows hot air
I'm carried away with it	He's a loud mouth
There's no telling how many	He's full of baloney or malarkey
He has a dirty mouth	He talks a big game
He's a Doubting Thomas	He's a big showoff
He's a put on; he puts on airs	He tells tales
He has a short fuse	He's stuck up
You put words in my mouth	He's an apple polisher
Think before you speak	He sweet talks
He's more bark than bite	He's windy
It's like rubbing salt on a wound	He puts on airs

He hit a sore spot	The play of words
Read all about it	He's gilding the lily
Another voice heard from	He's a rumor mill
You can't fool me	It's a big to-do about nothing
You don't know the half of it	Tough talk; sweet talk.
He's sour as a pickle	There are words for it
Why are you singing the blues?	He didn't mince words
He had to eat his words	I wish you had never said that
Keep your mouth shut	He talks through his nose
Don't gossip	The written word is silent
Don't monkey around with me	He has a way with words
Keep a stiff upper lip	Damning with faint praise
Screaming bloody murder	Don't talk back
Chew on this	Talk, talk, talk
Ranting and raving	She talked a blue streak
Abusing free speech	She never stopped talking
She flew right into him	She will talk your head off
She made the feathers fly	After all is said and done
She's mad as a wet hen	She talked down to me
She skinned him alive	She told him off good
Mum's the word	A closed mouth gathers no foot
Speaking volumes	Giving him a say
A lot of hoop-la	To hear him tell it
He pops off too much	Don't give me any lip
Keep your damn mouth shut	His silence says a lot
I'm not talking or saying (a denial)	They are not talking to each other
Hard words seldom hurt anyone	Silence is more eloquent than words
A closed mouth catches no flies	He had nothing to say and he said it
You may have to eat those words	A good speaker is first a good listener
Logorrhea: Excessive flow of words	Never tell a lie. Never tell on brother.
When I was so rudely interrupted	The insider was singing (to the judge)
Scholars talk books, butchers talk pigs	Take that and smoke it in your pipe
I'm going to wash your mouth out	Speak of the devil and he will appear
Some things are easier said than done	He's long on words, short on facts
Shut your mouth, save your breath	The squeaky wheel gets the grease

An honest man's word is his bond

Nothing asked, nothing gained

It takes two to start an argument

He pointed an accusing finger at me

They are holding his feet to the fire

From the heart speaketh the mouth

An argument never convinced anyone

here are two sides to every question

She gave him a raking over the coals

She had him eating out of her hand

Gabs; chatters; rattles; fusses; cries

Give your word and keep it

Keep your words soft; tomorrow you may need to swallow them

I don't like big words; they are left for scholars

Your mouth looks pretty when it's closed

Writing is a way of talking without being interrupted. (A Word a Day)

Two good talkers are not worth one good listener

What a spendthrift he is of his tongue. (Shakespeare)

Diarrhea of the mouth, constipation of the brain

You never learn a thing while you are talking

There's gonna be some ass-kicking around here

He's barking at the moon—up a tree; up the wrong tree

If you don't say anything, it can't be repeated

In the next breath she's saying the exact opposite

Nearly everything that comes out of his mouth is untrue

He not only talked the talk, he walked the walk

Talk softly and carry a big stick. (Theodore Roosevelt)

She was the queen of mirth. (Liz Carpenter)

Don't make a mountain out of a molehill

The whole truth and nothing but the truth

Out of the abundance of his heart the mouth speaketh

Your smile says a lot before you start talking

Instead of offering advice, offer your ear

An honest politician is one who when bought, stays bought, said about a congressman

When people tell you that you look good, they're telling you how old you are

A secret is something you tell others because you can't keep it to yourself

A nasty tongue is worse than a wicked hand

A hypocrite with his tongue destroyeth his neighbor

The tongue can no man tame. It is an unruly evil full of deadly poison.

If you don't stop crying, I'll give you something to cry about

A prophet is without honor in his own hometown

If one knows, it's a secret; if two, it's public

If you can't say something nice, don't say anything

There is a time to speak and a time to be silent

People who live in glass houses should never throw stones

What the child hears at home is soon known outside

Sticks and stones will break your bones, but words will never hurt you

A third ear hears what's not been said

It's a balancing act to please everyone

Get the lowdown— the skinny, the inside scoop)

That's one thing that you won't get out of my mouth

A word in earnest is as good as a speech. (Charles Dickens)

Holler calf-rope—holler uncle (give up in a fight)

You can't put those words in my mouth

She could do long division with her eyes shut (Leon Hale)

She could spell the covers off the book (Leon Hale)

There's many a slip between the cup and the lip

Making promises and keeping them are two different things

Ask me no questions and I'll tell you no lies

He not only talked the talk but walked the walk

That's how the cow bit the cabbage

He would tell a lie when the truth would serve him better

Mumbles; stutters; yells; screams; whispers

Most people want to know only to talk

An honest man is able to speak for himself. (Shakespeare)

Some think too little and talk too much

What a spendthrift he is of his tongue. (Shakespeare)

I have often regretted my speech, but never my silence

It's easy for a man to speak one thing and mean another

Silence is the most perfect expression of scorn

It's not every question that needs an answer

How sweet sounds the voice of a good woman

Silence is one of the hardest arguments to refute

Their very silence is a loud cry. (Cicero 106-63 BC)

Often silence is the wisest thing for a man to heed. (Pindar 552-492 BC)

It's difficult to keep quiet when you have nothing to say

Let any man speak long enough and he will get believers

You have not convinced a man because you have silenced him

A gift of words indicates a dearth of knowledge

Not even a fish gets in trouble if it keeps its mouth shut

A silent man is the best one to listen to

There are just two kinds of people in the world—talkers and non-talkers

Most talkers are non-listeners; some non-talkers are non-listeners

She breaks down her conversation into small pieces

Being silent isn't the same thing as listening

Thoughts that break and words that burn

An honest tale speeds best by being plainly told (Shakespeare)

A sage has large ears and a small mouth

The silence of the dead was overwhelming (after the earthquakes in Haiti)

Oh, God, that men should put an enemy in their mouth to steal away the brain (Shakespeare)

I love words but I don't like strange ones; you don't understand them and they don't understand you. Old words are like old friends, you know 'em the minute you see 'em. (Will Rogers)

No one has prosperity so high and firm that two or three words can't dishearten it; There is no calamity which right words will not begin to redress. (Emerson)

To think like a wise man and communicate in the words of the people (A Word a Day)

Once a word leaves your mouth, you cannot chase it back, even with the swiftest horse. (Chinese proverb)

Sam was seeking a divorce because his wife was talking too much. Judge: Sam, what does she talk about? Sam: Well, judge, she don't say.

SOME RETORTS

The gloves are off	It's a pipe dream
Quit rattling off; quit your yakking.	You make me laugh
It's a gimmick	He laid an egg
Who's running this show anyway?	He's out in left field
I told you so	Sure enough, now come?
He's puffed up like a toad	I wouldn't bet on it
Throw smoke at him	I'll believe it when I see it

Was you there, Charlie?	I don't believe a word you say
He left a foul odor	I couldn't care less
It smells; I smell a rat	This could go on forever
Well, I'll be a monkey's uncle	Watch your mouth
Hog wash! Shut your face.	I'll wash your mouth
She had her say	Think before you speak
Put your money where your mouth is	Keep quiet about it
It's no big deal	Keep your mouth shut
It's a pie in the sky	Quit popping off
Of all things!	It's too horrible to imagine
Well I'll be!	Such nonsense!
Watch out, he's a dog in the manger	I don't get it
Come down off your high horse	Who said so? Says who?
He blowing off	You don't say
He dropped the ball	You're kidding. Don't kid yourself
He welches on her	It's no laughing matter
Watch out, he's a snake in the grass	We broke up

SOME PHRASES

Nary a word	Street smarts
A spoonful of charity	Wagging tongues
A wake up call	On thin ice
An educated guess	Breaking the ice
Dirty words	Rumor mill
Lazy rhetoric	Right pert
That is to say	Riled up
I allowed that	Crabby; cranky
I figured (figgered)	Touchy; touchous
I'll relate (what he did)	If stares could kill
Stirring up trouble	By word of mouth
Dog eat dog	The gift of gab
Puts the spotlight on	The last word
Touching a sore spot	Famous last words
Damned with faint praise	Poking fun
After all is said and done	As I was saying

As sure as shooting	Barbs fly
Preaching to deaf ears	In his own words
On the soap box	Verbal fireworks
Going to great lengths	Stop ranting
A whale of a tale	Another voice heard
Pearls of wisdom	Body language
The jewel in his crown	A play of words
As a matter of fact	Bragging rights
The moment of truth	Small talk. Straight talk.
The unvarnished truth	A loose tongue
Little white lies	Tongue in cheek
Tough talk; trash talk.	Snake oil
Paying lip service	

Mavis Kelsey while Dean—Postgraduate School of Medicine, University of Texas and Professor of Medicine at U.T. in 1952.

Admonitions, Advice, Directives & Commands

BE SURE YOU ARE RIGHT, THEN GO AHEAD.
(David Crockett)

There's a lot of good advice in these sayings. People have always been willing to give advice and recommendations or admonish their children, friends, employees and the general public. But when advice is ignored, commands are sometimes given. There are many well-known words of advice, most well-meaning. Children grew up responding to these admonitions and pass on these same sayings. The sayings become part of the vocabulary as they pass from generation to generation. The Bible contains many that have been around for 2,000 years in various forms. Reading these quotes reveals the challenges of parents' in their efforts to build character and keep children out of trouble. If you read these quotes, it will also help you stay out of trouble, live a better life and contribute to society.

First there are directions for children to behave properly: To **not talk too much**; **not eat too much**; **clean your plate**; **clean up your mess**; **be nice to mother**; **and don't sass her. Don't pout**; **put aside your childish ways**; **quit hurting your sister**; and **try to settle down. Make up your bed**; **read good books**; **use your head**; and **be careful what you say**.

Then comes advice for the grownups: **It's time to get moving**; **make yourself useful**; **roll up your sleeves**; and **put your shoulder to the wheel. Don't fight**; **keep your chin up**; and **keep your cool. Don't make excuses. Don't nag** or **knock it. Take aim**; **steer a steady course. Mind your own business**; **save your money. Deal yourself in**; **seize opportunity**; **stay out of trouble.** Finally, **you can take it easy**; **don't judge others**; **see the world**; **take time to smell the roses. Batten down the hatches and hope for the best but prepare for the worst. Be slow to make a promise and swift to keep it.**

- An admonition, according to Webster, is "a gentle or friendly reproof or warning; counseling against fault or oversight."
- Advice is a "recommendation for a decision or course of conduct."
- A directive "points out direction, guidance or authoritative instructions."
- A command "directs authoritatively or orders."

Let your conscience be your guide	Listen to the voice of experience
Give it your best shot	Get your numbers straight
Live a happy, healthy and hopeful life	Don't rock the boat
Give a little, get a lot	Talk with people, not at people
Count your daily blessings	Don't act out and act up; be good
Respect Mother Earth	Leave well enough alone
Let's get down to earth about this	Show a little more backbone
Go ahead, make my day	Make up your mind
Don't back out on me	Get down to business
Don't let me down	Watch your language
Try not to get so worked up	Grit your teeth and bear it
Let her rip	If the shoe fits, wear it
Say it with a smile	Put it on the line
Think good thoughts	Stay on your toes

Do your own thinking	Don't make a fuss about it
Get your head and game together	Don't get your hackles up
Don't believe everything you hear	Showcase your wares
Tell it like it is; never tell a lie	Come as you are
Stay out of trouble	Batten down the hatches
Roll up your sleeves and get at it	Clean up your own mess
Cool your heels; settle down	Deal me in
Dig yourself out	Hash it out
Don't forget your manners	No excuses accepted
Don't get so antsy	Lend a hand
Don't get your hopes up	Don't hog the road
Don't get all fired up	Don't drive drunk
Don't get yourself in hot water	Get going
Give him a little slack.	Go help
Hold your horses	Go West, young man
Keep the lid on	If you don't like it, lump it
Leave well enough alone	In Rome do as the Romans do
Pull in your reins; wrap it up	Judge not lest you be judged
Be still; quit showing off	Let's get going
Hang in there; finish what you start	Let's stay on the same page
Wipe that smile off your face	Put your shoulder to the wheel
Don't make a pig of yourself	Put yourself in another's shoes
Limber up; get in shape	Take a hard look
Keep your thoughts to yourself	Spread the word—the news
Save for a rainy day	Stay put; steer clear
Don't stretch your luck too far	Watch your step
Know where to draw the line	Pony up
Stick to your story	Step up to the bat or to the plate
Do the right thing.	Turn on the heat
Be polite and don't have an attitude	You made your bed, now lie in it
Try your best, even if it isn't enough	Tend to your own business
Have a good cry	Don't rock the boat
Eat less, move more	Get it right the first time
Don't get your ass in a sling	Get the ball rolling
Act your age	Stay in touch

Call a spade a spade	Get into the swing of things
Do the best you can every day	Don't ask, don't tell
Don't bite the hand that feeds you	Don't tease me
Don't fool around	Don't toy with me
Don't give up without a fight	Abandon ship. Fire!
Don't be a poor loser	Make yourself scarce
Don't cry for him	Don't cross my path
Don't judge a book by its cover	Go climb a tree
Don't kick a man when he's down	Don't jump on me
Don't look a gift horse in the mouth	Quit dragging your feet, or heels
Don't monkey around with me	Don't give me any lip
Don't rat on me	Face the music
Don't sell yourself down the river	Hurry and ketch up
Don't tell tales out of school	Get a move on
If you can't lick 'em, join 'em	Lay off
Keep a stiff upper lip	Back up
Keep your chin up	Now git!
Let bygones be bygones	Stop, halt, whoa
Keep your cool; take it easy	Pipe down; shut up
Make haste slowly	Pull your horns in
Never give up	Stop messing up
Practice what you preach	Quit foolin' around
Seize the moment	Sit down
Take the bad with the good	Quiet down
Take it or leave it	Zip your lip
Take time to smell the roses	Use your head
Think before you speak	Quit bellyaching
You be careful	You better watch out
You can't say it often enough	Take that and smoke it in your pipe
Light a shuck; shake a leg; high tail it	Don't put the cart before the horse
Shut your mouth and eat your supper	Use your head; Quit bellyaching
Quit picking on me; quit pestering me	Don't get all wrought up about it
Never awaken a sleeping baby, or dog	Live well, laugh often and love much
If first you don't succeed, try, try again	Put it in black and white (record it)
Speak now or forever hold your peace	

Dr. Mavis P. Kelsey, right, and his brother John R. Kelsey, Jr., at ground breaking of main campus building, Kelsey-Seybold Clinic in 1998.

I would like a drink; your wish is my command

Take care, my friend; don't be hard on yourself

Stick to your principles; remember where you came from

Take smaller steps; take it one step at a time—one day at a time

Be sure you're right, then go ahead (David Crockett)

Don't fib me; don't soft soap me; don't rag me; don't knock it

Don't tease me; don't kid me; don't bug me; don't spoof me

Don't try to get by with a bunch of excuses.

Don't throw the baby out with the bath water

Keep your mouth shut; hush your mouth

Don't tell on your brother; Mama, make him stay away

Just wait until we get home! You're going to get it when we get home.

Determine never to be idle (Donald Dyal)

If you don't straighten up, I'm going to knock you into the middle of next week

Don't bite off more than you can chew

Don't get your panties in a bunch (Vicki Buxton)

Don't lend salt; it will break up a friendship

Don't make a mountain out of a molehill

It's a great world; see it before you leave it

Live it up; live and let live; Live one day at a time

Never let a kiss fool you or a fool kiss you

Give to the poor and take from the rich

Let not the sun go down on your wrath

Leave well enough alone; let sleeping dogs lie

Keep your promises; Play fair; Tell the truth

Don't write what you would not want to read yourself

Don't get riled up about it; don't get lathered up; don't get edgy

Quit meddling in other people's business

Get your act together; get real; get regular; get your ducks in a row

Don't sit around and feel sorry for yourself

Close your eyes and open your mouth

Hope for the best; prepare for the worst

Make hay while the sun shines; make yourself useful

Don't even think about parking here (Dumas County Courthouse, 1992)

Strike that word from your vocabulary

Twenty-three skidoo; get out; skedaddle; scram; get lost; drop dead; disappear

If you can't push, pull. If you can't pull, get out of the way.

Listen to Mother; you be careful; stop acting like your father; don't sass your mother

Don't get your meat where you get your bread (don't chase the girls in the office)

Do the right thing. It will gratify some people and astonish the rest (Mark Twain—a favorite saying of George Bush)

Put up your dukes; Say you didn't mean it; put up or shut up; don't give me any sass or backtalk

CHAPTER FIFTEEN

A Texas Ranger from Harper's Weekly, July 6, 1961.
Judge James G. Thompson, great grandfather of Mary Wilson Kelsey,
was a Ranger in the Texas Republic in 1838.

Humor, Wit & Common Sense

JEST OFTEN DECIDES MATTERS OF IMPORTANCE MORE EFFECTIVELY THAN SERIOUSNESS.
Horace (65 BC – 8 AD)

There's often humor in sayings, intended or not. Many writers, especially humorists such as Mark Twain have taken pleasure in producing humorous aphorisms, wisecracks, quips, limericks, and the like.

People enjoy facts stated in funny, ludicrous or absurd terms. They enjoy witty, quick and clever remarks. People sometimes express tragedy or sadness with grim humor. Philosophy, common sense or the profound are often stated in humorous terms.

For laughing out loud	He was afraid of his own shadow
Life is sexually transmitted	I did it just for the hell of it
He could sell socks to a snake	Wearing glasses that are too rosy
Bubbling over with joy	I just can't help it, I like the guy
I wish I knew how to quit you	Battling the bulge (dieting)
Kiss me, you fool!	Who stole my cheese?
Heads I win; tails you lose	She's too hot to handle
Honk if you're horny	Once it's gone, it's gone
The won't-grow-up modern male	Common sense is not so common
It's not over till the fat lady sings	Cold ain't so hot
He's painted himself into a corner	To be chic is not to be chic
Mistaking vulgarity as for wit	Wrinkles don't hurt
You may have to eat those words	A girl in a very attractive package
The lead dog has the best view	You never finish writing a book
Don't jump to conclusions	Stirring up apathy
That secret leaks like a sieve	I could do without you
My knees are barking. (Leon Hale)	We were nosed out by a landslide
We parked the dog. (Leon Hale)	Life is a bowl of cherries
Laughter is the mind sneezing	Everybody's got to be somewhere
A love letter from the IRS	Eggs cannot be unscrambled
Wise as a tree full of owls	It isn't easy being beautiful
Studying to be a half-wit	Use good ole common sense
If you've got it flaunt it	Than which there is no whicher
When you are in love it shows	Boys are nature's raw material
When I win the lottery	Experience is in short supply
Do whatever you do best better.	It's colder than a witches tit
Not till Sitting Bull stands up	A rich uncle named Sam
It rang a bell in my memory archives	There's only one number one
Barefoot boys with cheeks of tan	Humor: that leavening subtle uniter
Men are rapidly becoming obsolete	Don't judge him till you kiss him
Banal questions are best met with a little humor	
Looking out for number one isn't all that bad	
Laughter brings comfort during troubled times	
A doctor who treats himself has a fool for a patient	
A bargain is something you cannot use at a price you cannot resist	

How can I drain the swamp when I'm up to my ass in alligators?

Comedy is a funny way of being serious

Last but not least, avoid clichés like the plague

Humility is one thing I've always prided myself on

What a child hears at home is public the next day

A secret is what you tell someone not to tell because you can't keep it secret

I'm not hard of hearing; I'm hard of listening (Denton Cooley)

Make sure you wear clean underwear in case you're in an accident

Never let a kiss fool you or a fool kiss you

I like to be loved as I love when I love (saying on a Faberge egg – Gaye Kelsey)

Experience is something you get when you don't get what you want

Experience is something you get just after you need it

The crowd was seven people deep

The sun has riz and the sun has set and here we is in Texas yet

A guest and dead fish stink on the third day

Dally not with other folk's women or money (Benjamin Franklin)

I can't get along with you and I can't get along without you

I feel so miserable without you; it's almost like you being here

Pity the poor pelican. His beak holds more than his belly can

I'm a lover and a fighter and a wild horse rider and a pretty good windmill fixer

You don't have to go home, but you can't stay here (Gaye Kelsey)

Old age and treachery always overcome youth and skill (Willie Nelson)

Wash your face and comb your hair and get yourself ready for the Dallas Fair

A reply to a letter to Dad for money: Too bad, so sad, your dad

Indian word for vegetarian: a bad hunter

It's nice to be at the top of the food chain

He who hesitates is poor (Mel Brooks)

He committed suicide by falling off his ego (Earl Brewer)

You can be right or you can be happy. Choose happy.

Get your hands in gear to wash the dishes.

The economy of lies: when cronies collude (*Wall Street Journal*)

Good health is the slowest possible way by which one can die

If you can't do anything about it, relax and enjoy it (Clayton Williams)

You gotta be a little crazy to stay happy (Mary Patino)

They (women) come in handy (from a friend not named)

He opened his mouth and put his foot in it

When you come to a fork in the road, take it.(Yogi Berra)

It's only a short trip from the top of his brain to the tip of his tongue.

No matter where I am, there I am.(Peggy Noonan)

You caught me red-handed—with my pants down

If you don't watch out, he'll get in your pants

You better get out while the gettin's good.

I wonder what my stomach thinks about this

Heaven is for real and there is a Santa Claus

When it comes to getting to the bathroom, every hundredth of a second counts

He made his statement by building a huge house (architect Virginia Kelsey)

I wouldn't give you hay if you were a cow in a concrete pasture

There will be a hot time in the old town tonight

The best way to win a friend is to ask his advice

The more I see of other countries the more I love my own.

That favorite subject, Myself (James Boswell)

Civilized men cannot live without cooks

You can lead a horse to water but you have to have a horse.

Spring travels north at fifteen miles a day (Mrs. James Cooke Wilson Sr.)

She's so fast she catches herself coming back

When does an atheist pray? When his life is endangered.

You're gonna freeze your butt off—tits off

You go first. No, no, after you.

Being moral: doing the right thing while no one is watching

If the United States sneezes the rest of the world gets double pneumonia

He's so sissy he has to squat to pee

I could write a hundred acres about it

Not tonight Josephine (said Napoleon)

Reach in your pocket and pull out the dough

Hurry up and wait (World War II expression)

Half the lies that people tell are not true

You can live without sex, but you can't live without your glasses

Instead of asking for permission, ask for forgiveness later (Sheldon Ericson)

My mind wandered all night about absolutely nothing

She smells as sweet as a peach—as an orchard hog

Our annual going out of business sale

Diarrhea of the mouth is bad, but constipation of the brain is worse

It went through him like Grant took Richmond

It's better to be open than closed (about diarrhea)

I know some things I wish I didn't know

Those kind words make me feel like I'm somebody

When there's a little money I buy a book; if there is any leftover I buy food.

History is one damn lie after another (Winston Churchill)

History is a bunch of lies (Mark Twain)

He used language I wouldn't take from anybody but my wife (Ramon Adams)

He's as welcome as a polecat at a picnic

He's so thin he has to stand up twice to make a shadow (Ramon Adams)

Familiar flavors bring back childhood memories

He was grinning like a calf eating briars (Jim Kemper)

I owe my career to my first wife and my second wife to my career.

There's only one chance to make a first impression (Wendy Kelsey)

He's not from another country, he's from another galaxy

A somebody was once a nobody who wanted to and did

Elitism is the slur directed at merit by mediocrity (A Word a Day)

You can't walk and chew gum at the same time

How do you screw a porcupine? Very, very carefully.

When Adam saw Eve a thought popped through his mind

Privacy as we once knew it is dead, just ask Google

How do you titillate an ocelot? You osculate its tit a lot. (tongue twister)

Such trouble has smoke coming out of my ears

Why are we here? Because we are here, that's all, 'nuff said.

When I'm good, I'm very good. When I'm bad, I'm better.

Too much of a good thing is too much

You can't teach taste (Julia Childs)

Being in love is a wretched state when it is not reciprocated

Marriage is either a blessing or a dismal failure

Busier than a jump cable at a negro picnic

Restraint was thrown in the ash can

I'll scratch your back if you will scratch mine

When I do good I feel good, when I do bad I feel bad (Abraham Lincoln)

A pat down; having your genital area patted against your will

Imagination is the workshop of your mind

The sum of the parts is greater than the whole

People give to people (Ross McKnight)

Don't take the easy way out; take the right way (Ross McKnight)

Getting suited up (getting drunk for the party) (an AKK saying)

Sex is like air: It's not that important unless you aren't getting any

If you think no one cares, try missing a couple of mortgage payments

Some days you are the dog; some days you are the tree

There are two excellent theories for arguing with women; neither one works

Idleness like kisses, to be sweet must be stolen (A Word a Day)

Hogging the road; he took his half in the middle

The room was so small I had to walk in and back out to turn around

My mother had morning sickness after I was born

It's cold enough to freeze the balls off a monkey

Step down immediately but not right now (Obama to Mubarak)

Worry gives wrinkles which give you something to worry about

Nothing is as important as you think it is when you are thinking about it

April showers bring the Spring time and the flowers

They say money can't buy happiness; yeah?

Your report of my burial is an exaggeration (Mark Twain)

Take an aspirin and call me in the morning

The bad man will get you if you don't watch out

Want to live longer? Take nap. (Chinese)

Don't saw the limb off your sitting on

Don't say money cannot bring happiness; what about food, clothing and shelter?

Physical disability makes you appreciate what you once took for granted

Expressions and sayings take the place of big words

I like pretty words that are passed on outside of the classroom

I drink to the general joy of the whole table. (Shakespeare)

A minor operation is one performed on somebody else

Getting what you deserve and deserving what you get are not the same

Eyes on the road and fingers off the phone

Quit trying to jam too many tasks into so little time

Hang a mark on the things you take for granted

It takes an hour to have a five minute conversation with her

I may be crazy but I'm not stupid (Gaye Kelsey)

One man is good as another and a good deal better

The clock keeps insisting its 5:15. My Timex says its 10:15. (Leon Hale)

Here comes the baby; out goes the marriage

Through the lips and over the gums, look out stomach, here it comes

If gold is Monte Carlo; silver is a slot machine in Las Vegas

Instead of mounting a dunghill and crowing

Don't fall into the trap that newer is better

Nobody goes there anymore, it's too crowded (Yogi Berra)

Stylish guys steal short sleeves from nerds

It gets late early out here (Yogi Berra)

I'd rather be right than President. You don't need to worry, you'll never be either

There are no good deeds that go unpunished

Enough butter to choke an artery (Leon Hale)

All men are created equal, some are just more equal

He's working like he still needs the money

Look at the dirt on the back of your neck

She smiles like a baby and bites like an alligator

Now you're getting a dose of your own medicine

Opportunities are never lost; someone else will take the ones you miss

Everyone needs a friend to goof off with

Here's looking up your kilt (Angus Anderson)

The best barbeque in the world or anywhere else (Swazey's BBQ, 1949)

Life is the art of living without using an eraser

The mind cannot absorb what the seat will not endure

When good enough just isn't good enough

Wine and cheese are ageless companions

It's colder than a well digger's ass in Alaska

Save your food so you don't throw away any dough

No matter how important you are, you may get measles

A verbal contract is not worth the paper it is printed on

Ridicule: The Washington Compost and the New York Slime

I love hard labor; I could watch it all day

You begin cutting your wisdom teeth the day you can chew

The best remedy for a short temper is a long walk

If I told you once I told you a thousand times not to exaggerate

He was so narrow-minded he could look through a keyhole with both eyes

He was so thin he had to stand up twice to cast a shadow

It's not your aptitude but your attitude that determines your altitude in life.

He doesn't know the difference between chicken salad and chicken doo.

Give it (the news) to him in little pieces

He's so lazy he hurries up to do nothing

If there's a 50-50 chance things will go wrong, nine times out of ten they will

Some people can stay longer in an hour than others can in a week

A man chases a woman until she catches him (Jamie Griffith)

Half the lies that people tell us are not true

That's as rare as horse manure in a garage (Dr. Al Snell, Mayo Clinic)

He couldn't get as far as you could throw a bull by its tail

Adults only (pornography—it abuses the word adult)

It's hotter than a whorehouse on nickel night

At the end of the day write down three gratitudes (M. D. Anderson Analog)

Be good and you will be lonesome (Mark Twain)

The grocery bag that breaks will be the one with the eggs

Don't let the facts get in the way of a good story

Don't trouble trouble till trouble troubles you

Try to reason about love and you will lose your reason

Choose neither a woman or linen by candlelight (Chinese proverb)

If I am king and you are king, who fetches the water? (Chinese)

It may take a year to build a friendship but only an hour to lose one

Apple blossoms are beautiful but rice dumplings are better (Chinese)

I'm no longer a spring chicken; I'm just an old hen (Wanda Newton)

A mosquito in a nudist camp: I know what to do but I don't know where to start

The patient told the doctor: I'm having memory trouble. The doctor asked: How long have you had this problem? The patient replied: What problem, doctor?

If you lend someone $20.00 and never see him again, it was well worth it

Instead of loving your enemy, why don't you try treating your friends a little better?

Bush took the "Is" out of his speeches (I-ectomies) Obama put the "Is" in (I-implants)

I'll never have a baby for fear it will fall off the top of the car (George Peterkin)

As subtle as an army tank rolling down a cobblestone road on a Sunday morning

I don't deserve this honor, but I have arthritis and I don't deserve it (Jack Benny)

I've been busier than a one-legged man with one hoe and two rattlesnakes (Ladybird Johnson)

May your fair ass always be shining (Eleanor Roosevelt to Gypsy Rose Lee, 1959)

Remember, son, if you ever need a helping hand you'll find it on the end of your arms

A person without a sense of humor is like a wagon without wheels—jolted by every pebble on the road. (Beecher in A Word a Day)

Nothing helps scenery like bacon and eggs. (Mark Twain)

There's no such thing as a new joke. (Mark Twain)

It's human to exaggerate the merits of the dead. (Mark Twain)

Don't put off till tomorrow what can be put off until day after tomorrow. (Mark Twain)

He's useless on top of the ground, he ought to be under it inspiring the cabbage. (Mark Twain)

Man is the reasoning animal. Such is the claim. I think it is open to dispute. (Mark Twain)

Clothes make the man. Naked people have little or no influence in society. (Mark Twain)

After three days men grow weary of a wench, a guest and rainy weather. (Benjamin Franklin)

Neither a fortress nor a maidenhead will hold out long after they begin to parley. (Benjamin Franklin)

Abstract art: a product of the untalented, sold by the unprincipled to the utterly bewildered. (Al Capp)

When you see what some girls marry, you realize how they must hate to work. (Helen Rowland)

Two fish swimming in a river ran into a concrete wall. "Dam," one said. (Mark Schmidt)

Choose a job you like and you'll never have to work a day in your life. (Mark Schmidt)

Ham and eggs: A day's work for a chicken, a lifetime commitment for a pig. (Mark Schmidt)

There is something in the misfortune of others, even our best friends, that does not wholly displeasure us. (He had it coming to him)

If people don't want to come out to the ballpark, nobody is going to stop them. (Yogi Berra)

A man can't have too much red wine, too many books or too much ammunition. (Rudyard Kipling)

There's nothing more agreeable than to make peace with the establishment and nothing more corrupting

If we condensed the life of the universe to twelve hours on a clock, humans appeared 3/10 of a second before twelve. (The Episcopalian)

The only time a woman will admit her age is when she can get something for nothing (like social security) (Wanda Newton)

Boys walk down the street holding up baggy pants with one hand and holding a cell phone with the other (Wanda Newton)

When I want a lemonade, I'll ask for it (When a bartender twisted lemon peel in his martini)

Some people have become so expert at reading between the lines, they don't read the lines. (A Word a Day)

I know this isn't true but rumor has it that ... (Lyndon Johnson who knew all the time the guy was guilty. Saying something that means the opposite.)

I'd rather have someone in the tent pissing out than someone outside the tent pissing in (Lyndon Johnson)

These are not books, lumps or lifeless paper, but minds alive on the shelves. (A Word a Day)

Damon Runyon's Law. The race is not always to the swiftest nor the battle to the strong but that's the way to bet.

Human wandering through a zoo: What do your cousins think of you? Am I my keeper's brother (a monkey's thought)

The pessimist sees the difficulty in every opportunity; the optimist sees the opportunity in every difficulty. (Winston Churchill)

Philanthropy is the most selfish thing you can do; it makes you feel better than any other way. (Ross McKnight)

You won't be judged by the hand you are dealt, but by the way you play the hand. (Ross McKnight)

Give a man a fish and he will eat for a day; teach him how to fish and he will sit in a boat and drink beer all day (a paraprosdokian)

We are born naked, wet and hungry, and get slapped on the ass, then things just keep getting worse

Wild animals never kill for sport; man is the only one to whom the torture of fellow creatures is amusing in itself. (A Word a Day)

My husband and I have decided to have a family while our parents are still young enough to take care of them (a paraprosdokian)

My friends keep wanting to show me films of their babies birth. No thanks, but I'll look at a video on the conception if you have one.

POSH Portside outward, stern side home: Luxury of sailing from Britain to India in 19th Century)

Never write metropolis for seven cents, when you can write city and be paid the same. (Mark Twain)

You wanted it in the first place because you didn't have it, now that you have it you no longer want it (*Wall Street Journal*)

Happiness is a butterfly which, when pursued is always out of your grasp, but when you sit down quietly may light upon you

What are you having? Calf brains and oxtail soup. Well that's one way to make ends meet.

Water is like sex or money; when there's plenty of it you don't think twice, when there's not you can't think of anything else

Around her neck she wore a yellow ribbon. She wore it for her lover who was far, far away (saying revived during the War with Iraq)

If writers were good businessmen, they'd have too much sense to be writers. (Irvin Cobb in A Word a Day)

All our problems would be solved if they came in our teens when we know everything.

They killed can't and beat couldn't 'til he could (what you're told if you say you can't). (Keats Tyler)

The woman who tells her age is either too young to have anything to lose or too old to have anything to gain

She learned not to take more than one drink at a party; two drinks put her under the table and three drinks put her under her boss.

Kelsey's Return: Walking home with your guest and he walks halfway back with you. (Old Scottish saying)

A government program is the closest thing to eternal life that I know (Ronald Reagan)

We devour a book, digest raw facts, regurgitate other people's ideas, even though they are half baked

The trail boss gave us two hours to get a full night's sleep. (Ramon Adams)

He's so clean his folks wouldn't know him either from sight or smell. (Ramon Adams)

He didn't last as long as two bits in a poker game. (Ramon Adams)

It's just right, if it was any worse I couldn't eat it, if it was any better you wouldn't have given it to me

Lady, the only gas leak you should have in your house is your husband. (Tom Kelsey, from a plumber's billboard sign)

Beans are like people; they often talk behind your back (Mary Wallace)

HUMOR – ENTERTAINMENT FROM DONALD DYAL'S COLLECTION

Never test the water with both feet	Never kick a cow chip on a hot day
A work free drug place	It's bad luck to be superstitious
Determine never to be idle	Every artist was first an amateur
Never miss a good chance to shut up	A closed mouth gathers no foot
He who laughs last thinks slowest	Tracers work both ways

We plan for the future, we don't defend the past

If a teacher insists on discipline and respect she is guilty of child abuse.

If a teacher can't get kids to work she's a babysitter

If a teacher makes a child stay in to get his lessons done,
she's guilty of child abuse

If you throw enough dirt, some of it will stick

Never take a sleeping pill and a laxative on the same night

If at first you don't succeed, sky diving is not for you

You will always be late for the previous train and in time for the next.

Why not go out on a limb; that's where the fruit is

Some people think they are worth a lot of money because they have it

If you don't run your own life someone else will

Amateur shows enable people without talent to show it

What people say behind your back is your standing in the community

He that is good at making excuses is seldom good at anything else

If you're not making any mistakes then you're not trying hard enough

Even if you're on the right track you'll get run over; if you just sit there

People who complain they don't get all they deserve should
congratulate themselves

I couldn't carry a tune in a bucket or hand basket

Sometimes the Republicans seem to be machine-gunning themselves in the foot

Good judgment comes from bad experience and a lot of that comes
from bad judgment

The quickest way to double your money is to fold it in half
and put it in your pocket

Everyone seems normal until you get to know them

On the other hand you have different fingers

When you wrestle with a pig the pig has fun and you get dirty

If the enemy is in range so are you

Always forgive your enemies; nothing annoys them so much

There's two kind of dirt; the dark you get on light clothing, and the light that you get on dark clothing

Never criticize someone unless you walk a mile in their shoes. Then you are a mile away and have their shoes.

Some people say I'm overweight, but after looking at the charts I prefer to say I'm six inches too short

Mary Wilson Kelsey, 1970

CHAPTER SIXTEEN

Metaphors

YOU CAN'T TEACH AN OLD DOG NEW TRICKS.

B riefly stated, a metaphor is using a word for something it isn't to describe something that it is. Metaphors are used because they can save a lot of words in getting to the point. We have collected a carload full and haven't scratched the surface. Anytime you want to see a metaphor, look at the headlines and texts of your daily newspaper. Headline writers couldn't survive without them. You will also see old hackneyed ones, many as clichés, and a few made up for the occasion.

There are many famous metaphors. Metaphors have been used for at least 3,000 years when Solomon said, "There is nothing new under the sun."

There are metaphor writers for the government, for advertising, marketing and annual reports. They are experts in the use of euphemisms to make things seem better than they really are. Subjects where metaphors are frequently used are evasions, exaggerations, repetitions to emphasize and misleading expressions to mean the opposite.

John Geary, an expert in metaphors, says there are usually two metaphors for every twenty-five words written. Simple metaphors are so common that we don't notice them. There are some metaphors that are used by millions of people.

A good metaphor is fun. People like metaphors which are humorous or surprising and which carry an obvious meaning.

SOME METAPHORS COLLECTED FROM A THOUSAND SAYINGS

A raft of trouble	Within a gnat's hair
People flock to the fair	A long drive to disaster
Sinking the Astros (sports)	A barrel of fun
Ripe for the picking	The jury is still out
Chasing rabbits (wasting time)	His was a blank slate
Catching some z's	Rubbing salt in the wound
The probe eyes a big deal	After the dust settles
Etched on his mind	When the gloves come off
Putting the squeeze on him	A chip off the old block
I'm in the dark about it	Many bridges to cross
Don't rock the boat	The fly in the ointment
Circling the wagons	Let the air out of his tires
His career is frozen	Barking up the wrong tree
He walks off the field	In the doghouse
Pouring cold water on the plan	Too much on his plate
Banks open the spigot	Taken to the woodshed
Keeping darkness at bay	Got her tits in a wringer
The roadmap to success	All that glitters is not gold
The key to success	Batten down the hatches
It's time to change the guard	Hold your horses
Battle lines are drawn	Pull in your reins
Escaping the ax (not fired)	Lower the boom
They gave him an earful	The fruit of their labors
A smash hit	In one ear and out the other

It's a jungle out there	Has the stomach to do it
He immersed himself in it	My tail is dragging
Do it on your own nickel	Without missing a lick
Giving him a run for his money	A powerful soapbox
Saved by the bell	Sandwiched in
Way off track	Packing heat
Throwing a wet blanket on it	Just scratched the surface
The watchdog (inspector)	A close shave
In uncharted waters	Sucking hind tit
The columnist hit a homerun	Went to bat for him
We turn the page	Not a drop in the bucket
Giving the team a facelift	Toot my own horn
Exiting the stage	In the driver's seat
Wipe Israel off the map (Iran)	Until hell freezes over
Sweetening the pot	Hotter than a burning stump
Sharp elbows fly	He carries no partisan baggage
Cut from the same cloth	The school of hard knocks
The ripple effect	He's in a pickle
On the slippery slope	Draining the swamp
Sour grapes	A one-two punch to the gut
He can wallow in the mud	The melting pot
A love affair with letters	A half-baked idea
Muddying the waters	Overplayed his hand
Riding out the storm	A new law kicks in
He cast a long shadow	The missing link
Dishing it out	A nightcap
Hitting a stone wall	Pushing the envelope
A pretty thick skin	Born into a different world
The fat is in the fire	Let sleeping dogs lie
Tightening the noose	Shining a spotlight on it
Hauled off in cuff links	It's not written in stone
He can't hit the curve ball	The well went dry (out of money)
The story is not yet written	Missing the mark
Feeling the pinch	A new sheriff in town
Ready for a liftoff	The road ahead

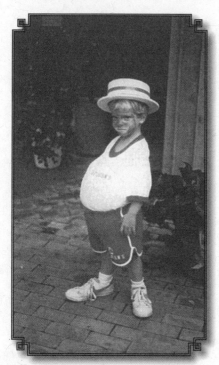

*Cooke Wilson Kelsey, age four,
the son of Mavis P. Kelsey, Jr.*

Sticky fingers	He wants to feather his own nest
A firestorm over prices	It's an albatross around his neck
He's not out of the woods yet	The company plows ahead
It's in the cards	Smearing his opponent
Putting the heat on	He screwed things up
Stuck in the Stone Age	He's hell on wheels
Give him a little slack	On the cusp of power
Cut a little more off the top	It's lonely at the top
I'll chew over it awhile	The icing on the cake
She has a sweet tooth	The fleet's in
Dodging the bullet	It's a one-way street
The early bird gets the worm	That puts a new face on it
A prescription for financial pain	He's gone to pot
His future is up in the air	Coming into sharper focus
This watchdog has lost his teeth	Made it out of thin air
He was hung out to dry	In the fast lane
Chew on this	The wrecking crew
He's cleared for takeoff	Stuck in first gear
High flyers	Chewing the fat
Bitten by the gold bug	It's a fishing expedition
Hounded by taxes	Oil-thirsty America
Hogs at the public trough	Got his tail kicked
A sour reception	A giant step backward
Getting our grip on reality	Stirring the pot
The undercurrents of thought	Head for the hills
Sniffing them out	Fires a salvo
Greasing the skids	Cutting ties
As the clock ticks	I caught his eye
A wild card	On the right track
As the world turns	Keep the lid on
Tapping into it	She navigates her own course
Hitting pay dirt	It's one step in the right direction
Relaxing the law	It's in the ballpark
Prime the pump	My phone is ringing off the hook
I put my finger on it	He's putting words in my mouth

The gnarled hand of labor	The underdog
You hit the nail on the head	A queer duck
A comeback to a grander perch	Walking on air
Yachts get tax break	Blaze claims mother and daughter
Breaking the mold	The day went swimmingly
It brought the town to its knees	The jail cancels visitations
Slam on the brakes	Slapped with sanctions
Lobbing full blown lies	A house of cards
Harnessing the nation's will	The amen corner
They paved the way for me	Lean years
He has the teeth to succeed	A big jump in output
He likes to shoot the breeze	Funds slide on a slippery slope
They nailed Tom DeLay	He jumped into the race
The domino effect	It's ripe fruit ready to fall
He looked the other way	Buckets full of love, or tears
Trampling the opposition	It's a tough nut to crack
Using the rearview mirror	He devours the offer
He paints a dark picture	The world is your oyster
For the long haul	Life is a cherry
Taking the bait	Money is as beautiful as a rose
He landed on his feet	Shaving off expenses
Let your mind wander	A built-in bear trap
The game of his life	He bit the dust
Fodder for gossip	A portrait of the future
The white elephant	Kiss pain goodbye
Cooking or kicking up a storm	He balks at quitting
Sneaking a peep	A snake eating its own tail
A peeping Tom	He's got a full plate
They whitewashed it	The fox in the henhouse
Sowed seeds of fear	Hints are piling up
Show me the ropes	Turning the tide on him
His savings flew out the window	It's on the front burner
Came to a screeching halt	Stick a fork in it. It's done.
He steps into the opponent's trap	Bursting the housing bubble
He walks a fine line	Taking a bite out of the apple

Got him on-the-hook	East meets West
Getting inside her head	The waves kissing my feet
Don't lose the ball	A flood of water problems
Leading the charge	Snatching power out of the air
His pants are on fire	Bringing in the beans
Sheds light on it	In the lap of luxury
Losing steam	Closing a bloody chapter
Taking pot shots	Turning the tide of events
Tightened his grip	Coming out of the closet
A shot in the arm	Pulling out the weeds
Derailing the opponent	It just doesn't wash
Drain your lizard	Riding the tiger
Shake the dew off your lily	He dropped the lawsuit
Barbs are flying	Trading barbs
Cowed by public opinion	Faced with the problem
Making a big splash	Frugalities spread
A horse of a different color	A flea market
The tide has turned	Playing chicken
Papering over a mess	Who blinked first?
It doesn't pass the smell test	He wrote the book on it
A pipe dream	He didn't show his face
Smooth sailing	A chip on his shoulder
Swooped down on him	A little bird told me
Freshens up	Her act may backfire on her
He rode the range	In the dumps
Learning the ropes	Bringing home the bacon
Getting a bite	Spilling the beans
Clutching at straws	Playing with fire
Riding shotgun	The elephant in the living room
Reading her face	He's barking up the wrong tree
Gobbling up time	Running while standing still
Hitting where it hurts	Their rivalry heats up
A blot on his record	The economy is losing its cushion
Plugging the leaks	He holds the key to the solution
Ushered into womanhood	He buys drinks all around

Sounding a retreat	Crooked as a dog's hind leg
He can't find the off-switch	The milk of human kindness
Touching all the bases	He ripped his britches with me
Upped the ante	It's a black eye for us
Blowing kisses	Keep your powder dry
Scorched earth war	Wash your dirty linen at home
In the eye of the storm	Calling a spade a spade
The pot boils over	A stitch in time saves nine
Put a lid on it	Every rose has its thorns
Drawing a line in the sand	Out of the frying pan, into the fire
I'm snake-bit	Up the creek without a paddle
The nation must sober up	Not a snowball's chance in hell
A good first step	My hands are tied
Facing headwinds	Extend the olive branch
On a wing and a prayer	She's the bell cow
Pumping up your willpower	Fish or cut bait
He sparks a backlash	Spread too thin
A window of opportunity	It's a pig sty
I'm running out of gas	He's playing with half a deck
Wrestling with a decision	The die is cast
He dropped the ball	If the shoe fits, wear it
He's walking on thin ice	He can't hold his tongue
Money laundering	He's a fifth wheel
It's time to clean house	Money talks, history walks
Up from the ashes	He's got bigger fish to fry
Born in the state of flux	His eye is on the sparrow
They're circling the wagons	You reap what you sow
Open war on cancer	Let the cat out of the bag
His effort is bearing fruit	Throw the book at him
Opening old wounds	Don't open up a can of worms
Reigniting controversy	She spilled the beans
Hooked on drugs	Zip up your lip
Sucking the blood from taxpayers	Face the music
Pull out all stops	He hit the nail on the head
Push the pedal to the metal	Shoot the breeze

I've seen this movie before	Full of baloney
Smile, you're on camera	He listens to his own drum
Birds do it, bees do it	Touching a sore spot
It will grab you by the throat.	Pearls of wisdom
He put his foot in it	Wagging tongues
Another brick in the wall	Whistling in the dark
The slippery slope	He's a big wheel
The battle rages	He made a bold statement
Burning bridges behind him	He's bad news
Hung out to dry	You've got egg on your face
Bumps in the road	His wife wore the britches
He runs a tight ship	He can fry in his own grease
Too big for his britches	Fear the Greeks who bring gifts
Hit the jackpot	Every cloud has a silver lining
Lighting the match to it	Fight fire with fire
Easy on the trigger	Blood is thicker than water
The empty saddle	A legislative log jam
Don't fiddle with it	A law with teeth in it
Singing to the choir	Take a bead on costs
They split the blanket (divorced)	We ran the traps
Trim your sails	A political piñata (victim)
Get in the swing of things	Ending on a high note
He was led to the slaughter	He can't cut the mustard
Every dog has his day	A place in my heart
He buried his head in the sand	Haven't scratched the surface
Grist for the rumor mill	The pissants will finally get us
That line is wearing thin	Light a shuck
His swan song	Make hay while the sun shines
Showing her claws	The marrow of the bone
Facing an uphill fight	The first domino to fall
It blew up in his face	Window of opportunity
We shepherd our own flock	On death's doorstep
His nose is out of joint	Add fuel to the fire
Kiss your dream car goodbye	Taken to the cleaners
When you're thrown a curve	A clean sweep

She swept it under the rug	Up to snuff
Tighten your belt	Speaks volumes
He's on the fast track	Chart a new course
A thaw in relationships	Real estate bubble
It's up in the air	Cliff-hanger
Seize control of these monsters	Take aim at
Blowing off steam	Get some nibbles
Only scratched the surface	Back on track
Bridging the gap	News makes a big splash
A breath of fresh air	Voters are hamstrung
Red carpet treatment	Root out
Playing Russian Roulette	A bitter pill
Stuck in the slow lane	Riding the waves of chance
Throwing caution to the wind	A bottleneck
When Jim Crow still ruled	Step up to the plate
Handed over the keys	Licked his wounds
They're launching a new fund	Sowing his wild oats
A social butterfly	That ship has sailed
He worked off the fly	It slipped under the radar
He's polishing his image	He fell off the wagon
A smoking gun	A political tidal wave
He laid an egg	The bleeding has slowed
A kettle of fish	The movement takes root
Asleep at the switch	Throw down the gauntlet
Quaking in their boots	Put yourself in another's shoes
Paints a disturbing picture	Too many irons in the fire
Violence spills over	Preaching to deaf ears
A different ball of wax	A pig in a poke
They poured out their grief	He swallowed every word
He had to eat his words	Hard as a rock '
Fat as a pig	Sweet as sugar
Slick as grease	Old as the hills
Green as grass	Dry as a bone
Weak as a kitten	Happy as a lark
Light as a feather	Dumb as a doorknob

Smooth as silk	Dirty as a dog
Tough as a boot	Black as the ace of spades
Playing second fiddle	His shadow still lingers
A turf battle	It's a walk in the park
She stole the show	A dirty mouth; flannel mouth.
Getting a handle on it	He's wool gathering
Even a blind hog can find an acorn	He's reading between the lines
The squeaky wheel gets the grease	China loses its moral compass
In Rome, do as the Romans do	He's stewing in his own juice
Gather flowers while the sun shines	I lit a fire under him
There's always room at the top	That put a hole in the budget
A rolling stone gathers no moss	His skin is three inches thick
Make hay while the sun shines	Left out in the cold—dark
Little strokes fell great oaks	Keeping the wolves at bay
Too many cooks spoil the broth	There's little left in the tank
Cheney stirred up a hornet's nest	Don't wait until the eleventh hour
We're up to our ass in alligators	He made it up out of whole cloth
Cigarettes are coffin nails	He's at the helm of the company
He threatens to jump ship	He's shooting blanks (impotent)
The deck is stacked against us	He doesn't have a leg to stand on
No more than you can grab smoke	I haven't seen you in a coon's age
Knocked from his pedestal	Gadhafi's grip on power crumbles
Scared the daylights out of me	The elephant in the living room
Birds of a feather flock together	Sweet as sugar; happy as a lark.
Don't put the cart before the horse	Slick as grease; fat as a pig.
There's a skeleton in every house	Light as a feather; smooth as silk.
Every family has its black sheep	Working to put food on the table
It's a boil that needs to be lanced.	He unloaded both barrels on me.
Nobody knows what's over the hill	Let's kill this turkey before it breeds
He's up the creek without a paddle	Home sales are still in the drought
It's like pouring salt on the wound	Standing on the shoulders of giants
Both are tarred with the same brush	The window for peace is closing
Unlocking your subconscious desires	Here it is right in our own backyard
The proof of the pudding is in the eating	Shut your mouth, save your breath
He opened up a whole can of worms.	The invisible hand that moves people

You can't teach an old dog new tricks

He didn't amount to a hill of beans

He's a pain in the ass (or in the neck)

That's how the cow bit the cabbage

Put your money where your mouth is

All the world's a stage (Shakespeare)

The grass is greener on the other side

You made the mess; now sleep in it

There's more than one way to skin a cat

Rode a wave of sentiment to victory

Seeing the light at the end of the tunnel

Always grasping at the tender reeds

Shines like a dead fish in the moonlight

With the hair of the dog that bit you

A third ear hears what's not been said

Separating the wheat from the chaff

The higher they rise, the steeper they fall

Born with a silver spoon in his mouth

Whoever wins, America is already lost

Bringing home a rabbit, or the bacon

A bucket of cash can douse a wildfire

He swallowed it hook, line and sinker

Turmoil has reached the boiling point

He knows which side his bread is buttered on

Cooke Wilson Kelsey, son of Mavis and Mary Kelsey. 1942-1957.

He bit off more than he could chew

The straw that broke the camel's back

Getting half a loaf is better than getting no loaf at all

The pressure cooker (the CEO's job)

Company raised its voice (complained)

The chase comes to an end, or at least for a rest

The best of the litter. The runt of the litter.

It's a gem (or jewel) of a restaurant

Company risks whether to eat or be eaten

The rug was pulled from under him

Wiping the cobwebs out of an aging mind

Gains in income are not lifting all boats

Is that a bull or a bear in the cornfield?

He hitched his wagon (to the wrong issue)

Will the last one to leave turn off the lights?

Japan's shattered mirror (earthquake)

He couldn't see the forest for the trees

My love is a red, red rose (Robert Burns)

The sands are shifting for the Middle East

He pulled himself up by his bootstraps

Intimidation is spilling over the borders

The foul output of sneering anti-Americanism

Normal people don't wear green eyelashes

Keeping kids from landing in the trash pile

Don't cross that bridge until you get to it

The landscape is littered with dashed hopes

Don't count your chickens before they hatch

A bird in the hand is worth two in the bush

Your chickens (curses) come home to roost

There's many a slip between the cup and the lip

Don't cut off your nose to spite your face

Honey catches more flies than vinegar

We will all hang together or will all hang apart

Don't have a fox to watch the henhouse

You can't make a silk purse out of a sow's ear

He can't see the forest for the trees

The way to the heart is through the stomach

He's not worth the powder to blow him to hell

Snake in the grass. Dog in the manger.

He's dealing from the bottom of the deck

When the cat's away, the mice will play

He who pays the piper, calls the tunes

He knows which side his bread is buttered on

Never look a gift horse in the mouth

An apple does not fall far from the tree

You can't have your cake and eat it too

An ounce of prevention is worth a pound of cure

You can't squeeze blood out of a turnip

I didn't fall off the turnip wagon yesterday

Water under the bridge (or over the dam)

Bears and bulls make money while the hogs lose

He couldn't tell his ass from a bull fiddle

Mapping out the route (making plans)

Overalls to coveralls in three generations

Closing the barn door after the horse is out

The fun ended when the music stopped

Pass the smelling salts; we just fainted

It straddles two nations (the Rio Grande)

We need someone to step into her shoes

He's trying not to step on somebody's toes

The porch light is on but nobody answers

Swift currents sweep away the opposition

The banks open the spigots (make more loans)

If a story can get legs it can determine the election

A gourmet kitchen at blue plate price (an ad)

They killed the goose that laid the golden egg

There's gonna be some ass kicking around here

Put some lead in that pencil (Wendy Kelsey)

I'm going to take you out to the woodshed

Events cast a new light on the subject

Basking in the glow of a job well done

Wall Street pit bulls make a big killing

We hammered out a plan (George Bush)

They skimmed the cream off—the good stuff off

Texas is on the front line in the war against cancer

People are keeping a tight grip on their wallets

Chilly weather heats up demand for heaters

Leavening fear with the yeast of optimism

Sitting on his hands (not doing anything about it)

Separating the wheat from the chaff

The sage has large ears and a small mouth. (China)

I'm left with a sour taste in my mouth

Places left unfinished at the time of creation

Cuba is dipping its toes into capitalism

Hospitals pursue a slice of a billion dollar pie

You do the cooking, we'll do the dishes

Kepler blew the lid off of everything we knew about the stars

We've been beating our heads against a wall

The first amendment is not a blanket that smothers debate

You can lead a horse to water but you can't make him drink

As long as the music is playing, you've got to get up and dance

Hard as a rock. Weak as a kitten. Tough as a boot.

Old as the hills. Dry as a bone. Dumb as a doorknob.

Dirty as a dog. Black as the ace of spades. Green as grass.

Environmentalists have a nose for controversy to raise money

Would the "real" religion please stand up? (*Houston Chronicle*)

It's like the frog in the pot which is slowly being boiled to death

Political parties veered to extreme right and extreme left

Ireland embarks on a bleak journey (to overcome financial depression)

Mercury can't decide what to do (the weather keeps changing)

That's the way the cookie crumbles (Angus Anderson)

The corpse sits up in its coffin (a project which was given up for dead)

A bag drag (politicians raising money in one state to spend in another)

In hot water, we're about to boil over. (Peggy Noonan)

Metaphors are things we pass down through generations. (David Brooks)

Obama hopes to harness some of the unity caused by Bin Laden's death

Moved the goal post; raised the bar; leveled the playing field; sat on the sideline

A man who carries a cat by the tail learns something he can't learn any other way. (Mark Twain from John W. Kelsey)

Euphemisms for the toilet: the outhouse, the privy, the restroom, the powder room, the ladies and gents rooms, His and Hers; the little boy's room, going to see a man about a dog

Expressions for being fired: Laid off, became redundant, got the boot, got kicked out, got pink slipped, is stepping down, was shown the door, pushed out the door, heads rolled

METAPHORS FOR EXAGGERATION

If you want something you will do a thousand things to achieve it.
If you don't, you will give a thousand excuses to refrain from it.

WILD EXAGGERATIONS TO PROVE OR PROMOTE A POINT

He worked tons of hours	It's priority one, two and three
Hotter than the hinges of hell	She shed buckets of tears
She skinned him alive	A raft of bad news
He will break his neck trying	A flood of propaganda
I'll never say another word	She bawled her head off
The whole kit and caboodle	A barrel of love
I would die for a martini	A mountain of red tape
I have all the time in the world	There is a flood of water trouble
To infinity and beyond	All the world and her brother
Too little, way way too late	Big is too small a word for it
She's one in a million; thanks a million.	The letter is too long by a half a mile
I'm dying from starvation; let's eat.	He would break his neck to help out

If I said it to you once, I said it a million times

If I had a thousand dollars for every time you said that

I could write a thousand page book about it— a thousand acres

Scarce as hen's teeth or horse manure in a garage

He waited for eons and eons (he hesitated)

It's worth more than all the tea in China

He's got a roll of dough that would choke an ox

That's the last thing on earth I would do

A nickname is the heaviest stone that can be thrown at a man

There's no weapon that slays its victim more than praise

Selfishness is the greatest curse of the human race

The heaviest burden you can carry is a chip on your shoulder

I stuck my neck out a mile (House Speaker John Boehner)

There's no tonic so powerful as the expectation of better times

The whole world benefitted—waited

It took him forever to make up his mind

Since the creation of the world there's been no greater tyrant than intemperance

If you don't straighten up I'm going to knock you into the middle of next week

One of the worst plagues on the world of society is this; thoughtless inexhaustible verbosity

METAPHORS ABOUT THE EYE AND VISION

"Why do you behold the mote in your neighbor's eye but do not consider the beam in your own eye?" (Matthew 7:3) may be the best known Biblical metaphor about the human body. People are very aware of seeing and being alive. There are more sayings about the eyes and the heart than about all other members of the body.

Vision is the most important human sense. It has been the source of sayings since creation. As God made the world, He said, "Let there be light." (Genesis 1:3)

It's a great world. See it before you leave it.

THE EYES AND VISION

Open your eyes to the facts	Keep your eyes peeled
Before your very eyes	Eyeball it
Poked in the eye	She's making eyes at me
My eyes feasted on it	She eyes them
A feast (or treat) for sore eyes	Money-eyed interests
Cast an eye	When Irish eyes are smiling
Double eyes	More than meets the eye
Four eyes (wearing glasses)	In the twinkling of an eye
Smiling eyes	A bird's eye view
He looked me in the eye	Keep your eagle eyes out
Keep an eye out	As far as the eye can see
Eye to eye	A wandering eye

She pulled the wool over my eyes	Raised eyebrows
Stars in their eyes	Down to a gnat's eyelash
A good eye and a steady hand	It's eyewash
I never laid eyes on him	A sharp eye
What's going on behind those eyes?	Casting a nervous eye
A joy to my eyes	The nation's eyes are on him
The apple of my eye	She caught his eye
She cried her eyes out	All eyes are on her
Go at it with your eyes wide open	A stye on the eye
Bright-eyed and bushy-tailed	Eyeing the opportunities
All eyes are on her	Eye-opening evidence
It's more than meets the eye	She gets starry-eyed
She had a good eye for art	It brings tears to my eyes
His eyes rest on politics	I looked him in the eye
His eyes probe a big deal (*Wall Street Journal*)	He's eye is on the future
Making goo-goo eyes	My two eyes make one of sight
His eyes are bigger than his belly	His eyes fix on it—gaze on it
Drink to me only with thine eyes	Our eyes locked together
I've seen it all	The world's eye
Eyes bugged out	Keep your eye on the prize
Eyes flashing	Turning a blind eye
I'll keep an eye on her	It's a black eye for us
Cast your eyes on this	Rolled her eyeballs
Evil eye	A private eye
They rolled their eyes	We saw eye to eye
A twinkle of the eye	Keeping your eyes open
In the public eye	I felt every eye was on me
I caught his eye	The naked eye and the open ear
She has her eyes on him	It raised some eyebrows
In the eyes of the beholder	Keep your eyes on the lookout
She's an eye opener—an eye full	Before your very eyes
He viewed it with a jaundiced eye	Staring you in the face
He turned a blind eye to the problem	Close your eyes and cover your ears
I watched out of the corner of my eye	Tears are the language of the eyes
The eyes of Texas are upon you	He pulled the wool over my eyes

His eye is on the sparrow and I know He watches me

Keep your eyes wide open before you marry and half closed after you marry

An eye for an eye and a tooth for a tooth (Bible)

We have two eyes and one mouth that we may see more and talk less

Ears are the eyes to the blind (Sophocles, 496-400 BC)

Keep your eyes on the road—on the ball

Those little girls and their own little eyes

Her eyes are fixed (on the flooded river)

SEEING

See what I say	Seeing the future
I've seen it all	I've seen this movie before
Seeing is believing	Seeing straight through him
I'll believe it when I see it	I can see what's going to happen
He will never see the light of day	I saw the light
They come to see and be seen	He sees gold in it
We see eye to eye	I see what you mean
The retrospectroscope	Seeing the threat
I won't believe it until I see it	When you look but can't see
A person you look forward to seeing	Seeing my way through
Seeing the light; seeing the way	Seeing his light shine
Now you see him; now you don't	We'll see; See here
He couldn't see the forest for the trees	Seeing is understanding—is knowing
Even if you haven't seen it, you've seen it	I saw you out of the corner of my eye

Vision is the art of seeing things not visible to the eye

There are none so blind as those who will not see

Better once to see than many times to hear

What you see is what you get (Barbara Bush)

Seeing the world through rose-colored glasses

LOOKING

Never look back	The company looks abroad
You look good	It looks like rain
Don't look at me like that	It doesn't look right
Look out	I don't like the looks of them

Be on the lookout	Looks alone don't tell
Look both ways	What's cookin', good lookin'?
He looked the other way	Well, look who's here
It looks easy	When you look but can't see
Looks deceive	Take a deeper look
Take another look	Looking for a good deal
Looks don't deceive	An honest look
Look at me	Slow looking
Don't look now	The looks of things
Look after the kids	A sunny outlook
Looka' here	A fresh look
Look around	The company looks ahead
Look out	Look after the poor
Looking to the future	There's no looking back
Never look back	Keep watching

Mary Wilson Kelsey and Mavis P. Kelsey at 100th Anniversary Celebration of UTMB viewing an art exhibition at the Rosenberg Library in Galveston, Texas.

Look before you leap	Look what you've done
From the looks of things	Look before you leap
Someone to look up to	If looks could kill
Look the other way	I like your looks
The weather doesn't look so good	Looking on the bright side
Look for the bright side	A look-see
By the looks of things	Stop, look and listen
Take a second look	An unvarnished look
Your mouth looks good when it's closed	
Observe all men, thyself first (Benjamin Franklin)	

LIGHT AND DARKNESS

In the center of the spotlight	Let more light in
A moment in the spotlight	Lighting the way
She saw the light	He hid his light under a bushel
Blindsided him	Lighting up the scoreboard
Come daylight	He's overshadowed by worry
A shady deal	The outlook darkens
The sunny side	The blind leading the blind
Shedding light on it	Love is blind
The light of day	The end is in sight
He sets his sights high	As different as daylight and dark
Left in the dark	I'm in the dark about it
A bright spot in my life	Getting the green light
Casting a shadow	Using the rearview mirror
The crack of dawn	The outlook darkens
He was afraid of his own shadow	Setting your sights
He cast a long shadow	Taking in the sights
Throw on the dimmer switch	It put me in a bad light
Keep darkness at bay	Sight is the highest body privilege
We will keep the lights on for you	In the light of day
I couldn't hold a candle to him	On cloud nine
This country girl loves the night lights	In a bad light
Light out for it	In the public spotlight
He cast a cloud over it	A bright spot in my life

Shedding light on it	Lighting up the scoreboard
He hid his light under a bushel	Her smile would light up a room
Seen in a different light	Light the way
Seeing the light at the end of the tunnel	More light, less heat on the subject
He can't tell the light from the darkness	He knocked the daylights out of him
Darkness is a luxurious cloak of comfort	
He's afraid of the dark (nyctophobia)	

MORE ABOUT VISION AND EYES

He's gaze was fixed	Get a glimpse
Blinkers	Lurking in the shadows
A peeping Tom	On the sunny side of the street
What a view	A twisted view
A close peek inside	Get some "Z" time
The dark side. The light side	An upbeat view
The big picture	Asleep at the switch—or the job
Watch your step	Get some shuteye
In plain sight	Taking forty winks
On the verge of tears	Keeping darkness at bay
Don't start crying; bust out crying.	A behind-the-scenes view
A glimmer of hope	He's in the dark about it
Who blinked first?	Made in the shade
Crystal clear	He enters the picture
Lit up like a country church	Picture perfect
Stepping out of the shadows	The bigger picture
The knothole gang	A birdseye view
The window for peace is closing	Painted with broad strokes
I have a dream	A spitting image
A cloudy future	It clears the air
Staring you in the face	A slim outlook
I'm picturing a bright future	Embracing our vision
Quick as a wink	Seen in a different light
Quit staring at me	Give it a close read
The picture sharpens	Gangs own the night
A trail of tears	Walls have ears as doors have eyes

Watch out; watch what you're doing

When the groundhog sees his shadow

Look at that dirt on the back of your neck

A black eye; a black-eyed pea; black-eyed Susans

METAPHORS OF GENERICS

Generics are sayings that use a name, place or thing to identify or express a meaning.

Get your ducks in a row.

ANIMALS	PEOPLE
A lame duck	Good time Charlie
A horse of a different color	Jim Dandy
Scarce as hen's teeth	Real McCoy
Horse feathers	Peeping Tom
Playing possum	Joe Six-pack
Buffaloed by it	A cup of Joe
An eager beaver	An Uncle Tom
A dirty dog	Average Joe
The bell cow	A Gloomy Gus
A dumb ox	Johnny come lately
A pussy cat	Ready Freddie
Stubborn as a mule	Hobson's choice
The lions share	John bull
An old goat	Davy Jones locker
Gentle as a lamb	Tight as Dick's hatband
A frog in my throat	Doubting Thomas
A dark horse	Life of Riley
A stalking horse	Dead beat dad
Monkey business	French leave

A cash cow	Mexican standoff
A pack rat	Indian giver
A snake in the grass	Dutch treat
Crooked as a snake	Dutch uncle
You silly goose	Proud as a peacock
Strong as a bull	Big as a whale
A lone wolf	The ugly duckling
A wildcat	

METAPHORS FOR LIES AND EVASIONS

Many expressions are used to avoid the words lie or liar. Calling someone a liar is serious business. More than a few people have been killed for it. If you want to know more, read some Wild West novels like *The Virginian*.

Don't let the facts get in the way of a good story.

LIES

She tricked him	A falsehood.; little white lies
The truth is not in him	Bearing false witness
Telling a windy—a fib—a whopper	Making a mockery of the truth
A liar must have a good memory	Never tell a lie; never trust a liar
Come clean; there's no way around it.	He can't handle the truth
Exercised bad judgment	Fabricated; misled.
He double-crossed me; he's a crook.	He's dishonest; he's a liar
He sneaked one by me; he put one over on me	
He pulled a fast one on me; he snookered me	
He would lie when the truth would serve him better	
A liar will not be believed when he speaks the truth	
There's lies and there's damn lies; it's a bald faced lie	
Nearly everything that comes out of his mouth is not true	
I had to bite my tongue a little (telling an untruth)	
Truth telling is greater than sulking around in the dark	

That's a damn lie; don't lie to me.

A hair perhaps divides the false and the true (Omar Khayyam, 1070-1123)

EVASIONS

From Webster's Dictionary: an evasion is to use sophistry or trickery in avoidance or escape; not being frank; evading the truth or point at issue, as a subterfuge.

He put a spin on it; he's less than candid.	I will think about it
There's no one who doesn't exaggerate	He sidetracked it
He's not forthcoming; he stonewalled it.	The silent treatment
He's tempted by the devil	The devil is in the details
Straying from the truth	A sliver of truth
It doesn't add up	He's beating around the bush
Stretching the truth; bending the laws	Truths that are not quite true
An insincere apology	Made bad choices
Misrepresented; Whitewashed it	Was less than honest—equivocated
Not being factual; In denial	He has less than perfect credit

Give him the runaround. Pussy-footing around.

It makes no sense. It doesn't have the ring of truth.

A loophole you could drive an eighteen-wheeler through

Maybe is a sneaky way to say no

Maybe doesn't mean maybe anymore; it means no

Stretching the truth; embellishing the truth

Playing games; twisting the news; spinning a yarn

He has amnesia for the facts; he's not upfront.

It just doesn't hold water; it doesn't ring true

Embellished the truth; Exaggerated; Misspeaks

He didn't lie; he misstated

Quit playing around it; quit stalling; quit beating around the bush

The most dangerous of all falsehoods is a slightly distorted truth

When you say you agree with something in principle, you have not the slightest intention of carrying it out. (Bismark from A Word a Day)

METAPHORS IN OXYMORONS

Oxymorons are a combination of words for epigrammatic effect of contradictory or incongruous words. They are popular phrases or sayings of paradoxical meaning, often used by humorists. They also crop up in ordinary conversations. Many oxymorons have become well known sayings. Dr. Marde Grothe has written a book containing hundreds of oxymorons expressed by prominent people. He listed several by George H. W. Bush, including one that states **"I have strong opinions of my own, but I don't always agree with them."**

I'm in favor of free speech as long as it's kept strictly under control.

Deeply superficial	Shenanigans aren't amusing
An authentic phony	A well-meaning pain in the ass
Deadly serious comedy	Ostentatious simplicity
Grim humor, darkly comic	Deep down he's shallow
Perfectly rotten	A sweet little vicious old lady
Magnificently ugly	Tough love, cruel kindness
Genuinely bogus	The unwelcome guest of honor
Pretty ugly	Jumbo shrimp
Health food makes me sick	Free love is too expensive
She's not happy unless she's mad	A life of ease is a difficult pursuit
A cold welcome	Stocks add to their loses
I am an atheist and thank God for it	The high cost of cheap money
Free love is too expensive	Keeping cool is a hot topic
It's fun to do the impossible	I'm slowing down fast
To lead the people, walk behind them	He had nothing to say and he said it
She don't say what she's talking about	I'm an atheist and I thank God for it
An obedient wife commands her husband	I'll give you a definite perhaps

I didn't like some of the good old days

There is a lot of lies going around and half of them are true

It's difficult to keep quiet if you have nothing to say

The secret to life is honesty; if you can fake it you've got it made

If you think health care is expensive now, wait until it's free

Success has ruined many a man (Benjamin Franklin)

The richer your friends the more they will cost you

I've seen more than I remember and remember more than I've seen

A verbal contract isn't worth the paper it's printed on

People that go to a psychiatrist ought to have their heads examined

The best cure for insomnia is to get a good night's sleep

If there's a fifty-fifty chance that something will go wrong, then nine times out of ten it will

Some people can stay longer in an hour than others can in a week.

I'm often wrong but never in doubt (Jamie Griffith)

We always weaken what we exaggerate

The end of the human race will be that it will eventually die of civilization

Where people are least sure they are most dogmatic

People have one thing in common: they are all different

A man chases a woman until she catches him

A man's best fortune, or his worst, is his wife

When a man steals your wife, there is no better revenge than to let him keep her

When a man brings his wife flowers for no reason (there is a reason)

When love is concerned too much is not enough

The love we give away is the only love we keep

My mother had a lot of trouble with me but I think she enjoyed it

Two important things to teach a child: to do and to do without

If you are a parent it helps if you are a grownup

Not to speak is to speak, not to act is to act

Pain and debt are the luxuries of living (Steve Smith)

With friends like these who needs enemies?

We cannot afford much success at this price

It takes him an hour to make a five minute statement

METAPHORS IN RHYMES

A rhyme is a composition in verse having correspondence of terminal sounds, chiefly poetry. People like to go out of their way to express their thoughts in poetry and rhymes. Rhymes are easy and pleasant to remember. Great philosophy can be found in poetry. There have always been poets, many famous ones.

I would have made a rhyme if I had thought of it in time.

Zip your lip	You snooze you lose
Sit or git	Fewer makers, more takers
So sad, your dad	Don't flub your dub
She's hot to trot	Long awaited, much debated
What's buzzin', cousin	The military: stride with pride
See you later alligator	Snail mail
In a while crocodile	Loose lips sink ships
Put up or shut up	A wheeler and a dealer
What's cooking, good looking?	It's news you can use
Beat a retreat	Those who wait may be too late
East or West, home is best	She shopped till she dropped
Push the pedal to the metal	We've got it made in the shade
No pains, no gains	People said no to the status quo
Use it or lose it	It comes about without a doubt
Rootin', tootin', high falutin'	The price to pay, while being gay
Stash cash	As snug as a bug in a rug
Good deal, Lucille	What's the tale, nightingale?
Be wise, immunize	Man proposes—but God disposes
Haste makes waste	A fault confessed is half redressed
Too sweet to beat	The record shows I took the blows
Finders keepers, losers weepers	Keep your eyes on the prize
Worry, worry, quite contrary	A show down on the low down
An apple a day keeps the doctor away	A pint's a pound, the world around
A diller, a dollar a ten o'clock scholar	Wham, bam, thank you ma'am
A new face in the race	A man with a plan

In silk and scarlet, walks many a harlot

Candy is dandy, but liquor is quicker

He takes a lickin' but keeps on kickin'

Finders keepers, losers weepers

Wives must be had, be they good or bad

When prices drop, people are opt to shop

Pity the poor pelican whose bill holds more than his belly can (also a pun)

It's better than riches to scratch where it itches

A couch slouch (formerly a couch potato)

While the bees are making honey, the banks are making money

The sun has riz and the sun has set and here we is in Texas yet

I'm a lover and a fighter, and a wild horse rider; and a pretty good windmill fixer

Wash your face and comb your hair and get yourself ready for the Dallas fair

Advice is least heeded when it is most needed

Early to bed and early to rise, makes a man healthy, wealthy and wise

He that fights and runs away lives to fight another day

Yours is not to answer why, yours is but to do and die

It don't mean a thing (if ain't got that swing) (Elvis Presley)

The dollar slide is felt far and wide (*Wall Street Journal*)

Go to the stock and get some rock (cocaine)

Breathes there a man, with hide so tough, who says two sexes aren't enough

Blessed is the wooing which is not long a doing

Men should choose with careful eye, the things to be remembered by

As they open chests, so letters open breasts

Men seldom make passes at girls who wear glasses

A little nonsense now and then is relished by the wisest of men

When I am dead it will be said, his sins were scarlet but his books were read

Through the lips and over the gums, look out stomach, here it comes

Two small words with the greatest meaning: If it is to be, it's up to me

Rain, rain, go away; come again another day

Texas, where oil wells flow and millionaires grow

The cow is of the bovine ilk—one end is moo, the other is milk

What a sticky mess we may create when with good intent we legislate

Some like it hot, some like it cold and some like it in the pot nine days old

School days, school days—good old golden rule days

What men call gallantry and gods call adultery is much more common where the climate is sultry (Lord Byron)

Let's get to drinkin' said ole Abe Linkin, cause a little bit of drinkin' does a world of good (a favorite fraternity song)

We may live without friends, we may live without books but civilized man cannot live without cooks

Reading and writing and arithmetic (or readin', writin' and 'rithmetic) taught to the tune of a hickory stick

METAPHORS ABOUT TIME

TIME: There is an appointed time for everything. And there is a time for every event under heaven—A time to give birth and a time to die; a time to plant and a time to uproot what is planted. A time to kill and a time to heal; A time to tear down and a time to build up. A time to weep and a time to laugh; A time to mourn and a time to dance. A time to throw stones and a time to gather stones; A time to embrace and a time to shun embracing. A time to search and a time to give up as lost; A time to keep and a time to throw away. A time to tear apart and a time to sew together; A time to be silent and a time to speak. A time to love and a time to hate; A time for war and a time for peace. Ecclesiastes 3:1-8

Take time to smell the roses.

IT'S ABOUT TIME

A good time was had by all	Staying on the same time line
Time keeps zooming by	In the flash of a split second
Time just keeps roaring by	As the years roll by
Time is the devourer of things	I'm having the time of my life
You can't turn back the clock	A hell of a time
There's good and bad times	At the drop of a hat
Love, not time, heals all wounds	Making time. Gaining time
Time is money	Equal time
Many a time. Many's the time	Time weary
It's about time. It's time to go	Slow times. Old times
He's racing against time	Time after time. A lifetime
It's a waste of time	I can't find time
Lost time. I'm killing time	Tomorrow never comes

A long time coming	Carve out time for it
It's time to move on	It's time to shine
It's high time	Now it's my time
It's no time to panic	Time consuming
Crowded for time	From here to eternity
Seize the moment	Time on my hands
Passing the time of day	Just in time
Give me some time	Crunch time
Take some time off	Daybreak; sunup; sunrise
You can't go back in time	As time runs out
Don't rush; take your time	It's a matter of time
Time stays, we go	Time stands still
Father Time, the ravager of time	Withstand the test of time
Never is a long time	I don't have enough time
Timing is everything	Punching the clock
Tempus fugit	As the years roll by
Take time to think things out	Making time
It's about time	Gaining time
Our time has come	Time out
It's payback time	Old times
It's time to go	Time after time
Time is running out	A lifetime
He's a slave to time	I'm killing time
It's just a question of time	A race against time
Carve out time for it	He's right on time
Crunch time	In the nick of time
Time is on (or not on) our side	Take your time
The time is ripe	Free time, me time
At the crack of dawn	Stingy with time
It's time to take a fresh look	She gave him a hard time
It's time to pay the piper	They stopped the clock
It's time to go	Only a snap in time
Time in the trenches	She takes her own sweet time
Busy all the time	The best of times
A brief moment in time	Times are tight

Times are changing	Wasting time
Time waits for no man	Time will tell
The time of my life	For as long as I can remember
Time marches on	Procrastination is the thief of time
In the time it takes to pluck a chicken	
It's time to make a move or to move ahead	
Quicker than you can say Jack Robinson	
The clock ticks on toward the deadline; the tyranny of time	
In the presence of eternity, mountains are as transient as clouds	
Coming events cast their shadow before them	
Time does not become sacred to us until we have lived it	
She doesn't have time for such nonsense (Leon Hale)	
There's a time for everything: hog killing time, cotton picking time, tea time, dinner time, supper time, bedtime	

Lt. Col. Mavis P. Kelsey, Sr in U.S. Airforce, 1941-1945 in World War II

METAPHORS ABOUT TRAVEL AND MOTION

There are many metaphors using forms of travel by different means and down many paths.

One generation opens the road for other generations to travel. (Chinese)

TRAVELING

A back-seat driver	Derailing his opponent
He took a hard right turn	It's one step in the right direction
Making a beeline for it	Drawing a line in the sand
I ain't getting nowhere	Sounding a retreat
All systems go	I'm running out of gas
On the dodge; on the lam	He took the other way
On the go; on the run	Using the rear view mirror
Grinding to a halt; narrowing the gap	They're circling the wagons
Fast track it; step lively	Slamming on the brakes
Going full throttle; hit his stride.	My free ride is over

Cut out for home	He threatened to derail the train
Hightailing it; hot foot it	Going south in a hurry
On the war path	Moving full speed ahead
Navigating the way	Getting off on the right foot
Staying the course	Criss-crossed the country
He's in the driver's seat	Picking up steam; riding the rails
The long journey home	Off and running
Hitting head winds	I'm in a rut
Heading into parts unknown	Coming full circle
Up and raring to go	Reaching a milestone
Hitting on all six; kicked into gear.	Crossing the hurdles
Greasing the wheels or the skids	A souped up engine
A U turn on global warming	By air, by sea, by land
The economy shifts into low gear	A late start
Leapfrog ahead of the competition	Went full throttle
Asleep at the switch—wheel	Running while standing still
Put the brakes on it; hit the brakes.	Getting out from behind the wheel
Taken for a ride	They took his car keys away
The gravy train	There's no turning back
Going nowhere fast	That stopped me in my tracks
Coming to a grinding halt	Watch where you are going
A step backward or forward	Starting from scratch
Always on the go	Running in circles
Running on all four	Right down (or up) my alley
We're just rolling and rolling	It's a step in the right direction
It was all downhill	You've come a long way, baby
Running with the big dogs	He goes out of his way for me
As the years roll by	Trail blazers; pathfinders.
He carries a big load	He clears the way; paved the way.
Taking it to the streets	It's an uphill drive, road
A running start; a rough start	It's slow going; at a snail's pace
Upsetting the apple cart	It was just yonder a few steps
By shanks mare	Step on it; a race to the top.
Screeched to a halt	Ambulance chaser
He blew into town	Take a powder

Riding freight trains; hitching rides	Raring to go; all Aboard
Grease the wheels	Tough sledding
A lazy man's load	Get out of my way, you jerk
He's ginning along; he's in a rut	In the last stretch
In the long haul; in the long run	I'm ready to roll; run for your life
She's coming round the bend	Getting over the hump
Covering all the bases	Getting off on the wrong foot
Going to great lengths	Walking a fine line
Along for the ride	Keep on trucking
A step in the right direction	He ran out of gas
Running wild, at break neck speed	One giant step forward
It's like carrying coals to Newcastle	Crank it up
You can't get there from here	Every step of the way
He's running on empty	Out for a spin; hit the road.
It's a race to the finish	He shifts into high gear
Hit the road; he hit the skids	Putting the brakes on
He fell by the wayside	Revving up his engine
Running out of gas, or out of steam	It's time to go; getting into gear
Don't spare the horses	Leading the way
Don't tailgate me	Taking a step backward
On the move; hit the pavement	A brake on the economy
Hit the ground running	He lost his way
Every sign had led to here	He ran the gamut
He hit the ground stumbling	A journey across the landscape
Put the pedal to the metal	Showing me the way
In the driver's seat	Searching for the next step
Stuck in the slow lane	Racing against time
The wheel of fortune	Heading for the hills
Grab it and run	Take your foot off the gas
He came barreling down the pike	Stuck in reverse
Car makers make U-turn	She pulled out of town
Heading for parts unknown	He's racing against time
When the rubber meets the road	The engine shifts into high gear
Riding shotgun; he rode the range	Shifting into neutral
Stuck in first gear	Amtrak chugs into the red

Keep on going, one foot at a time	Facing the long haul
He's hell on wheels	She's hot to trot
Soft pedal it	A leap forward; hitting on all six.
At breakneck speed	Inching forward
He's up and raring to go	On a mad dash
Hitting on all cylinders	Chugging along
Making the leap	What's around the corner?
Breezing through; throttling back	Kicked into high gear
Riding off into the sunset	It's like the end of a journey
Off to a good start—a great step	He's long gone
Traveling light	A slow start
Running rough shod over them	Cover your tracks
He roared past the opposition	One more hoop to jump through
He's going downhill	The hub of activities
VW guns to win	He switched lanes on me
Hot on his trail; the race to the top.	At breakneck speed
His track record	Mapping it out
On the run, ready to run	Getting up speed
Let's go riding	Gas up your car
Off to a slow start	Picking up speed
Foot on the pedal	Kiss your dream car goodbye
He rides the gravy train	His tail over the dashboard
Life is a journey—a battle; a play	Off in the wide blue yonder
Going nowhere fast; a leap forward.	Where the next horizon beckoned
Nobody knows what's over the hill	Put your best foot forward
Going where others fear to tread	Every path has its puddles
Running on empty; he ran out of gas	Might nigh onto a quarter of a mile
Full steam ahead; building up steam	The job engine shifts into high gear
Put the brakes on; release the brakes	Come hell or high water, I'll be there
He left his tracks; the inside track.	Our country is on the wrong track
The first to arrive, the last to leave	One is never lost on a straight road
The liberals are stepping on the gas	There are different paths to success
Let's hit the road and go somewhere	Picking up steam; picking up speed
The fool wanders, the wise man travels	
Keep on going, one step at a time—one day at a time	

Even if you're on the right track you'll get run over if you just sit still

The chase comes to an end, or at least to a rest

A gentleman man ought to travel but dwell at home

Staying the course; off course; changing the course.

It's a great world—see it before you leave it

One for the money, two for the show, three to get ready and four to go

He went through like Grant took Richmond

Hang on to your hats; hang on for a fast ride

He couldn't get as far as I could throw a bull by the tail

Everyone is jumping on the band wagon

The road is not long in the company of friends (Chinese)

His own decision carried him down this sorry lane

She'll be coming round the mountain when she comes

Traveling with the patient through the twists and turns of his health

Traveling off on a windy track of delusion

Pointed in the right direction (David Brooks)

Come by and pick me up, I'll be waiting outside

There are people in the cart and there are people pulling the cart

A traffic hazard: a teenaged boy driving with a cell phone

Swing low, sweet chariot, coming for to carry me home

She'll be coming round the mountain when she comes

If you don't know where you're going you will probably end up somewhere else

Look what gasoline has done to global warming

Traveling with the patient through the twists and turns of their illness

A globe-trotter; gadabout; vagabond; a tramp; airing out; swagger

Joy ride; gallivanting; foot-loose and fancy-free

He road in on the first load of timber and he rode out with the last load of pipe

Do not walk behind me, I may not lead. Do not walk in front of me, I may not follow. Do not walk beside me, the path is narrow. In fact, just leave me alone.

Not to go back is somewhat to advance; if you don't move forward you are losing; he who moves not forward moves backward.

ON THE ROAD

A bumpy ride on a bumpy road	The trail of tears
He's following the money trail	The roadway for recovery
Taking the high road	Down memory lane

Clearing the tracks	Few career paths remain open
Every step of the way	The rocky road
Twelve miles from nowhere	A rocky road paved with perils
The fast track; in the fast lane.	All roads lead to Heaven
I camped on his trail	She hit the ground running
Ready to hit the road	The comeback trail
At the end of the road	On the road to stardom
Concrete paths	Walking down the same lane
Finding the road back	The avenue to success
The road to the top	Paving the way
I'm on the road again	It's the end of the road for him
A step in the right direction	The end of the trail is clear
On the straight and narrow paths	He's running on all cylinders
A road block to justice	Off and running
I've made tracks to the restaurant	A road block to success
Hit the road	A path to sanctification
A wide place in road	Rules of the road
What's around the corner	The road map to success
On the right road	From street to street
The end of the road or trail	The road to recovery
Rivers are moving roads	The road ends here
I'm on his trail	Road block to justice
Back on track	The road not taken
Over hill, over dell	Riding the rails
A turn in the road, a U-turn	The road to respectability
A long thorny path to success	It's the end of the road
A rocky road, a winding road	Another path appears
He paved the way	The road to success
A stop on the way	He gassed up; fill her up
On the highway	The path has been cleared
The road to ruin	Another path opens
The white man's road	The straight and narrow path
Getting in the groove	She's on the road to stardom
We're on the right track	Off the beaten path
The primrose path	Staying on track

A stop on the road to success	The long road back
Beating the path	A road never before traveled
It's a long road ahead	On the road again
Down lover's lane	Life's highway
Leading one up the garden path	Keep your eyes on the road
On easy street; an easy road.	On the war path
Facing a rough road	He took the long way around
Diverging paths	What lies down the path?
Catching a ride	Cranking up the opera
Running the traps	Getting lost on the road back
On the road to ruin	The road never before traveled
Chug holes; bogged down	At the end of life's journey
The road ahead, or back	Camping on his trail
They paved the way for me	Up the road a piece
Riding the wave of discontent	The road to nowhere
It left a trail of blood	Bridging the gap
Taking the right path	U-turn on global warming
Stay on the right road—track	I'm ready to hit the road
The path I chose not to follow	He went lumbering down the road
Our country is on the wrong track	On the right track; off the track.
It's the first step in a long journey	He went lumbering down the road
Running rough shod over people	He pointed the way, along the way
They sprinkled her path with roses	He beats a path; beating a path
The perilous path across an abyss	I'm shifting into neutral on that one

The road gets bumpy for GM in China

Better times down the road—around the corner

His own decision carried him down this sorry road.

The road to equality is paved with detours

The road to status in Nigeria is a secondhand car

The road to the White House is full of risks

Hogging the road; he took his half in the middle

Wide is the gate and broad is the road to destruction

The road to hell is paved with good intensions

Along the way; lead the way; block the way

A long, long road a winding to the girl in my dreams

They sprinkled her path with rose petals

It's not like I had been down that road before

He paved the way—crossed the line

He's on the fast track, on the right track

The paths to the priesthood (and many others)

I've been helped down the road a little

Traveling on a winding road of delusion

Westward, the course of empire takes it way

I'll take the high road; you take the low road and I'll get to Dublin before you

Lonesome road—the people on the road are lonesome

Traveling off on a windy road of delusion

Let me live by the side of the road, and be a friend of man

The road to equality is paved with detours

PROVERBS AND AXIOMS ABOUT TRAVEL

There are different paths to success.

The path to wisdom is a crooked one (*Pharos* magazine)

A merry heart goes a long way, a sad one tires in a mile

The road to hell is paved with good intensions

A journey of a thousand miles starts with one step

People may come, people may go; but life goes on forever

It's sometimes safer to pull your freight than to pull your gun

Art is a bridge between heaven and earth

We must not shrink from what's ahead

I have crossed the Rubicon, the point of no return

TRAVEL ON THE WATER

Sailing rough waters	Riding out of storm
Sold down the river	Rowing upstream
Up the creek; down the river	He sailed under false colors
Smooth sailing ahead	Rowing up Salt Creek
Up the creek without a paddle	It's a long voyage ahead
At the helm	You can circumnavigate them
She navigates her own course	Homeward bound; outward bound
In the channel, navigating the channel	
It's difficult to go with the flow when you're swimming upstream	
On the road to Mandalay, where the flying fishes play. (Rudyard Kipling)	

CHAPTER SEVENTEEN

Le Caprice,
Wilson beach house, at Caplen,
Bolivar Peninsula, Texas, 1939

Texas Brags

TEXAS IS THE PLACE WHERE YOU CAN DREAM BIG DREAMS
WITH THE CHANCE TO ACHIEVE THEM. *(George W. Bush)*

Texas has a reputation for bragging. It has a lot to brag about. **If you've got it, flaunt it.** *A lot of people criticize Texas for bragging but* **they live in glass houses and shouldn't throw stones.** *They should remember the biblical saying,* "**He who is without sin, cast the first stone.î**

Texas bragged about being the largest state until Alaska, more than twice the size of Texas, was admitted to the Union. Anyway, Texas is about 800 miles across from Texarkana to El Paso or from the top of the Panhandle to Brownsville. Texarkana is closer to Chicago than it is to El Paso. El Paso is closer to Los Angeles than it is Texarkana. While crossing Texas in a covered wagon on the way to the California gold rush, the travelers complained: **The sun has riz and the sun has set and here we is in Texas yet.**

Texas has a perimeter of 3,822 miles and covers over 268,000 square miles. Texas has been populated at least 11,000 years and since 1528 has been under six flags: Spain, France, Mexico, Republic of Texas, the United States and the Confederacy. The last battle of the Civil War was fought in Texas. Texas has had six capitols: Washington-on-the-Brazos, Harrisburg/Houston (Harrisburg became part of Houston), Galveston, Velasco, West Columbia and Austin.

Texas has 254 counties with many famous courthouses. Most counties have something unique to brag about. For example, Culbertson County has six mountains with peaks over 8,000 feet high and Brewster County is as big as Connecticut and Rhode Island put together. In fact, the average size of a Texas county is about the size of Rhode Island. If each county could send two senators to Washington like Rhode Island does, we would be represented by 508 senators.

The Texas state flower is the bluebonnet; the state bird is the mockingbird; the state tree the pecan; and the state reptile is the horned lizard.

Texas is said to have the most diverse racial population of the United States. It serves the greatest variety of foods also known in Texas vernacular as **vittles**, **eats**, **grub**, **chuck**, **chow**, **slumgullion**, and other names. The food includes that of the Indians, the pioneers, the Old South, the blacks, the Cajuns, the Creoles, and the Mexicans. Later were added the cuisine of the French, Italians, Germans, Chinese, Japanese, East Indians, Middle Easterners and Africans.

Chili originated among the street vendors of San Antonio. It sometimes had doubtful contents. Albert Maverick told me that if you found a dog tooth in a bowl of chili they would give you another bowl free. The Gebhardts were the first to can and sell chili, making it a national dish.

Hamburgers originated at a train stop in Athens, Texas where they were sold as **ground beef sandwiches** to the passengers. They were made popular in 1903 when they were sold at the World's Fair in St. Louis which celebrated the centennial of the Louisiana Purchase. It was there that they were first called hamburgers. Some other cities claim falsely that they sold the first hamburgers. The first drive-in restaurant was said to be the Pig Stand in Dallas.

There are some who claim Texas for the origin of **corndogs**, **margaritas** and **Ruby Red grapefruit**.

For those of you who have never traveled in Texas, cattle guards are horizontal steel rails placed at fence openings in the roads adjacent to highways to prevent cattle from crossing over that area. For some reason the cattle will not step on the "guardsî. Recently President Obama was reading a report that there were over 100,000 cattle guards in Texas. The ranchers had protested his proposed changes in grazing policies, so he ordered the Secretary of the Interior to fire half of the "cattle" guards. Before the Secretary of the Interior could respond, Vice-President Joe Biden intervened with a request that before any "cattle" guards were fired, they be given six months of retraining. This was a joke on the Internet.

Mary Wilson and Mavis Kelsey on Joe Darby's horse at Le Caprice in 1939

LE CAPRICE

Le Caprice was the beach house of J. Cooke Wilson, Sr. built in 1936 at Caplen on the Boliver Peninsula. There were large screened porches on the two floors, each of which faced the beach and the Gulf of Mexico. Each floor contained sitting areas, several swinging beds suspended from the ceiling, a large sitting room with a fireplace, and bedrooms on each side. The house could sleep twenty-four people comfortably. It was usually full during the summer months. The beach house was completely destroyed by Hurricane Carla in 1963.

On the walls along the ceiling throughout the house many sayings were printed. Mary Wilson, who would become my wife, provided most of these sayings and helped paint these sayings on the walls. The house became famous for these sayings. Listed here are the sayings which I can remember.

In love of home, love of country has its rise

Follow principle and the rest unties itself

Let thy discontent be thy secret

Better say nothing than not to the point

A fool and his money are soon parted

The way to a man's heart is through his stomach

A merry heart goes all the way, a sad one tires in a mile

A laugh is worth a hundred groans in any market

A good name is worth more than a girdle of gold

It's the flight, not the cry of the wild goose, that leads the flock to fly and follow

A journey of a thousand miles starts with one step

An empty gourd makes the loudest noise

De Gustibus non disputandum (Of taste there is no dispute)

Chacun à son goût (Each to his own taste)

To err is human, to forgive is divine

The smallest good deed is better than the greatest intention

Pearls unpolished shine not

A hint to the wise is sufficient

Flowers die, birds fly, new days, new ways, but love stays

A nation's wisdom is in its proverbs

People who never do more than they get paid for never get paid for more than they do

Politeness is to do and say the kindest thing in the kindest way

He who knows and knows not he knows is asleep; awaken him

I admire those who know more than I do and pity those who know less

Failures are the pillars of success (Oilmen have several failures and/or dry holes before they succeed to strike it rich—Cooke Wilson's interpretation.)

The people who reorganized Humble Oil Company in 1918. James Cooke Wilson Sr. is second from the left in the top row.

FREQUENT SAYINGS IN TEXAS

Small town Texas values	A wagon sheet
East Texas hillbilly	Crop failure
Drugstore cowboy	Rare as hen's teeth
A cowpoke	A wampus cat
A bronco buster	The calaboose
Tex-Mex food	La Cucaracha
Tall tales of Texas	Cash on the barrelhead
Along about 1900	In the doghouse
Texas two step	Wild west shootout
A Texas sized advantage	Wild West
Texan to his toenails	Up to snuff

A smooth talking Texan	Bragging rights
Texas twang	A full house
Bedding down	A dinky town
A Texas size showdown	Full of beans
The Runaway Scrape	A holdover
Texas-sized woes	Shooting the bull
Round up time	Chewing the fat
A shooting iron	On his high horse
Painting the town red	From pillar to post
Up the road a piece	Talking turkey
Fixing dinner	Full as a tick
Puts on a show	Dyed in the wool
Screwed up, messed up	A weekend rancher
Greased the skids	He jumped the gun
He got his dander up	Saddle up; pony up
A string of bad luck	Hands up
Shoofly pie	Go west, young man
A one-horse town	Buckle up; brace up
Roping off bad banks	Don't tailgate me
Sucking hind tit	Take an axe to it
A tough titty	No bull
A whole string of problems	Give Houston a big hand
Ready for lift off	Tightening the noose
Filthy rich	His word is his bond
In high cotton	Rise and shine
A crook	I'm buffaloed
A sissy	He's a wet blanket
A tomboy	I'm farm raised
He rules the roost	A colored gal
He talks a big game	Straw boss
Remember the Alamo	A wrangler
Don't Mess With Texas	Gunslinger
It's where I hang my hat	A cotton picker
Come spring	A spick
I savvy	A young whippersnapper

He's a dandy	Yellow dog Democrat
Not worth a red cent	A blue dog Republican
Worth every penny	The bell cow
Ladies and gents	The pick of the litter
She's knocked up	A shine ass; an ass kisser.
Red light district	Big spender
A hard row to hoe	Dirt poor
He's right smart	Mean as the devil
Making good money	Fair-to-middling
I spotted him	A big taste of Texas
Blind tiger	Down the chute
He's running wild	Horn in
He draws fire	Real raunchy
Fair game	A posse
Jumping off place	Bull rider
Shooting craps	Hot diggity
He bluffed us	Going Texan
No matter where	Howdy partner
He gritted his teeth	Cattle kings and barons
A shotgun wedding	Born to fight
The wild bunch	Slap dab in the middle
I'm here to tell you	White-faced cows
In a manner of speaking	Prairie schooner
His heart belongs to Texas	A road runner (paisano)
Don't get worked up in a lather	A tinhorn
Red as a turkey gobbler's neck	A mule skinner
He was strung up on a limb	Kangaroo court
I got him by the ying-yang	Horseface
Rich as six feet up a hog's ass	Just around the corner
Hogs at the public trough	Full of piss and vinegar
Help yourself to seconds	A ten-gallon hat
Lit up like a country church	A jamboree
Come down off your high horse	Pissed off
Grab opportunity by the horns.	The crack of dawn
A frying-size boy; a young sprout	300 head of cows

Sink your teeth into it	Cow puncher, cowpoke
He's tight as the bark on a tree	Cattle rustler
Getting hitched (to marry)	A tenderfoot
Straight from the horse's mouth	Dress up clothes
Texas tea is not what it used to be	A sombrero, a ten gallon hat
Everything is bigger in Texas	Smack dab in the middle of Texas
I couldn't take it no longer	Texas is like a whole other country
She led a fast life	Where the West begins
Shoot Luke or give up the gun	He has deep Texas roots
A run-down-at-the-heels-farmer	He has the Midas touch
The Bowie knife	I'll clean your plow (J. R. Kelsey)
A knock down drag out fight	A Texas good old boy
He shoots from the hip	They polished him off
He runs me ragged	He didn't know what hit him
So many cotton picking times	Between a rock and a hard place
Running off at the mouth	He flew the coop
She bawled her head off	Being country; Getting citified
Welcome as a polecat at a picnic	Spoken from the heart (Laura Bush)
Strutting around like a turkey gobbler	BOI—Born on the island (Galveston)
A Texas norther	A Texas dust storm
A Texas tornado	A Texas cyclone
A mail order cowboy	A drugstore cowboy
An honest-to-God cowboy	
I don't talk his language, he don't talk mine	
The bigger the hat, the smaller the herd	
If you ain't from Texas, you ain't (bumper sticker)	
The Old Three Hundred (Austin's colony)	
It was so dark you could feel it (Ramon Adams)	
The Law West of the Pecos—Judge Roy Bean	
A Texian (in Texas before Texas statehood)	
It's just two hoots and a holler from here	
A wide place in the road (small town)	
Restraint was thrown in the ash can (from *Gay as a Grig*)	
He was sniffing like a hound dog picking up a scent	
Texas looms loud on the political scene	

He throws his weight around; puts on a show

She cooked a mess of mustard greens and cornbread

Dallas for education, Ft. Worth for fun

Hasta la vista (Until we meet again or See you later)

They are like two bulls in one pasture

Caramba; mas o menos; mi casa es su casa

All hat and no cattle; the larger the hat, the smaller the herd

He's welcome as a polecat at a picnic

Hunt up somebody you can use for a backbone

He's strutting around like a turkey gobbler

I knocked the whey (or piss or Hell) out of him

She's fixing dinner (instead of cooking)

High-Low-Jick-Jack and Game (poker)

Taking up a collection; passing the plate

I never met a man I didn't like. (Will Rogers)

In the second place behind God he loved ranching

She cooked me a mess of turnip greens and cornbread

He's a thorn in my side; a burr under my saddle

Burnet County, Texas; It's Burnet, durn it, not Bur-net

They looked plumb civilized (Shine Phillips)

The sun has riz and the sun has set and here we is in Texas yet

I'm a lover and a fighter and a wild horse rider and a pretty good windmill fixer

Wash your face and comb your hair and get yourself ready for the Dallas Fair

Republicans tighten their grip on Texas; Texas has spoken

Fall-off-the-bone good ribs chased down with a peach cobbler

You can't clear the water until you get the hogs out of the creek

An Indian killed a white man for pissing in the spring (into the toilet bowl)

He couldn't pour water out of a boot with the directions printed on the heel

He couldn't pour water downhill

An honest politician is one who when bought stays bought (Simon Cameron)

There's nothing more sacred to a Texan than his word (Frost Bank)

George Bush was born with a silver foot in his mouth (Ann Richards)

Ladybird finished the course and kept the faith (Bill Hobby)

He's not worth a bucket of spit (Vice President John Nance Garner)

It's better to be in the tent passing out than it is to be outside pissing in (LBJ)

*J. Cooke Wilson, Sr. and
Mary Wilson Kelsey at
Spindletop Monument, 1941*

I've been busier than a one-legged man with one hoe and two rattlesnakes (Ladybird Johnson)

There's no fertilizer like the footsteps of the owner (Alfred Glassell)

Bitten by the political bug (Oveta Culp Hobby)

How the West was won: Bible, fist and gun

He reared back like he had corn to sell (Julie Kemper)

She's running around like a chicken with its head cut off (Julie Kemper)

That's as rare as horse manure in a garage (Dr. Al Snell, Mayo Clinic)

I was raised in the town of Throckmorton, Texas (Ross McKnight)

I'm for gun control; use both hands. (Rick Perry)

I'm a big boy and I know how to play the game (Rick Perry)

I could whip him with my eyes closed and one hand tied behind my back. (Rick Perry)

The boss gave us two hours to get a good night's sleep

Crawl off and feed your tapeworm. (Ramon Adams)

It's water but you've got to chew it before you swallow it. (Ramon Adams)

He didn't last as long as two bits in a poker game. (Ramon Adams)

He wouldn't ride nothing wilder than a wheelchair. (Ramon Adams)

He's so thin he has to stand up twice to make a shadow. (Ramon Adams)

I wouldn't give a nickel for them but I wouldn't sell them for a million dollars. (Clare Glassell)

Born in the middle of nowhere (Dr. May Owens)

The better you take care of your land, the better it takes care of you (Ross McKnight)

Bill Hobby knows the nuts and bolts of Texas politics

Caro did a hatchet job on LBJ when he wrote his biography (Bill Hobby)

What's the difference between gonorrhea and Austin? You can cure gonorrhea. (Bill Hobby)

They spoke with their pocketbooks. (Bill Hobby)

A mule could do it if he had one hand. (Bill Hobby)

The only difference between a coon ass and a horse's ass is the Sabine River. (Bill Hobby)

Bad fences make bad neighbors. (George W. Bush)

To whom much has been given, much is required. (from the Bible, often quoted by George W. Bush)

Throwing stones at the sideline (George W. Bush)

The way to increase revenue is to grow the economy. (George W. Bush)

Deposit that information in your memory bank. (George W. Bush)

Stability can't be earned at the price of liberty. (George W. Bush)

Where his dog made his deposits on the lawn (George W. Bush)

The shadow of Bush looms large

We had a front seat to history. (Susan G. Baker)

Texas is on the frontline to cure cancer. (Susan G. Baker)

Never ask a man if he's a Texan. If he is, he will tell you. If he isn't, don't embarrass him.

Any jackass can kick a barn down, but it takes a carpenter to build one. (Sam Rayburn)

You'll never get mixed up if you tell the truth. (Sam Rayburn)

No one has a finer command of the language than the man who keeps his mouth shut. (Sam Rayburn)

Home, Home on the Range: Oh, give me a home where the buffaloes roam and the sky is not cloudy all day

We don't eat cow, we eat beef: we don't eat pigs, we eat pork; we don't eat sheep, we eat lamb; we don't eat goats, we eat cabrito

Chuck wagon food: mountain oysters, son-of-a gun stew, whistle berries (beans), sow belly, potluck; son of a gun stew; sinkers (biscuits)

Old time Texas food prices: a Coke and a hamburger—a nickel and a dime; a dozen hot tamales—two bits; chicken fried steak and cream gravy—four bits; a porterhouse steak—a buck

A topwater: a novice or incompetent person (saying originated in East Texas from shiner minnows swimming near the surface)

There never was a rider who couldn't get throwed; there never was a horse that couldn't get rode

A snow bird comes to the Texas Rio Grande valley in a tee shirt with a ten dollar bill and never changes either one

Snowbirds: Northerners who spend the winter in the Texas Rio Grande River Valley

No one could get the mule to work until I hit him over the head with a two-by-four. Reason: no one had ever explained it to the mule before.

Insects: Katydids, July flies, skeeters, chiggers, grasshoppers, boll weevils, wasps, screw worms, bumble bees, horn flies, heel flies, tarantulas, Daddy long legs, scorpions, ticks

You are the master of the spoken word and you are the slave of the written word; so don't write something you wouldn't say

The Texan was good natured and likeable but in three days no one could stand him (in *Catch-22*)

The frontier is won by those who dare to take the first step when no one can. (Owen Wister in *The Virginian*)

We're building a country out here and there's no place for weakness. (Owen Wister)

Inject a few raisins into the tasteless dough of conversation (Texas humorist O. Henry, pseudonym for Gene Stratton Porter)

POPULAR SONGS I REMEMBER IN TEXAS

Turkey in the Straw	Dixieland
Alexander's Ragtime Band	Old San Antonio Rose
My Old Kentucky Home	Old McDonald Had a Farm
The Wabash Cannonball	The Red River Valley
In the Land of Dixie	Home on the Range
My Blue Heaven	The Eyes of Texas
Take Me Out to the Ballgame	Texas, Our Texas (state song)
Polly Wolly Doodle All Day	Oh, Pretty Woman
The Yellow Rose of Texas	Deep in the Heart of Texas
Buffalo Gal	A Ding Dong Daddy from Dumas
Cielita Linda	The Wreck of the Old Ninety-Nine

Bury Me Not on the Lone Prairie

Eighter from Decatur (county seat of Wise)

The Old Grey Mare, She Ain't What She Used to Be

The Moon Shines Bright on Pretty Redwing

Willie Nelson songs: All My Exes Live in Texas, Hello Walls, Crazy, Time Slips Away, Blue Eyes Crying in the Rain, Red-Headed Stranger, One the Road Again, Who Will Buy My Memories; Mama, Don't Let Your Babies Grow Up to Be Cowboys

SOME OIL PATCH SAYINGS

Mary Wilson Kelsey's father, James Cooke Wilson, came to Spindletop during the first year of the discovery well drilled by Anthony Lucas in 1901. Cooke represented a syndicate of investors from Meridian, Mississippi, who sent him to Spindletop to take part in the boom. He drilled the twenty-seventh well on Spindletop. The well was a gusher. Cooke spent the rest of his life in Beaumont where he organized the Wilson Broach Oil Company and drilled wells in Texas, Louisiana and Oklahoma. He spent time in many oil camps. One night the tent in which he slept was punctured by bullets. In 1908, at twenty-nine years of age, he had become very wealthy and married Mary Bradley Randolph. In 1918 he was one of the organizers of the Humble Oil Company, later to become Exxon.

Cooke Wilson was acquainted with the other pioneers of Spindletop, including the Hammil brothers who actually did the drilling of the first well. Years later when most of the oil had been produced, Cooke bought the leases on Spindletop and produced oil from numerous stripper wells. He then produced sulfur from Spindletop.

After Cooke's death in 1944, his family continued operating the company until the 1970s when it was dissolved. His fortune has continued to this day to finance many charities and educate his numerous descendants.

Struck it rich is an old saying, frequently used in the **oil patch** to describe people who discovered oil and suddenly became rich. In the 1930s I met an oilman who was a friend of the Cooke Wilson, Sr., family of Beaumont, Texas. He made a good living in the oil patch but never struck it rich. He left his heirs several oil royalties which never produced any income. These royalties were completely forgotten and his children didn't know they even existed until sixty years later when a huge gas field was discovered on the land. I'm told that the heirs are each receiving a royalty payment of more than $100,000 each month. That's **striking it rich**! We have a few of these old royalties but, so far, the most Mary's estate ever received is about $100 per month.

The well blew out—blew in

The price (of oil) caved in

He got his money's worth

He struck it rich

Spudding a well; a wildcatter.

I lost my shirt on a dry hole

I'm in the oil business

I'm an oil man

Oil money; drowning in oil; hot oil

I wanted water but they gave me oil. Damn the oil; give me water. (Waggoner)

Wilson-Broach Oil Company, Beaumont, Texas stock certificate for Mary Wilson Kelsey 1962

The Lucas Gusher at Spindletop, 1901

Spindletop blew in on January 10, 1901

Spindletop Lucus Gusher (the most famous oil well in the world)

Texas, where oil wells blow and millionaires grow

The hole; the drilling bit; roller bit; making hole

Christmas Tree (valves that control the flow of an oil well)

Doodlebug (a fake instrument for finding oil)

Dry hole; duster (no oil found; a blowout)

The oil company branches out with its roots in Texas

Cable tool drilling; rotary rig drilling; casing the well

Alas, most wildcat wells come in a duster

He bought a whispering interest in a wildcat drilling venture

If you don't have an oil well, get one (Bill Hobby)

He rode into the boom on the first load of timber and he rode it out with the last load of pipe

The big inch (twenty-four-inch pipeline from Texas to the northeast to supply oil during WWII while German submarines were sinking the oil tankers

More oilfield terms: An oil town, an oil boom, we struck oil, we hit a gusher, we got production, we had a blow out, the well caved in

Some oilfield workers: roughneck, roustabout, tool pusher, derrick man, sharp shooter, oil rig worker, a backup man, fireman, nitroglycerine shooter, a boll weevil, a pipe hand, snapper

Oil patch words used to describe Spindletop oil drilling, 1901-1906: Hit the ball, a real pipe hand, sharp shooter, got production, a duster, a gusher; a boom, dry hole, cratered, blow out, roughneck, roustabout, tool pusher, rotary rig, a gusher, struck oil, struck it rich, oil boom, boom town, oil town, hot oil out of East Texas

The oil camp mess hall: In 1926 we ate in the Humble Oil mess hall on the Parrott Ranch during the oil boom and saw a gusher come in and a well that was a duster. This ranch is still producing oil eighty-five years later. It helped pay for my college and medical school education. Dad gave our interest back to the Parrott family. A cousin in Beaumont in still receiving modest royalty payments from it.

QUOTES FROM DR. DONALD DYAL, FORMERLY DIRECTOR OF SPECIAL COLLECTIONS, CUSHING LIBRARY AT TEXAS A&M, AND DEAN OF LIBRARIES AT TEXAS TECH UNIVERSITY

Why not go out on a limb; that's where the fruit is

What people say behind your back is your standing in the community

Never miss a good chance to shut up

He who laughs last thinks slowest

If the enemy is in range, so are you

Almost anything is easier to get into than get out of

Ten small words with the greatest meaning: If it is to be, it's up to me

Words are like toothpaste. Once you get them out you can't put them back.

Sex is like air; it's not that important unless you aren't getting any

Experience is something you get just after you need it

Don't test the water with both feet

The nice thing about egotists: They don't talk about other people

If at first you don't succeed, skydiving is not for you

Never take a sleeping pill and a laxative the same night

Never test the water with both feet

You will always be late for the previous train and in time for the next

The law of unintended consequences

It's bad luck to be superstitious

Even if you're on the right track, you'll get run over if you just sit still

The quickest way to double your money is to fold it in half and put it in your pocket

Never criticize someone unless you walk a mile in their shoes, then you are a mile away and have their shoes

The Lucas Gusher Monument at Spindletop, was dedicated October 9, 1941, and was named for Anthony F. Lucas whose untiring efforts led to Spindletop discovery well.

SAYINGS OF DAVID CROCKETT

Davy Crockett was a folk hero, even before he was killed in 1836 at the Battle of the Alamo. He was famous as a hunter, having killed one hundred bears in one year. He was a politician. Since he had virtually no formal education and was illiterate, he decided he needed to learn to read and write when he ran for election to the United States Congress. So his wife taught him to read and write and he won election. He became famous for his speeches. He published his autobiography in 1834. It contained many of his sayings, among which was his favorite, **"Be sure you are right, then go ahead."** When about to swim across a swollen stream, he said, **"I was born to be hanged so I knew I wouldn't drown."**

These sayings are in *King of the Wild Frontier, An Autobiography of Davy* Crockett, by David Crockett, 1834 (an unabridged edition by Dover Publications, 2010).

The hard times and plenty of them	Cut out for home
Set on him like a wildcat	When I turn my memory back
In a devil of a hobble	The doing of the Almighty
Makes the fur fly	To lift up the voice of complaint
A jolly good man	As sly as a fox
The devil take the hindmost	About two hours before day
Wet as a drowned rat	Took too many horns (drinks)
Got a bad name	The jib was up with me
She was as ugly as a stone fence	He has a stiff upper lip
Barking up the wrong tree	As good luck would have it
My dander was up	Rained riproariously
Having a shake with him	Set out for
Of the real grit	I didn't believe the half of this
He was on the wrong scent	Raised a fuss
Necessity is not very particular	The very picture of hard times
Lock, shot and barrel	I took a notion to hunt bears

It was a punishment on them (for leaving me)

The second epistle of Noah's freshet (a flood)

He whipt me an eternal sight worse

Puffing and blowing as though his steam was high enough to burst the boilers

Hang on like a turtle does to a fisherman's toe

Gave me the devil in three or four different ways

I would have given the world if it had belonged to me

A little of the Creator (a shot of whiskey)

Understand which way the wind blows

It wasn't the thing it was cracked up to be

My pluck is never to seek and never decline office

An empty purse is as near the devil as anything else I've seen

Fed the hungry and covered the naked

Reeled about like a cow with the blind staggers

My face looked like it had been half soled with brown paper

Vines so thick that a good fat coon couldn't much more than get along

The briars had worked on me such rate that I felt like I needed sewing up

So tired I could hardly work my jaws to eat

The old Serpent Himself (the Devil)

I asked the bears for no favors, no way

The dogs so poor they would almost have to lean up against a tree to take a rest

Others that have more learning than me

She gave me the whole bottle and thought if it killed me I was going to die anyway

I was determined to give him salt and vinegar

Death, that cruel leveler, entered my humble cottage and tore from my children an affectionate mother

I reckon he didn't fancy the business of gathering grapes in an out-of-the-way thicket again soon (when a man disappeared).

There was as good fish in the sea as had ever been caught out of it (consolation for loss of a sweetheart)

When David Crockett lost an election for Congress he said, "You can go to Hell, I am going to Texas"

CHAPTER EIGHTEEN

Roger and Bonita Kelsey,
parents of Mavis P. Kelsey, Sr.

Sayings *of the* Ancients & Greats

❖

**WHAT HAS BEEN WILL BE AGAIN. WHAT HAS BEEN DONE WILL BE DONE AGAIN.
THERE IS NOTHING NEW UNDER THE SUN.** *Eccl. 1:9, Solomon (1011 BC – 931 BC)*

P*eople were using sayings in the earliest days of the written word, and many are as true today as they were thousands of years ago. For example: Sayings like Solomon's* **"There's nothing new under the sun."** *The first sayings we have are Sumerian, 5000 – 3500 BC. It was in Sumer (modern day Iraq) where the first written word was engraved on clay cylinders. One writer has said the ancients have stolen our sayings. Don't say the ancients weren't smart. Sumerian and Sanskrit are dead languages but their sayings live on forever. There's no telling how long some sayings existed before there was a written language. Most of these sayings were taken from* **Roget's Thesaurus.**

Sumerian (5000-3500 BC)
Wealth is hard to come by but poverty is always close.
Possessions are sparrows in flight that can find no place to land.

Sanskrit (3000 BC)
There is pain in acquiring wealth, pain in keeping it, pain in spending it, pain in losing it; why so much sorrow?

The Bible (3000 BC-200 AD)
Many are called but few are chosen.
What a man soweth, that shall he reap.
Lay up for yourself treasures in heaven.

The Talmud (3000 BC to 1 AD)
Who wins through evil loses.

Homer (750 BC)
The raging impotence of woe.

Aesop (620-560 BC)
Outside show is a poor substitute for inner worth.
It's easy to despise what you cannot get.
We often give our enemies the means for our destruction.

Pindar (552-492 BC)
Often silence is the wisest thing for a man to heed.
Please all and please none.

Heraclitus (5th Century BC)
Religion is a disease but it is a noble disease.

Confucius (551-478 BC)
If you call a stinkweed a rose, it will smell the same.
The cautious seldom err.
Real knowledge is to know the extent of your own ignorance.

Aeschylus (525-465 BC)
He who knows useful things, not many things, is wise.

Sophocles (496-406 BC)
Ears are eyes to the blind.
None love the messenger who brings bad news.

Herodotus (484-424 BC)
Nor snow, nor rain, nor heat, nor gloom of night stays these couriers from the swift completion of their rounds (Source of motto once used by the U. S. Postal Service).

Socrates (469-399 BC)
Excellence is not an art but a quality.

Plato (428-347 BC)
Those who have torches will pass them on to others.

Aristotle (384-322 BC)
There are instances of men who have been ruined by their money or killed by their courage.

The excellent soul is exempt from a mixture of madness.
Beginning, as the proverb says, is half the battle.

Cleanthes (300-220 BC)
Fate leads the willing, drags the unwilling.

Archimedes (287-212 BC)
Give me a lever long enough and a fulcrum strong enough and I can move the world.

Plautus (254-184 BC)
A woman smells good when she smells of nothing.

Cicero (106-43 BC)
The beginning of all things is small.
Honor is the reward of valor.
Extreme justice is extreme injustice.
A room without books is a body without soul.
The greater the difficulty the greater the glory.
Peace is liberty in tranquility.
Their very silence is a loud cry.

Julius Caesar (102 – 44 BC)
I came, I saw, I conquered.
Hasten slowly.

Virgil (70-19 BC)
Training is of great importance in early years.
The Lord delights in odd numbers.
A woman is ever a fickle and changeable thing.
They are because they think they can.
Earth's noblest thing, a woman perfected.
The wound unuttered lies deeply in the soul.
Vice is nourished by secrecy.
Each one is carried away by his own desires.

Horace (65 BC-8 AD)
Jest often decides matters of importance more effectively than seriousness.
He who begins has half the work done.
A word once spoken flies away, never to be called back.
Words spoken can never be recalled. Once you've said it, you're stuck with it.
Training is of great importance in the early years.
Whatever advice you give, be brief.

Pliny (62 BC – 113 AD)
His only fault is that he has no fault.

Juvenal (60 BC -140 AD)
Who will guard the guards?

Livy (59 -17 BC)
In great attempts it is glorious to fall.
She is only constant in her inconsistency.
A merry companion is as good as a wagon.

Mavis P. Kelsey, age 98. May 18, 2011, Houston, Texas.

Seneca (54 BC-39 AD)
I was shipwrecked before I got aboard.
Age is an incurable disease.
Life is most delightful when it's on the downward slope.
What happens also ends.

Ovid (43 BC-18 AD)
Add a little to a little and there will be a great heap.
Time is the devourer of things.
Have patience and endure.
If you wish to marry well, marry your equal.
The art of medicine is usually a matter of time.
He who is not prepared today will be less so tomorrow.

Publilius (1st century BC)
To do two things at once is to do nothing.
Practice is the best of all instructions. (Note: This is rote memory which has been abandoned in today's education.)

Lucian (c120-180)
You may lead an ass to knowledge but you can't make him think.
If you think to grow a beard is to acquire wisdom, a goat is at once a complete Plato.

Marcus Aurelius (121-150 AD)
Even a palace life may be well lived.

Omar Khayyam (1048-1131 AD)
A hair perhaps divides the false form the true.

Chaucer (1390-1400)
Examine well your own thoughts.

Montaigne (1533-1593)
Nothing is so firmly believed as that we least know.

Cervantes (1547-1616)
Let the guts be full; it's they that carry the legs.

John Lyly (1554-1600)
The empty vessel giveth a greater sound than a full barrel.

Shakespeare (1564 – 1616)
What a spendthrift he is of his tongue.
A great man is the man who made a thing for the first time.
Oh, villain, villain, smiling damn villain
I drink to the general joy of the whole table.
Thereby hangs a tale.
An honest tale speeds best by being plainly told.
Out damned spot, out I say.
All the world's a stage.
What's in a name? That which we call a rose; by another name would still smell as sweet.

George Herbert (1593-1633)
Lend only what you can afford to lose.

Voltaire (1694-1778)
If there were no god, it would be necessary to invent one.
The art of medicine consists of amusing the patient while nature cures the disease.

Benjamin Franklin (1706-1790)
Light purse, heavy heart
A full belly makes a dull brain.

Samuel Johnson (1709-1784)
Of all noises, I think music is the least disagreeable.

Thomas Jefferson (1743-1824)
We are not to expect to be transported from despotism to liberty in a feather bed.

Nathan Hale (1755-1776)
I have but one life to lose for my country.

Napoleon Bonaparte (1769-1824)
Imagination rules the world.

George Gordon, Lord Byron (1788-1824)
Be warm but pure, amorous but chaste.

John Keats (1795-1821)
There is no fiercer hell than the failure of a great object.

Anthony Trollope (1815-1882)
Of all the needs a book has, the chief need is that it be readable.

Friedrich Nietzsche (1846-1900)
Market ability is nothing more than refinement of piratical morality.

Mark Twain (1835-1910)
You've done yourself proud.
When in doubt, tell the truth.

Henry Adams (1838-1898)
A teacher affects eternity; he can never tell when his influence stops.

O. Henry (1862-1910)
Inject a few raisins of conversation into the tasteless dough of existence.

Carl Sandburg (1878 -1967)
An expert is a damned fool a long way from home.

Albert Einstein (1879-1955)
There's joy in creative expression and knowledge.

Will Rogers (1879-1935)
All I know is what I read in the papers.

Franklin Roosevelt (1888-1942)
The only thing we have to fear is fear itself.

Eleanor Roosevelt (1888-1962)
Words are the cruelest of weapons.
Not all wisdom is earned by winning a university degree.
A good listener can't be accused of rudeness.

Dwight Eisenhower (1890-1969)
We are going to have peace even if we have to fight for it.

CHAPTER NINETEEN

Mavis P. Kelsey, Sr., at Cushing Memorial Library, Spring 2010.

Proverbs, Axioms & Adages

YOU ARE THE MASTER OF THE SPOKEN WORD AND YOU ARE THE SLAVE OF THE WRITTEN WORD, SO DON'T WRITE SOMETHING YOU DON'T WANT YOUR PREACHER TO READ.

A *proverb is an epigrammatic saying that is popular. The Holy Bible contains many. An axiom is a statement of self-evident truth. Obviously many proverbs may be called axioms and vice versa. We have lumped together what some call proverbs and some call axioms. Other words denoting some of these sayings include maxim, quip, adage and aphorism.*

We live one day at a time	You are as good as you look
Out of place, out of mind	Here today and gone tomorrow
Nothing ventured, nothing gained	Every dog has his day
What you pay for is what you get	Time and tide wait for no man
Give credit where credit is due	Rome was not built in a day
Not doing is better than overdoing	To each his own
Gather flowers while the sun shines	Practice makes perfect
What I don't know doesn't worry me	Man is an animal of habit
Advice when needed is least heeded	Haste makes waste
A pint's a pound the world around	He who hesitates is lost
All your strength is in your union	History repeats itself
Honesty is the best policy	It's never too late to learn
A little learning is a dangerous thing	Better late than never
Better go than send	He laughs well who laughs last
Every little bit helps	Live and let live
The love of money corrupts	Everybody loves a lover
Laws are made to be broken	Love conquers all
Wisdom only comes with age	Learn to walk before you run
Believe not all you hear	Go with the flow
The best is the cheapest	Don't sweat the small stuff
It's better to beg than to steal	It's the little things that count
Beauty is but skin deep	Every cloud has a silver lining
Never look back	All's fair in love and war
Love is blind	Fight fire with fire
Boys will be boys	All men are created equal
Never say die	Blood is thicker than water
Figures don't lie	What fools these mortals be
Justice is blind	A stitch in time saves nine
Knowledge is power	Forgive and forget
Nothing stays the same	Tomorrow never comes
Your mistakes will follow you	The more the merrier
There's no time like the present	There's no magic wand
You can't live on promises	Don't push your luck
It's never too late to repent	Truth or consequences
Nothing succeeds like success	There is no easy ride

Failures are the pillars of success	Still water runs deep
Enough is enough	It's the thought that counts
Leave well enough alone	You can't change the past
Handle him with kid gloves	Past is past
Don't rock the boat	Justice is justice
We're all in the same boat	Time heals all wounds
To swear is unbecoming	Beauty endures
Variety is the spice of life	Size matters
The rich never lack relatives	You can't take it with you
One is young only once	You can't get away from yourself
Take the bad with the good	A word to the wise is sufficient
Accidents will happen	Rain falls on the just and unjust
It takes two to tango	Get it when (& where) you can
Beggars can't be choosers	All's well that ends well
Charity begins at home	Man cannot live by bread alone
Clothes make the man	Actions speak louder than words
Let bygones be bygones	A watched pot never boils
Time waits for no man	A good man is hard to find
Every rose has its thorns	Waste not, want not
Life is too short to waste	Live simply
Prayers can move mountains	Beauty is as beauty does
Exceptions prove the rule	All that glitters is not gold
Life is made up of interruptions	There's good in everybody
Opportunity makes a thief	The truth is in the details
Easy come, easy go	Better safe than sorry
Nobody's perfect	Pretty is as pretty does
Hope is the last thing to die	The good eventually win
Facts may be true or false	Time will tell
In the end is the beginning	Burned once, never again
If worse comes to worst	True love never dies
Ask and you shall receive	It's the money that talks
Take it one day at a time	Brevity is the soul of wit
It is what it is	Stupid is as stupid does
There is a reason for everything	There's no fool like an old fool
A rose is a rose by any other name	Handsome is as handsome does

It's hard to find a good man	The early bird catches the worm
It's how you finish	Every family has its black sheep
Never tell a lie	One good turn deserves another
There's always a deeper message	It's better to be safe than sorry
There's no place like home	There's strength in numbers
Truth is everlasting	United we stand, divided we fall
The show must go on	A woman's work is never done
Silence is golden	Love your neighbor as yourself
You can't keep a good man down	Two wrongs do not make a right
He's got a girl in every port	Faint heart never won fair lady
It's too much of a good thing	Cleanliness is next to godliness
Your presence is his present	The pissants will finally get us
It's an ill wind that blows no good	Penny wise and pound foolish
Stone walls do not a prison make	The best things in life are free
Love is a many splendored thing	Looks alone don't tell the story
It takes two to start a fight	Two's company; three's a crowd
Woe to those who call evil good	Think twice before you do it
Where there's a will there's a way	Advising is easier than helping
Parting is such sweet sorrow	Idleness is the Devil's workshop
It's bad luck to be superstitious	A fair bride needs little finery
What goes around comes around	Eggs cannot be unscrambled
Behavior has its consequences	Evil is him who evil thinks
His bark is worse than his bite	Believe in yourself
There's only one number one	To err is human, to forgive divine
Pride goeth before a fall	Don't believe all you see—hear
Everything comes to an end	We usually say what we mean
If you don't show up you are lost	Truth is stranger than fiction
Only death and taxes are certain	Confession is good for the soul
You can get used to anything	When it rains it rains on all alike
While there's breath there's life	If it's not online it doesn't exist
A rolling stone gathers no moss	Tall oaks from little acorns grow
A penny saved is a penny earned	A fool at forty is a fool indeed
There's a reason for everything	We get the leaders we deserve
There's no rest for the weary	The written word is silent
Familiarity breeds contempt	Image triumphs over information

You only believe what you want to	There will be a day of reckoning
Showing up is 85% of success	Necessity is the mother of invention
Opportunity only knocks once	Everything comes to him who waits
To the winner goes the spoils	Too many cooks spoil the broth
A friend in need is a friend indeed	To lead, one must follow the people
The best defense is a good offense	Silence is more eloquent than words
Let your conscience be your guide	We know the world by its stories
A flower by any name is still sweet	You can't be all things to all people
Every man is his own worst enemy	The rolling stone gathers no moss
Those absent always get the blame	Be sure your sins will find you out
You can't judge a book by its cover	A virtuous person sleeps well
Everyone has his price	Finger pointing is not the solution
Willful waste brings woeful want	To spread the news is to magnify it
Vows, like eggs, are easily broken	Thank God for small favors
Count your daily blessings	There are no guarantees in life
You can't keep a good idea down	Everyone has the right to be wrong
Rules are made to be broken	Stand up for what is right
To give is to receive	Slow and steady wins the race
Lead by example	There's no free ride
A thing of beauty is a joy forever	Never settle for one side of the story
Saying so doesn't make it so	From the heart speaketh the mouth
The more you have the more you want	No man is an island, entire of itself
All good things come to those who wait	Don't put all your eggs in one basket
The best gifts come in small packages	Don't put the cart before the horse
There's a tide in the affairs of man	The grass is greener on the other side
Words can be the cruelest of weapons	There are two sides to every question
You can't wash the spots off a leopard	A miss of an inch is a good as a mile
If first you don't succeed, try, try again	Being well-prepared is half the battle
An apple a day keeps the doctor away	Experience is better than knowledge
There's more than one way to skin a cat	In old age once again you are a child
Things are not always what they seem	Don't let a fox watch the hen house
Speak of the devil and he will appear	Work is my blessing, not my doom
If you want it done right, do it yourself	The pen is mightier than the sword
Honey catches more flies than vinegar	Keep your commitments (promises)
You can't be in two places at one time	Cut the coat according to the cloth

Silence in the face of evil is evil itself

Some things are easier said than done

Good fences make good neighbors

It's love that make the world go round

Practice is the best of all instructions

There's no such thing as a free lunch

Seeing is one thing, believing is another

Many famous men have a lowly origin

Saying and doing are two different things

God closes one door and opens another

Continuous dripping wears away stone

All excesses bring their own punishment

What resembles nothing does not exist

Let not the sun go down on your wrath

Hell hath no fury like a woman scorned

Forget the past and focus on the future

Life is just one damn thing after another

It always breaks just when you need it

The heaviest burden is an empty pocket

One man's trash is another man's treasure

Children should be seen and not heard

You know him by the company he keeps

The higher they rise the steeper they fall

A stopped clock is right two times a day

A little knowledge is a dangerous thing

You can't squeeze blood out of a turnip

He's known by the company he keeps

Ridicule is man's most potent weapon

It's never too late to find your true love

To do nothing is tiresome; you can't stop and rest

A truth is not hard to kill but a lie is immortal (Mark Twain)

One remembers hits but forgets misses

Heavy is the head that wears the crown

If you worship money you will always feel poor

Too much of a good thing can be too much

The glory of a house is its hospitality

You can't get something for nothing

All we know is that we know nothing

Always do what you say you will do

There are two sides to every story

Getting half a loaf is better than getting no loaf at all

Better be an hour early than a minute late

Don't give advice unless you're asked for it

Error has a life that truth can never reclaim

The Golden Rule: Do unto others as you would have them do onto you

The rich get richer while the poor get poorer

Price is what you pay; value is what you get

It's divine to give and graceful to receive

Only those who attempt the absurd will achieve the impossible

Character makes itself known in moments of hardship

Everything that goes up is bound to come down

Facts do not cease to exist because they are ignored

What the child hears at home is soon known outside

The best laid plans of mice and men often go awry

Don't put off until tomorrow what you can do today

Be it ever so humble, there's no place like home

The sins of the father are visited on the son

Where ignorance is bliss, tis folly to be wise

Lightning never strikes twice in the same place

One half doesn't know how the other half lives

Early to bed and early to rise makes a man healthy, wealthy and wise

Wish not so much to live long as to live well. (Benjamin Franklin)

Search others for their virtues, thyself for thy vices. (Benjamin Franklin)

The rotten apple spoils the barrel. (Benjamin Franklin)

Let thy discontent be thy secret. (Benjamin Franklin)

Forewarned, forearmed (Benjamin Franklin)

Lost time is never found (Benjamin Franklin)

All work and no play makes Jack a dull boy

It's too late to shut the gate when the horse is out

To promise is one thing, to keep it is another

We have all forgotten more than we remember

He that fights and runs away will live to fight another day

One hand doesn't know what the other hand does

A smile goes a long way in making friends

Parables are the chance to learn from somebody else's mistakes

A nasty tongue is worse than a wicked hand

We will all hang together or we will all hang apart

You may lead a horse to water but you can't make him drink

The heart of the wise man is like still water

Heaven hath no rage like love to hatred turned

The more it changes the more it stays the same

With malice toward none, with charity toward all. (Abraham Lincoln)

The highest result of education is tolerance. (Helen Keller)

The sayings of the people are the wisdom of the ages

Success has ruined many a man. (Benjamin Franklin)

Don't count your chickens before they hatch

Yours is not to know the reason why, but to do or die

Sticks and stones will break my bones but words will never hurt me

A fish doesn't know it is swimming until it comes out of the water

Of all the sad words of mouth or pen the saddest are these: It might have been

When the going gets tough the tough get going

He that boasts his ancestry confesses that he has no value to himself

They do not love who do not show their love. (Shakespeare)

Fools' names, as well as faces, are often seen in public places

Don't marry without love. Don't love without reason.

The road to Hell is paved with good intentions

As you did it to one of the least of these, you did it unto me. (Matthew 25:40)

The best place to hide anything is in plain sight. (Edgar Allen Poe)

It's not over till it's over (till the fat lady sings)

Take your pleasure in moderation. (Confucius)

You can call stinkweed a rose but it won't smell any better. (Chinese)

Getting old is not what it's cracked up to be

Doing nothing is hard work; it's hard to do nothing

Prepare for the worst and hope for the best

Those who ignore history are doomed to repeat it

If you are just staying even, you are losing (Ernie Cockrell)

Injustice cannot deflate injustice (Chinese)

The most important decisions in life are never easy

It's better to have loved and lost, than never to have loved at all

People may come and people may go, while life goes on forever

Fool me once, shame on you; fool me twice, shame on me

In life we don't know the end from the beginning

Never let our drive to fix problems create more problems to fix

Friendship in the end is what makes us happy

It's better to be alone than in bad company

Don't cross your bridges until you get to them

If you watch the pennies, the dollars will take care of themselves

Being a good listener is better than being a good talker

A short pencil is better than a long memory

An expert in one thing soon becomes an expert in everything

Don't swap horses in midstream (Abraham Lincoln in 1864)

Mass/energy cannot be created or destroyed

There are three sides to every story my side, your side and the truth

We are a part of nature, not above it (Kelly Kelsey)

Nature controls in the long run (Kelly Kelsey)

Families that pray together stay together

Walking is a man's best medicine (Hippocrates)

If you tell the truth, you don't have to remember anything

You can judge a man by his enemies as well as by his friends

There's no gathering the rose without being pricked by the thorns

Doubts are more cruel than the worst of truths

A place for everything and everything in its place

It's not what you like that puts meat on your bones

Not to speak is to speak; not to act is to act

Be not the first to try, or yet, the last to throw aside

The only thing of consequence is what we do (John Ruskin)

There is no such thing as too much (I don't believe this)

Darkness is a luxurious cloak of comfort

The strength of any organization is the quality of its people

There is no such thing as a day off (for a mother)

Dishonesty will stare down honesty and day of the week

If it looks like a duck and quacks like a duck, it's a duck

Faith springs eternal from the human breast

No fathers and mothers think their children are ugly

It's not the bark but the bite that counts

Mental and physical exercise keep you young

Sadness touches all our lives at different times

If you don't move forward you move backward

All through history the way of truth and love has always won

If an appointment isn't important enough to keep, it not worth rescheduling

Ontology recapulates phylogeny (A&M Comparative Anatomy Course, 1930)

If they are in your gun range, you are in theirs. (Donald Dyal)

Life is a bridge, pass over it but build no houses on it

Give me liberty or give me death. (Patrick Henry)

All men are created equal; some are just more equal

Duty is the sublimest word in the English language. (Robert E. Lee)

The hand that rocks the cradle rocks the world

There are old pilots, there are bold pilots but there are no old bold pilots

Treat your body as if it were the temple of God

Never fall into the trap that newer is always better

A single moment can make all the difference

Happy are those who have kept a middle course

Every sweet has it's sour, every evil it's good

Inferiors revolt to be equal, equals revolt to be superior

His eye is on the sparrow, I know he watches me

Allah knows every hair of your head. (Quran)

Get the job you like and you will never have to work again

Truth telling is greater than sulking around in the dark

Plan for the future and don't defend the past

You can't predict the future but you can plan for it

Everyone can have their own opinions but they can't have their own facts

Competition is the steady hand at our back

We are on the turning point of the rise and decline of planet Earth

Time does not become sacred to us until we have lived it

What God has put together let no man pull asunder

A good listener cannot be accused of rudeness

Several excuses are less convincing that one

Know the difference between right and wrong

Stand up and take responsibility for your actions

You miss 100% of the shots you don't take

You can't get everything you want in one package

Lilies that fester smell worse than weeds. (Shakespeare)

It takes spit and vinegar to change things around

Don't make a mountain out of a molehill

The only way to win a war is to prevent it. (General George Marshall)

The male is not like the female. (Quran 13:36)

History is a bunch of lies. (Mark Twain)

Let the Lord be thy quest. (Quran 94:8)

Success if built on the ability to do better, not just do good

The purpose of life is to enjoy every moment

It's easy to start a war but hard to stop it

If you don't say anything, it can't be repeated

Those with the least power are the first to exert it

The best prophet of the future is the past

The generous pocket will never be empty

To seek direction is the only way for forward

To whom you reveal your secrets you yield your liberty

The best memory is not as clear as faded ink

Better than to run is to start on time

Where there is sugar there is bound to be ants

No one knows the weight of another's burden

It's easier to dam a river than to stop the flow of gossip

You never know what is enough until you know what is more than enough

To appreciate your parents' love, bear children

From word to deeds is a great distance

Everyone is ignorant on different subjects

Either do not begin or, having begun, do not give up

To fall is not failure if you refuse to give up

He who runs fast will not run far

He who hurries does not walk with dignity

Before buying a house ask about the neighbors

Gold has its price, learning is beyond price

Don't believe all you hear or tell all you know

A little knowledge prompts conceit, abundance induces humility

All between the cradle and the coffin is uncertainty

A good sword is the one left in the scabbard

Consider the facts seven times before you suspect someone

To receive a favor is to sell one's liberty

Elitism is the slur directed at merit by mediocrity

Nature is nature and you can't beat nature. You can't beat God.

What is whispered in your ear is heard a thousand miles off

Eat thy bread with joy and drink they wine with a merry heart. (Ecc. 9:7)

In praising the son the father extols himself

Do the hard jobs first. The easy jobs will take care of themselves.

Character is much easier kept than recovered

Almost anything is easier to get into than to get out of

It's not only what you make but what you make of it

Time engraves our faces with all the tears we have not shed

How can we drain the swamp when we are up to our asses in alligators

There are people who want to be everywhere at once and then get nowhere

Education without values makes a man a more clever devil

Whether we like it or not, we're all in it together

Through writing one can change history. (Nobel Prize winner
Mario Vargas Llosa, 2010)

You will never find time for anything. If you want the time you have to make it

Ethnic pride and self-esteem: E. Pluribus Unum; more pluribus or more unum?

Sad is the day for any man when he becomes completely satisfied. (Lee Clark)

Make no little plans They have no magic to stir men's blood. (Lee Clark)

A pair of women's breasts has more pull than a pair of oxen. (Mexican)

A word in earnest is as good as a speech. (Charles Dickens-A Word a Day)

Whether you like it or not, everything in life is a compromise

The wind extinguishes candles while it kindles fire

Originality is the fine art of remembering

There is no labor a person does that is undignified if they do it right

Word of the ancients: Let food be your medicine. (Hippocrates, 400 BC)

A decent provision on the poor is the true test of civilization.
(A Word a Day)

Reading is sometimes a device for avoiding thought - (A Word a Day)

You can take a boy out of the country but you can't take the country out
of the boy

There comes a time when a man refuses his leader to answer to his own conscience

Man cannot discover new oceans unless he has the courage to lose sight of the shore

No one is useless in this world who lightens the load of anyone else (Charles Dickens)

No two men can be together but one becomes superior to the other. (Samuel Johnson)

Four things that cannot be retrieved are the spoken word, the spent arrow, the past life and the neglected opportunity

Refrain from doing all you can, spending all you have, believing all you hear and telling all you know

In picking up a sesame seed we can lose sight of a watermelon (being penny wise and pound foolish)

No man is an island, entire of itself; every man is a piece of the continent. (John Donne)

Any man's death diminished me...never to know for whom the bell tolls. (John Donne)

Everyone is kneaded out of the same dough but not cooked in the same oven (Yiddish)

Money rides, history walks (regarding preservation of archeological sites) (Keith Tyler)

Let food be your medicine; walking is the best medicine (Hippocrates, 400 BC)

When the lion has a historian, the hunter will no longer be the hero. (African proverb)

All men by nature are born unequal It is vain to treat them as if they were equal. (Roget's Thesaurus)

A man has to live life with himself and he should see to it that he always has good company

When poverty comes in the front door love flies out the back window. (Nancy Scanlan)

There are people in the cart and there are people pulling the cart. (those who don't pay taxes, those who do)

If you drink the right amount and the right kind of Scotch whiskey, you will live forever (Scottish saying)

You can fool some of the people all of the time. You can fool all of the people some of the time. But you can't fool all of the people all of the time.

There are three yous—what you think you are, what others think you are and what you really are

You must cultivate your friends like you cultivate your garden. (President Calvin Coolidge)

Nothing is important as you think it is when you are thinking about it. (Mavis Kelsey, Jr.)

The pessimist sees the difficulty in every opportunity, the optimist sees the opportunity in every difficulty

The measure of a man's real character is what he would do if he knew no one was watching. (A Word a Day)

For every addition of knowledge you forget something you knew. Therefore don't let useless facts elbow out the useful ones

If we condensed the life of the universe to twelve hours on the clock, humans appeared 3/10 of a second before twelve (The Texas Episcopalian)

It's amazing how much you can accomplish if you don't care who gets the credit. (J. Cooke Wilson, Sr.)

It's amazing how much you can accomplish if you don't care what the public thinks. (President Barack Obama)

You are the master of the spoken word you are the slave of the written word; so don't write something down you don't want the preacher to read. (Nancy Mitchell's mother)

Every man has his directions to which he turns: so be you forward with good work (Quran 2:148)

Friendship is the only cement that holds the world together. (President Woodrow Wilson, 1918)

In anger say what you want to say; tomorrow when your companions get drunk and argue, take up your hat and wish them a goodnight

The tree of liberty must be refreshed from time to time with the blood of patriots and tyrants. (Thomas Jefferson)

Drink no longer water; but use a little wine for thy stomach's sake and thine other infirmities. (Tim. 5:23)

CHINESE PROVERBS

Avoid the employment of servants too pleasing to the eye

If you wish to know the mind of a man, listen carefully to his words

There are no mistakes, only lessons

When we lose, we don't lose the lesson

Black cat or white cat: if it can catch mice, it's a good cat

Take a second look...it costs you nothing

Be kind to unkind people; they need it the most

A day of sorrow is longer than a month of joy

Attack is the best defense

Better to light a candle than to curse the darkness

The lean dog shames the master

With money you are a dragon; without—a worm

The tree casts its shadow, even on the woodcutter

When planning revenge, one should dig two graves

Jade is worthless before polishing

He who rides the tiger is afraid to dismount

He who commences many things completes only a few

A man will never change his mind who has no mind to change

He who has a trusted friend has no need for a mirror

The friendship of two requires the patience of one

Little is spent with difficulty, much with ease

Angus A. Anderson, 1916-2009, who contributed many sayings to Mavis P. Kelsey, Sr.

CHAPTER TWENTY

Dr. Peter M. Roget's Thesaurus

A HAIR PERHAPS DIVIDES THE FALSE AND THE TRUE.
(Omar Khayyam, 1070-1123)

Roget's International Thesaurus, The Complete Book of Synonyms and Antonyms and American and British Usages, *Thomas Y. Crowell Company, New York, 1946. 20th printing, 1966. New Edition Revised and reset First Edition, by Peter Mark. Roget's Thesaurus was first published in London in 1852. By 1966 there had been seven editions and thirty-two printings. Started by Roget in 1805 and increased ever since, the entries begin with sayings of the ancients and continue with sayings as late as 1961. The book contains many thousand entries and thousands of sayings, many annotated by their author's name. They reach back as far as 5000 BC, many of which are still as fresh today. We are listing a few, especially the ones from the ancients.*

A soft answer turneth away wrath	Actions speak louder than words
A man's house is his castle	Handsome is as handsome does
Good fences make good neighbors	The sad fatigue of idleness
Clothes make the man	Idleness is the root of all evil
Curved is the line of beauty	Never get hurried
A rolling stone gathers no moss	Haste makes waste
All lay the load on a willing horse	A skill is stronger than strength
Who is foremost leads the herd	It's easier said than done
From softness only softness comes	All for one—one for all
When it rains it rains on all alike	United we stand divided we fall
You cannot catch the wind in a net	War is hell
A man's a man for all o' that	Love is a malady without a cure
Man is a reasoning animal	There is no love lost between us
Silence gives consent	Marriages are made in heaven
The exception proves the rule	One good turn deserves another
It is easier to be critical than correct	Good to forgive, best to forget
Experience is the mother of wisdom	Envy is a proud weakness
Love truth but pardon error	Two wrongs do not make a right
Suspense in news is torture	This is adding insult to injury
The unexpected always happens	Laws were made to be broken
A fault confessed is half redressed	It takes a thief to catch a thief
Practice makes perfect	Money begets money
He who teaches is a learner	Debt is the worst poverty
A liar must have a good memory	You cannot make a cheap palace
Classic literature is always modern	What costs little is valued less
A picture is a silent poem	Have patience and endure (Ovid)
Of two evils chose neither	Joy rules the day and love the night
Nothing ventured nothing gained	Jesters often prove prophets
Rats desert a sinking ship	Sign no paper without reading it
It never rains but it pours	A good name is better than riches
Where there's life there's hope	The more noble, the more humble
The cure is worse than the disease	Rank imposes obligations
Forewarned is to be forearmed	Pride goeth before a fall
Stone walls do not a prison make	A man's style is part of him
Forbidden wares sell twice as dear	Bad luck often brings good luck

He who can does, he who can't teaches

Mediocre minds generally condemn everything that passes their understanding

We made war to the end, the very end

Duty is what one expects from others

The world has angels and too few, and heaven is overflowing

Whatever makes men good Christians makes them good citizens

The religion of one seems madness to another

Atheism is rather in the lip of many and never in the heart

I am an atheist and I thank God for it

What greater calamity can fall on a man than the loss of worship

Things do not happen in the world, they are brought about

Don't hit at all if it's possible to avoid it but never hit soft (Theodore Roosevelt)

Thrones sink to dust while nations pass away.

The pride of an ancestry increases in the ratio of distance

Nothing succeeds like excess; moderation is a fatal thing

Each man has an aptitude born within him

Right and victory don't always concur

The promised land always lies on the other side of the wilderness

God made the country and manmade the town

Be it ever so humble, there's no place like home

Heaven isn't built of country seats, but of queer suburban streets

A village is a hive of glass where nothing unobserved shall pass

Let the guts be full; it's they that carry the legs (Miguel de Cervantes)

A little body often harbors a great soul (Benjamin Franklin)

A good neighbor is a precious possession

Naked came we into the world and naked shall we part it

He is best dressed whose dress no one observes

Our course is chosen; all I ask is a tall ship and a star to steer her by

When left to herself nature is in no hurry

Have you not learned good lessons from those who rejected you?

There is a natural body and there is a spiritual body

We never know the worth of water until the well runs dry

The earth produces all things and returns all again

The richest soil if uncultivated produces the rankest weeds

Those who play with cats can expect to be scratched

What is a weed? A plant whose virtues have not yet been found

After all there is but one race—humanity

Man is as good as he has to be and a woman is as bad as she dares

Woman is ever a fickle and changeable thing. (Virgil, 70-10 BC)

Earth's noblest thing, a woman perfected. (Virgil, 70-10 BC)

There is nothing like an odor to stir memory

A little sweet will cure much bitterness

Music has charms to soothe the savage beast

Of all noises, music is the least disagreeable. (Samuel Johnson)

Give every man thy ear, but few my voice

None is so deaf as those who will not hear

Out damned spot, out I say. (William Shakespeare)

The heart's letter is read in the eyes

Though most be players, some must be spectators

Those that think must govern those who toil.

Who will guard the guards? (Juvenal 60-140 AD)

Whose most tender mercy is neglect (to leave me alone)

Examine well your own thoughts. (Geoffrey Chaucer 1340-1400)

The only way to get the best of an argument is to avoid it

Nonsense can only be defended by nonsense

What is now proved was once imagined

You have not converted a man because you have silenced him

Never judge until you've heard the other side

He who has imagination without learning has wings without feet

All I know is just what I read in the papers. (Will Rogers 1879-1935)

Truth is the object of philosophy but not always of philosophers

He who knows useful things, not many things, is wise. (Aeschylus 525-456 BC)

Fools rush in where angels fear to tread

No excellent soul is exempt from a mixture of madness. (Aristotle 384-322 BC)

None love the messenger who brings bad news

Oaths are but words; and words but wind

With just enough learning to misquote (George Gordon, Lord Byron)

The scholar is the student of the world

Self-education is fine if the pupil is a born educator

When in doubt, tell the truth (Mark Twain)

A liar will not be believed, even when he speaks the truth

A hair perhaps divides the false and the true. (Omar Khayyam, 1070-1123)

There is no one who does not exaggerate

The best witness is a written paper

A work of art should carry its justification in every line

Great art is an instant arrested in eternity

If you wish to be a good writer—write

Letter writing, that most delightful waste of time

A room without books is a body without soul. (Cicero 106-43 BC)

The true university these days is a collection of books

Of all the needs a book has, the chief need is that it is readable. (Anthony Trollope)

All the world's a stage, and all the men and women merely players.
(William Shakespeare)

Fate leads the willing, drags the unwilling. (Cleanthes 331-232 BC)

He that is born to be hanged shall never drown. (David Crockett)

I am the master of my fate; I am the captain of my soul

The best laid plans of mice and men are often gone awry

Fortune gives many too much, no one enough

Why then can one desire too much of a good thing?

Everything in the world is good for something

Trifles make perfection and perfection is no trifle

Rejoice that you are not a perfect thing

Dirt is not dirt but something in the wrong place

Culture would not be culture if it were not an acquired taste

Acorns were good until bread was found

The art of medicine is usually a matter of time (Ovid 43 BC-18 AD)

God heals and the doctor takes the fee. (Benjamin Franklin)

Early and provident fear is the mother of safety

He who is not prepared today will be less so tomorrow. (Ovid 43 BC-18 AD)

There is no fiercer hell than the failure of a great object

There is great benefit in making a few failures in early life

If first you don't succeed, try, try and try again

Those aren't weighed in the balance and found wanting. (Bible)

When good luck comes to thee, take it

Government of the people, by the people and for the people (Abraham Lincoln)

Some must follow and some must command

There's little hope of equity where rebellion reigns

Uneasy lies the head that wears a crown. (William Shakespeare)

Where liberty dwells, that is my country. (Benjamin Franklin)

To do nothing is the way to be nothing

Nothing ever was accomplished without enthusiasm

Sleep that knits the raveled sleeve of care

All work and no play makes Jack a dull boy

Those that govern the best make less noise

The gods help them that help themselves

An expert is a damned fool a long way from home. (Carl Sandburg)

Practical politics comes in ignoring facts

The greater the difficulty the greater the glory. (Cicero 106-43 BC)

Millions for defense but not a penny for tribute

Peace is liberty in tranquility. (Cicero 106-43 BC)

There never was a good war or a bad peace (Benjamin Franklin)

The reward of a thing well done is to have done it

I came, I saw, I conquered. (Julius Caesar)

An ounce of vanity destroys a hundred weight of merit

Never step over the bounds of modesty

Every braggart shall be found an ass. (William Shakespeare)

Many kiss the hand they wish to cut off

A friend to everybody is a friend to nobody

Better an open enemy than a false friend

In spring a young man's fancies turn to thoughts of love

A man in passion rides a wild horse

If you wish to marry well, marry your equal (Ovid)

Render me worthy of this noble wife. (William Shakespeare)

Marriage has many pains, but celibacy has no pleasures. (Samuel Johnson)

Threats without power are like powder without ball

Let me live by the side of the road and be a friend of man

Envy is the most corroding of vices, and also the greatest power in any land

It's easy to despise what you cannot get. (Aesop 620-560 BC)

There's no weapon that slays its victim so surely as praise

Censure is the tax a man has to pay the public for being eminent

We love flattery even when we are not deluded by it

The world delights to tarnish shining names

Justice without wisdom is impossible

Live and let live is the rule of common justice

The extremity of justice is extreme injustice

Selfishness is the greatest curse of the human race

Each one is carried away by his own desires. (Virgil)

If there were no bad people there would be no good lawyers

The worst of the law is that one suit breeds twenty

Lawsuits consume time and money and rest and friends

Few rich men own their property; their property owns them

Lend only what you can afford to loose

Lend and the chances are you lose a friend

Neither a lender or a borrower be (William Shakespeare)

Hang a thief when he is young and he'll not steal when he is old

Buy not what you want but what you need

Morality is nothing more than refinement of piratical morality.
(Friedrich Nietzsche)

Money is like manure—only good when spread around

Light purse, heavy heart (Benjamin Franklin)

The things that are most dear to us are the things that cost us the most

The art of pleasing is to seem pleased

Deep wounds never close without a scar

Laugh and the whole world laughs with you; weep and you weep alone

A man cannot spend all his life in frolic

One should be moderate in his jests. (Cicero)

Everything is funny as long as it happens to somebody else. (Will Rogers)

Fill a dull man with knowledge and he will not become less dull

He must not laugh at his own jokes

Beauty without grace is the hook without bait

Beauty is only skin deep but ugly goes to the bone

Ornamentation is the principal part of architecture

The finest clothes wear soonest out of fashion

The only thing we have to fear is fear itself. (Franklin Roosevelt)

The cautious seldom err. (Confucius)

Be not the first the new to try nor yet the last the old to throw aside

Discretion is the better part of valor

The only way to get rid of a temptation is to yield to it

There's none worse than a proud heart and a beggars purse

A word once spoken flies away, never to be called back (Horace, 65-8 BC)

If there were no God it would be necessary to invent one. (Voltaire 1694-1788)

Proverbs are short sentences drawn from long experiences.
(Miguel de Cervantes 1547-1616)

A retentive memory is a good thing but the ability to forget is a token of goodness

For all the sad words of tongue and pen the saddest are these:
It might have been

The common school is the greatest discovery made by man.
(H. Mann, 1796-1859)

To gild refined gold; to paint the lily, to throw a perfume on the violet.
(William Shakespeare)

Habit is a cable; we weave a thread of it every day and at last we cannot break it.

Greater love hath no man than this, that a man lay down his life
for his friend. (Bible)

And thou, son of man, take the barbers razor and cause it to pass upon thy
head, thy beard. (Bible)

It is the supreme art of the teacher to awaken joy in creative expression and
knowledge. (Albert Einstein)

Learn by heart or rote, commit to memory, wade through or burn the midnight
oil. A teacher affects eternity; he can never tell where his influence stops.
(Henry Adams 1838-1918)

And there the whining school boy with his satchel and shining morning face
(William Shakespeare)

To inject a few raisins of conversation into the tasteless dough of existence.
(O. Henry, 1862-1910—the pseudonym for William Sidney Porter of Texas)

Work is what you are obligated to do. Play is what you are not obligated to do.
(Mark Twain)

Nor snow, nor rain, nor heat, nor gloom of night stays these couriers from the
swift completion of their appointed rounds. (Herodotus, 484-424 BC)

There is something in the misfortune of even our best friend that does not
wholly displease us (He had it coming to him is another way to express it)

So much to do, so little done   Justice is blind; he knows nobody

Tears are the language of the eyes   Too swift arrives as lately as too slow

Dr. Lewis Stover, great, great grandfather of Dr. Mavis P. Kelsey, Sr.

21

Made-Up Words

FLABBERGASTED AND FLUMMOXED BY A FIDDLE FADDLE OF FLUNKY FLIM FLAM.

I *call these words made-up words. They are practical shortcuts in communication, especially when you are* **bumfuzzled** *about what a* **thingamagig** *or a* **whatjama-callit** *is. They are really meaningless words used when you want to be funny or you don't know how to describe or name something. Then they take on meaning. Bumfuzzled is meaningless until you use it to express confusion. There's no such thing as a* **magusa-lum** *but it is used to express the word "throat." They save printing space and save time that would be needed to find the correct name for an object or event. Most are common folk language.*

MADE UP WORDS

A boo boo	Bum fodder (toilet paper)
A knick knack	Bumf (junk mail)
A rippo (counterfeit; rip-off)	Bumfuzzled
A squidgen	Bunga bunga
Abracadabra	Bushwacker
Akimbo	Catty-cornered
Antigoglin	Cahoots
Balderdash	Caterwauling
Bamboozled	Cattywampus
Blahs	Caubunga; cuccadubinga
Blindsided	Chit-chat
Blooey, blotto	Chuckaluck
Blue john	Chugalug
Bodacious	Curlicue
Bohunkus	Claptrap
Boogaloo	Clip clop
Boogeyman	Cockalorum
Boondocks	Coldcocked
Boondoggle	Confab
Boonies	Coonass
Bragadocious	Crackaloo
Brouhaha	Crisscrossed
Buckaroo	Dilly dallying
Bugaboo	Ding dong
Bugger	Dingle berries
Discombobbulism	Guzzle
Dololley	Handy dandy
Dodads	Hanky panky
Dofunnies	Harum-scarum
Doofus	Heebie-jebbies
Doozy	Helter-skelter
Draggle-tailed	Hem and haw
Falderol	High falutin'
Fantabulous	High muckety-muck

Fiddle faddle	Hinky dink
Flabbergasted	Hip-hop
Flapdoodle	Hobbledehobly
Flim flam	Hocus pocus
Flip-flopping	Hodge podge
Floozy	Hoi polloi
Fluff-duff (fancy)	Hoity toity
Flummoxed	Honkytonk
Flunky	Hoo doo
Folderol	Hoochy kootchy
Fragged	Hoopla
Frigging	Hootennany
Frizzy	Hornswaggle
Frowsty (musty smell)	Hotsey-totsey
Funky	Howsomeever
Ga Ga	Huggermugger
Gadzok	Hullabaloo
Gallavanting	Humbug
Gallimaufry	Humdrum
Galonippers	Humongus
Geegaw	Hunky dory
Gibberish	Hurdy-gurdy
Gigity jig jig	Hush puppy
Gimmick	In a jiffy
Gizmo	In cahoots
Gobbley-gook	Jabberwocky
Gofer	Jambalaya (Cajun)
Goof-offs	Jazzercise
Groovy	Jigget-jiggle
Grungy	Kit and caboodle
Guffaws	Kooky
Gung-ho	Kowtowing
Kybosh	Ransacked
La la land	Ratty-tat-too
Lollapalooza	Razzledazzle

Larrapin	Rick-rack
Lollygagger	Riff raff
Lopsided	Rigmarole
Magusalom	Roastneers
Mish mash	Rootin', tootin', hi-falutin'
Mollycoddle	Rope-a-dope
Mumbo-jumbo	Rub a dub dub
Munchies	Salamugundi
Namby-pamby	Sashayed
Niffers	Schmoozed
Nitty-gritty	Schussing
Okel dokel yokel	Scrimpstion
Okey-dokey	Scruffion
Oogley	Scrumptious
Oops	Scrumpulescent
Out of kilter	Scrunched
Palaver	Scuttlebutt
Party pooper	Sexting
Pee-diddly-squat	Shenanigans
Pell-mell	Shilly-shally
Persnickety	Shimmington
Phishing	Shimmy
Phrick	Shindig
Pizzazz	Skeddadle
Podunk	Skidoo
Pollywog	Skookum
Poof	Skyped
Pooh-pooh	Slumgullion
Poppycock	Slurp-guzzle
Pow wow	Smidgen
Puckered up	Smithereens
Pyschobabble	Smooching
Quirky	Snazzy
Ragamuffin	Snockered
Rakehellion	Snoozing

Ramble-scramble	Southpaw
Rambunctious	Spiffy
Ramshackled	Spindizzies
Spooked	Wannabe
Squariferous	Washopper
Squiggle	Whatchamacallit
Squishy	Wee wow
Strill	Wham bam
Swazey	Whompy jawed
Switcheroo	Whangdooddle
Swooshed	Whanghide
Syfy	Whingding
Talleywhacker	Whippersnapper
Tantrum scantrum	Whirlamajig
Tee-hee	Willy-nilly
Teeny-weensy	Wishy-washy
Teeter-totter	Wonky
The whole shebang	Woozy
Thingamajigs	Wussee
Ticky tack	Yahoos
Tit for tat	Yak
Tommyrot	Yerp
Topsey Turvey	Yicky
Touchous	Ying yang
Tweedly dee and tweedly dum	Yippy-ka-ya
Tweeted	Yo-yoing
Twofers	Yucky
Vamoose	Yum
Vegans	Zigzag
Voo doo	Zilch
Vroom	Zings
Wacky	Zombie
Wampus cat	Zsa zsa

A FEW EXCLAMATIONS AND SLANG

Aw come on. Aw shucks	Judas priest
Aw shoot! Aw hogwash!	Leaping lizards
Bravo; by golly; by gosh	Let's get the hell outta here!
Lord 'a mercy; Man, oh man	Do tell! Don't tell me!
No fooling? No joke?	Doggone it; damn it; darn it
No problema; No way, man	For Pete's sake; fiddlesticks.
Oh my gosh	For the love of Mike
Oh my! Oh, yeah! Oh boy!	Fuddy duddy
Phooey; pshaw	Gee whiz; goldurn.
Praise the Lord	Gawdamighty
Right on	Good grief; golly Moses.
So what?	Hell no; hell fire; heck yes.
Son of a gun	Hi, folks; hey folks; hey man.
Sure as shooting; sure enough.	Holy Moses; holy cow.
Well, I swear! Well, I'll be!	Holy mackerel; holy smoke.
What a life	Horse feathers!
What the devil? What the hell?	Hot-diggity-dog. Hot dog.
Whatta you know! You don't say!	Howdy-do
You bet; you said it!	How are you all? How y'all?
You old so-and-so	I don't believe it!
You're not kidding!	
Dad blame it; dad rat it; dadburnit; dadgummit	

Bibliographical Notes

In 2009 I started writing down old sayings as they came to mind. When I told friends and family, they supplied more sayings. Right away my sons and their wives, John and Gaye Kelsey, Mavis, Jr., and Wendy Kelsey, and Tom and Ann Kelsey, and my niece Nancy Scanlan provided sayings. Former clinic administrator Vicki Buxton sent me a list of seventy-five sayings. My assistant Becky Lemoine Ayers provided sayings and also typed, edited and put this book together for me, for all of which I am deeply grateful.

David Chapman, Colleen Cook and Adele Huddleston at Texas A&M University libraries provided sayings. Dorothy Sloan, architect Virginia Kelsey, Angus Anderson, Bessie Liedtke, and Sandra Bryant are among many who jogged my memory with more sayings. Dr. Donald Dyal, head of libraries at Texas Tech University, supplied many sayings from his extensive collection. My niece, Mary Griffith Wallace, provided several books by Charles Earl Funk describing the origin of many sayings.

The recently published autobiographies of my friends Lieutenant Governor Bill Hobby and Susan G. Baker each contain many outstanding sayings. My 1961 edition of *Roget's Thesaurus* contains a collection of hundreds of sayings by great writers.

I read the *Houston Chronicle* and the *Wall Street Journal* every day and have hundreds of sayings from the headlines and columns. My old friend Leon Hale's column was one especially good source. Many of these sayings have been doctored up to bring out the point of the writer or fit today's advancing technology.

My memoirs, *The Making of a Doctor*, provided help in describing the activities of my youth. I have quoted *Webster's Collegiate Dictionary*, 1948, and *Roget's International Thesaurus*. I have copied proverbs from a King James Version of the Holy Bible and from a Bible given me by Becky Lemoine Ayers, the New International Version called *The Life Application Bible*, Wheaton, IL, Tyndale House Publishers, 1991.

There are many books published about the language of the time, some by accomplished linguists and lexicographers. There are books written whose authors reminisce about their youth in the early 1900s, the same time that I grew up. Two autobiographies I read recently by East Texas authors are replete with stories, lifestyle activities and speech of the early 1900s. The books are Oren Arnold's *A Boundless Privilege* and Mary Cimarolli's *The Bootlegger's Other Daughter*. I found many familiar Biblical quotations in Lester V. Berry's *A Treasury of Biblical Quotations* and *The Multicultural Dictionary of Proverbs* by Harold V. Cordry.

BOOKS WHICH WERE USEFUL INCLUDE:

Adams, Ramon F., *Cowboy Lingo* (Boston: Houghton Mifflin, 2000)

Adams, Ramon F., *Western Words, A Dictionary of the Old West* (Norman, OK: University of Oklahoma Press, 1998)

Arnold, Oren, *A Boundless Privilege* (Austin: Madrona Press, 1974)

Atwood, E. Bagby, *The Regional Vocabulary of Texas* (Austin, TX: University of Texas Press, 1962)

Baker, Susan Garrett, *Passing It On, An Autobiography with Spirit* (Houston, TX: Bright Sky Press, 2010)

Berry, Lester, V., *A Treasury of Biblical Quotations* (Mineola, NY: Dover Publications, 1948) (a reprint)

Blaisdell, Bob, Editor, *The Wit and Wisdom of Abraham Lincoln* (Mineola, NY: Dover Publications, 2005)

Bush, Laura, *Spoken from the Heart* (New York: Scribner, 2010)

Cimarolli, Mary, *The Bootlegger's Other Daughter* (College Station, TX: Texas A&M University Press, 2009)

Cordey, Harold V., *The Multicultural Dictionary of Proverbs and Over 20,000 Adages* (Jefferson, NC. and London: McFarland & Co., 1997)

Crockett, Davy, *King of the Wild Frontier, An Autobiography* (Mineola, NY: Dover Publications, 2010)

Dalzell, Tom, *Damn the Man Slang of the Depressed in America* (Mineola, NY: Dover Publications, 2010)

Dalzell, Tom, *Flappers 2 Rappers, American Youth Slang* (Mineola, NY: Dover Publications, 2010)

Dickson, Paul, *War Slang, American's Fighting Words and Phrases Since the Civil War* (Mineola, NY: Dover Publications, 2011)

Farnsworth, Ward, *Farnsworth's Classical English Rhetoric* (Boston, MA: David R. Govine Publisher, 2011)

Franklin, Benjamin, *Wit and Wisdom from Poor Richard's Almanac* (Mineola, NY: Dover Publications, 1999)

Funk, Charles Earl, *Thereby Hangs A Tale* (New York: HarperCollins Publishing, 1950)

Funk, Charles Earl, *A Hog on Ice* (New York: HarperCollins Publishing, 1955)

Funk, Charles Earl, *Heaven to Betsy* (New York: HarperCollins Publishing, 1955)

Funk, Charles Earl, *Horsefeathers and Other Curious Words* (New York: HarperCollins Publishing, 1958)

Geary, James, *1 is An Other, The Secret Life of Metaphors* (New York: Harper Collins, 2011)

Grothe, Dr. Mardy, *Oxymoronica* (New York: HarperCollins, 2004)

Herder, Ronald, *500 Best-Loved Song Lyrics* (Mineola, NY: Dover Publications, 1998)

Hobby, William P., Jr., *How Things Really Work, Lessons from a Life in Politics* (Austin, TX, University of Texas Press, 2010)

Keyes, Ralph, *Euphemania, Our Love Affair with Euphemisms* (New York: Little Brown & Co., 2010)

Miedar, Wolfgang, *The Prentice Hall Encyclopedia of World Proverbs* (New York: MVF Books, 1986)

Moss, Peter (Introduction), *Chinese Proverbs, Ancient Wisdom for the 21st Century* (Hong Kong: Form Asia Books Limited, 2010)

Moss, Peter (Introduction), *Asian Proverbs, Ancient Wisdom for the 21st Century* (Hong Kong: Form Asia Books Limited, 2011)

Oliver, Harry, *Black Cats, The Origin of Old Wives' Tales* (New York: Penguin Group, 2006)

Roget, Peter M., *Roget's International Thesaurus* (New York: Thomas Crowell Co., 1961)

Shakespeare, William, *Shakespeare, A Book of Quotations* (Mineola, NY: Dover Publications, 1998)

Spellman, Paul E., *Spindletop Boom Days* (College Station, TX: Texas A&M University Press, 2010)

Twain, Mark, *The Wit and Wisdom of Mark Twain* (Mineola, NY: Dover Publications, 1999)

Weaver, Bobby D., *Oilfield Trash, Life and Labor in the Oil Patch* (College Station, TX: Texas A&M University Press, 2010)

Webster, Noah, *Webster's Collegiate Dictionary*, Fifth Edition (Springfield, MA: Merriman Company, 1947)

About *the* Author

MAVIS PARROTT KELSEY, SR. *is founder and former chief of the renowned Kelsey-Seybold Clinic in Houston. A graduate and distinguished alumnus of both Texas A&M University and the University of Texas Medical School at Galveston, he is the author of numerous books on genealogy, history, medicine and art, including A Guide to the Courthouses of Texas and Twentieth-Century Doctor: House Calls to Space Medicine, His book Engraved Prints of Texas, 1554–1900 received the Philosophical Society of Texas Award of Merit. He lives in Houston.*